TOP SELLERS, U.S.A.

Also by Molly McGrath (with Norman McGrath)
CHILDREN'S SPACES (1978)

TOP SELLERS, U.S.A.

SUCCESS STORIES BEHIND
AMERICA'S BEST-SELLING PRODUCTS
FROM ALKA-SELTZER TO ZIPPO

Molly Wade McGrath

WILLIAM MORROW AND COMPANY, INC.

NEW YORK   1983

Grateful acknowledgment is made for permission to quote from the following:

"Animal Crackers" from *Chimney Smoke* by Christopher Morley.
Copyright 1917 by J. B. Lippincott, renewed 1945 by Christopher Morley.
Reprinted by permission of Harper & Row, Publishers, Inc.

"Levis, Plaid Shirt and Spurs" by John Stephens and Irving Bibo.
Copyright © 1949 Bibo Music Publishers. Copyright renewed %
The Welk Music Group, Santa Monica, Calif. 90401. International
copyright secured. All rights reserved. Used by permission.

Material on THE CUISINART from *Jean Anderson's* New *Processor
Cooking*. New York: William Morrow, 1983. Copyright © 1983 by
Jean Anderson.

Also for permission to use the following photographs:

Nabisco Brands, Inc., pages 70, 72, 95, 102, 103, 108, 110, 146,
color insert pages 1, 4, 8; Apple Computer, Inc., page 185; The
Gillette Company, page 82; Johnson Wax, S.C. Johnson & Son,
Inc., page 80; Kellogg Company, page 115; Miles Laboratories, Inc.,
page 164.

BAKER'S, LA BELLE CHOCOLATIÈRE, BIRDS EYE, JELL-O, MAXWELL
HOUSE, CUP AND DROP DEVICE, GOOD TO THE LAST DROP and
SANKA are registered trademarks of General Foods Corporation,
White Plains, New York.

Photographs on pages 20, 29, 45, 50, 63, 74, 88, 95, 109, 113,
125, 136, 145, 148, 152, 154, and 184 by Norman McGrath.

Library of Congress Cataloguing in Publication Data

McGrath, Molly Wade.
  Top sellers, U.S.A.

  Includes index.
  1. Commercial products—United States. 2. Success.
I. Title.
HF1042.M33 1983   338'.02'0973   83-13228
ISBN 0-688-02253-7

Printed in the United States of America

First Edition

1 2 3 4 5 6 7 8 9 10

BOOK DESIGN BY BLACKBIRCH GRAPHICS

To historians Margaret Wade Labarge and Hugh Mason Wade,
with all due respect

Acknowledgments

MANY THANKS TO EDITORS ELLEN JACOBSON LEVINE AND RUTH MILLER FITZGIBBONS WHO FIRST ASKED ME TO look at the background of top-selling products as the subject of a magazine article for *Cosmopolitan Living*.

Thanks, too, to neighbor Patricia Lynden in whose kitchen, over wineglasses, the list of items began to grow.

I am deeply indebted to Melvin J. Grayson, director of public relations for Nabisco Brands, and to other writers whose good copy about their companies' products became my primary source material. I wish to acknowledge also my two major reference sources, which were indispensably useful in providing details I had failed to elicit from the companies themselves: *Everybody's Business: An Almanac* edited by Milton Moskowitz, Michael Katz and Robert Levering (San Francisco: Harper & Row, 1980); *Great American Brands* by David Powers Cleary (New York: Fairchild Publications, 1981). Other sources are credited insofar as possible on pages 187–190.

My most grateful thanks to friends, relatives and acquaintances who were pressed into service as consultants in judging the appeal of the products I selected to study, and, finally, my apologies to everyone who has a favorite product with a story that I do not yet know, or could not include because of the limitations of space in one mere book.

—MOLLY WADE MCGRATH

New York
September 1982

Contents

PART FOUR

PART FIVE

PART SIX

TOP SELLERS, U.S.A.

Introduction

AMONG THE UNTOLD MILLIONS OF products created by entrepreneurial America, how do you single out those that are true TOP SELLERS? Early sales figures of a product often do not indicate that it will be a best-seller. JELL-O and BIRDS EYE frozen foods are examples of well-known products that did not make a major impression on the market for years after they first appeared. But once a best seller is accepted by the public, it seems to survive competition and rip-off, changing times and tastes.

In the first century B.C., Vitruvius, the architect and design theorist, attempted to pinpoint the characteristics of successful architecture. "All good buildings," he wrote, "must satisfy three conditions—convenience, durability and delight." His definition does not allude to *great* buildings nor does it suggest that a particularly splendid vaulted ceiling might redeem beyond the scope of his definition a structure that is otherwise flawed. Vitruvius was talking about buildings that serve the needs they were designed to meet, that stand the test of time, continuing to function efficiently and to please those who use them, when other monuments to trend and fashion appear briefly on the landscape, then disappear or are forgotten.

Successful products are something like the good buildings Vitruvius

discusses. Not all of them are classics in the design sense; few, in fact, can claim that distinction. Frequently, they are winners from the day they first appear on the market, but more important, they endure, becoming familiar, reassuring tokens of stability in the routine of our daily lives.

A true top seller is not usually born of a passing fad. A teakettle maker in Holland once struck it rich by producing a line of bottomless kettles in response to sudden demand when a popular rock singer and his fans took to wearing them as hats. The craze soon passed. Though the Dutch kettle maker garnered some extra guilders by sensing the market for a new version of his product, he had not created a top seller.

The bottomless teakettle was a short-lived folly, but real winners have sprung from equally unpredictable coincidences of demand, opportunity and someone's readiness to "mobilize." Rarely, it seems, is a best seller fully anticipated. When all the elements of the formula for a dynamic new product are carefully calculated in advance, the product, like the EDSEL, may inexplicably fail to please. When a great idea materializes, apparently out of nowhere, the result may be IVORY SOAP, the LOUISVILLE SLUGGER or even the OREO cookie.

It is not the purpose of this book to study corporations, except as it is necessary to understand how developments within companies reflected the times and lead to the introduction of certain products. We have chosen to consider mostly individual products, but some brand names, such as BIRDS EYE, have success stories behind them that we could not pass up. Sometimes, too, a character is so closely associated with a company that it becomes almost a product: AUNT JEMIMA, BETTY CROCKER, the AVON Lady. We will look at these because they are so much a part of what the company makes—an image, as well as consumer items.

There are certain categories of products that we expect to be accused of neglecting: automobiles, cosmetics, pharmaceuticals. Surprisingly, our research has shown that few products from these fields remain unchanged long enough to meet the criteria for inclusion in this book. References will be made to dramatic developments wrought by the growth of these industries, but we prefer to focus on the stories behind the items that have made their way into our social and economic history, and often into the language, adding to our sense of continuity with the past and heightening our expectations for America's future.

P A R T   O N E

1765–1812

The fledgling Republic had inaugurated its first President and set up the framework of government. For the next few years, George Washington would steer a precarious course between the perils of involvement in war abroad and divisive political squabbles at home. America's commercial development was still hampered by restrictive agreements with Britain, though by the time Washington began his second term there was a national bank to facilitate domestic and foreign trading, a tariff law covering thirty items and a lucrative new excise tax on liquor.

Waves of immigrants were spilling into the cities and rural areas. Their skills and resources generated new products for the increasingly lively marketplaces along the East Coast.

☞

BAKER'S CHOCOLATE

THE WALTER BAKER CHOCOLATE Company is the oldest concern in the United States with a record of having made the same type of product continuously in its original location.

The story begins with Dr. James Baker of Dorchester, Massachusetts, in the fall of 1764. The doctor had befriended a young Irish immigrant by the name of John Hannon, a chocolate maker by trade, who lamented the fact that no one had yet taken the initiative to set up a chocolate mill in the New World.

The doctor decided to help Hannon. He knew that James Boies's new mill on the Neponset River, in the heart of Dorchester, could be leased. He supplied the capital to get started, and together they obtained a run of millstones and a set of kettles. Early in 1765 the mill started production.

The new industry prospered in its early days until, just when everything was working smoothly,

John Hannon, bound for the West Indies to purchase cocoa beans, failed to reach his destination. Though he was presumed lost at sea, what actually happened is a mystery.

The following year Dr. Baker acquired full ownership of the plant and began making a blend of quality chocolate that he called BAKER'S. The mill continued as a family business for more than one hundred years. In 1927 it became part of General Foods, Inc.

It is not quite clear exactly how the figure of *La Belle Chocolatière* came to be associated with BAKER'S chocolate. We may assume that Walter Baker had a fondness for the painting, because an authentic replica of the original in the Dresden Gallery has, for generations, hung in Baker's administration building in Dorchester.

The tale behind that portrait resembles the plot of a Sigmund

Romberg operetta: Twenty years before Hannon's mill was started, young Prince Ditrichstein, an Austrian nobleman, ventured into one of Vienna's quaint chocolate shops to try the new beverage introduced from the western tropics. He enjoyed the hot chocolate, but for him a far more important discovery was Anna Baltauf, a waitress at the chocolate shop and daughter of Melchior, an impoverished knight. The prince fell in love with her, and later that year they were married.

As a wedding gift the prince had his bride's portrait drawn in pastel by Jean Étienne Liotard, a famous Swiss portrait painter. Liotard posed her in the chocolate server's dress she wore the day she met her husband-to-be. Today, because of a fascination with the maid on the part of Walter Baker or some other member of the Baker family, her picture has become one of the world's best-known, longest-enduring trademarks.

WITCH HAZEL

ACCORDING TO THE E. E. Dickinson Company, producers of WITCH HAZEL, it was the medicine men of the northeastern Indian tribes who first showed the Pilgrims how to boil the bark of the witch hazel shrub to make a natural extract useful in easing skin irritations and taking the ache out of bruises.

As the E. E. Dickinson people tell it, the Indians of the area that is now Connecticut became fascinated by the *Hamamelis virginiana* bush, which blossomed in delicate golden flowers late in autumn after the leaves had fallen and even its own branches were perfectly bare. The striking peculiarity of this bush, which appeared to defy the laws of

nature, led the Indians to believe that the Great Spirit wished to draw their attention to it. They collected a supply of the bush's twigs and boiled them in a caldron. Suddenly the phantomlike form of a beautiful maiden could be seen in the steam issuing from the caldron. Somehow—and there seems to be some allusion here to regional folklore in which witches figured prominently—the healing properties of boiled *Hamamelis* bark were attributed to the spirit of Witch Hazel, and the shrub came to be known as the Witch Hazel bush.

Early in the nineteenth century a man named Hawes, a missionary to the Indians, was so impressed with the effectiveness of witch hazel that he made a thorough study of its medicinal value. He concluded that it was indeed pure, astringent and soothing. Though Hawes did not choose to become involved in selling witch hazel, a few years later a clergyman named Thomas Newton Dickinson saw the prospect of a profitable market for it.

The descendant of a prosperous entrepreneurial family that had settled in New England during the Colonial period, Dickinson was a clergyman with a highly developed talent for business. He chose carefully the location for the plant that would distill witch hazel, selecting a site in Essex, Connecticut, on the banks of the Connecticut River and in the midst of fields with an abundant growth of fine-grade witch hazel shrubs. He devised a formula for making commercial witch hazel that proved so successful that it remains essentially unchanged today.

For many years after Dickinson's WITCH HAZEL came on the market in 1866, consumers watched their druggists draw a bottleful for them from kegs labeled with the "Bull's Eye" Dickinson trademark and the slogan, DOUBLE DISTILLED—NOT DOUBLE DILUTED. Since then, generations of women have discovered WITCH HAZEL's multitude of uses—not only as a

cleanser and astringent, but as an ingredient in facial masks and toners, and in hand lotions and, recently as a "dry" shampoo for corn-row hairdos.

The boom in highly promoted commercial cosmetics after World War II inevitably lured American women away from the old standbys of their mothers and grandmothers, but the resurgence of interest in

natural products during the sixties and seventies brought many customers back. Meanwhile, Dickinson has built up a good record of sales by shipping WITCH HAZEL in the modern equivalent of the "Bull's Eye" keg to cosmetic manufacturers, who rely on it as a key ingredient in their more elaborately packaged, expensive products.

HUDSON'S BAY POINT BLANKETS

HUDSON'S BAY POINT BLANKETS were early *North* American top sellers.

In the days before trade rules were clearly defined, some types of business were conducted informally, without benefit of tariffs or even monetary currency. Blankets, for example, were traded with the Indians through the Hudson's Bay Company in exchange for beaver pelts, highly coveted for making the stylish hats and warm coats popular in London and the evolving fashion worlds of America's new cities. The first recorded order dates back to December 22, 1779.

To make trading easier, the number of pelts required for a blanket was stitched in short, indigo-colored lines or "points," on the corner of each blanket. One short line and three longer ones meant one small and three large beaver skins; four lines meant four full-sized pelts were required.

Identical blankets, boldly striped and clearly marked with these particular points are today among the best sellers from L. L. Bean, Inc., in Freeport, Maine, and other stores specializing in high-quality classic merchandise. Points now indicate size and weight: three-and-a-half-point blankets measure sixty by eighty-six inches and weigh ten pounds per pair. Four-point blankets measure seventy-two by ninety inches and weigh twelve pounds per pair.

The sole distributor for POINT BLANKETS in the United States, Pearce Woolen Mills, Inc., in Woolrich, Pennsylvania, reports that they are chosen by many exploration parties. Admiral Byrd used them in the Antarctic, Colonel and Mrs. Charles Lindbergh flew in blanket coats, and they were part of the basic equipment on three Mount Everest expeditions.

Among the outstanding features of POINT BLANKETS is their durability. There are families currently using blankets purchased fifty or sixty years ago from Hudson's Bay Post stores: One owner claims to be using a blanket which was salvaged fifty years ago from a shipwreck in Lake Superior!

WEBSTER'S DICTIONARY

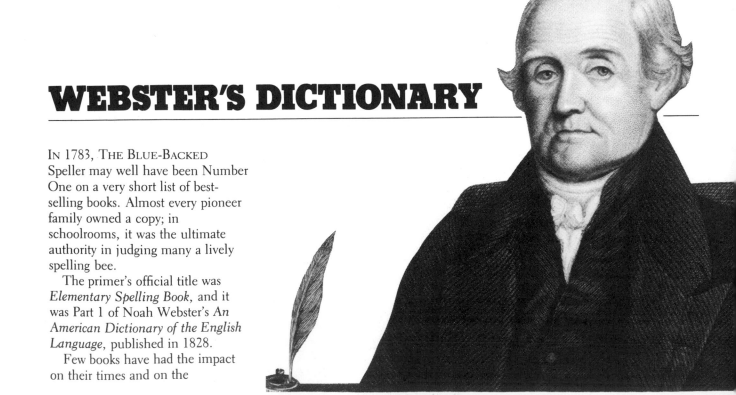

IN 1783, THE BLUE-BACKED Speller may well have been Number One on a very short list of best-selling books. Almost every pioneer family owned a copy; in schoolrooms, it was the ultimate authority in judging many a lively spelling bee.

The primer's official title was *Elementary Spelling Book,* and it was Part 1 of Noah Webster's *An American Dictionary of the English Language,* published in 1828.

Few books have had the impact on their times and on the

generations to follow as did this early dictionary, completed when its author was sixty-seven, after a quarter of a century of preparation. It contained some 70,000 entries, by far the largest number of any dictionary up to that time, and included an assortment of illustrative quotations as well as complete etymologies. Webster's book also embodied his ardent patriotic belief in the concept of a living *American* language. Its current successor, comparable in function, is WEBSTER'S NEW COLLEGIATE DICTIONARY which boasts more than 150,000 entries and is published today by the G. & C. Merriam Company, owner of the rights to WEBSTER'S DICTIONARY since 1843.

THE OLD FARMER'S ALMANAC

FOUNDED IN 1792 BY ROBERT B. Thomas of Massachusetts, THE OLD FARMER'S ALMANAC has appeared continuously for a longer time than any other publication in the United States. For 189 years, it has been America's best-selling annual, with readership numbering 3.5 million in 1981. The fact that the editors had to turn away twelve pages of advertising for the 1982 edition because it was fully subscribed is conclusive evidence of the little magazine's ongoing commercial success.

The first edition of THE OLD FARMER'S ALMANAC appeared without a single ad. Its purpose, as stated by its editor and publisher, was to offer useful astronomical facts, detailing their effect on the weather, and an assortment of "new, useful and entertaining matter" as well. The result was a potpourri of information ranging from a schedule of eclipses of the sun and moon for the coming year to Rules for Long Life ("by the learned Monsieur Comiers") and tips for removing corns from the feet: "Take the yeast of beer, and spread it on a linen rag, and apply it to the part affected; renew it once a day for three or four weeks; it will cure."

Testimonials to the value of THE ALMANAC have always abounded. For example, it is alleged that Abraham Lincoln consulted it for evidence to win a murder trial. In the fall of 1857, Lincoln acted as attorney for a man named Armstrong, accused of murdering a man with a slingshot on the night of August 29, 1857, in Cass County, Illinois. At one point in the trial, Lincoln called for what was later described as "a popular and well-known family Almanac for 1857." According to THE FARMER'S ALMANAC, on the night of August 29, 1857, the moon was "riding low." On the strength of this information, Lincoln pointed out to

[Nº. I.]

THE

FARMER's ALMANAC,

CALCULATED ON A NEW AND IMPROVED PLAN,

FOR THE YEAR OF OUR LORD

1793 :

Being the first after Leap Year, and seventeenth of the Independence of America.

Fitted to the town of BOSTON, but will ferve for any of the adjoining States.

Containing, befides the large number of ASTRO-NOMICAL CALCULATIONS and FARMER'S CALENDAR for every month in the year, as great a variety as are to be found in any other Almanac, *Of* NEW, USEFUL, *and* ENTERTAINING MATTER.

BY ROBERT B. THOMAS.

" While the bright radient fun in centre glows,
The earth, in annual motion round it goes ;
At the fame time on its own axis reels,
And gives us change of feafons as it wheels."

Publifhed according to Act of Congrefs.

PRINTED AT THE Apollo Prefs, IN BOSTON,
BY BELKNAP AND HALL,
Sold at their Office, State Street ; alfo, by the *Author*
and *M. Smith*, Sterling.
[*Sixpence fingle,* 4s. *per dozen,* 40s. *per groce.*]

the jury that there would not have been sufficient light for Armstrong to take accurate aim with his slingshot. No one even considered doubting the accuracy of the statement in THE FARMER'S ALMANAC regarding the inadequate moonlight on the night of the fatal crime. Armstrong was acquitted.

For a short time in 1944 publication of THE OLD FARMER'S ALMANAC was actually banned. After apprehending an agent from a German U-boat on a Long Island beach with a copy of the 1943 ALMANAC in his pocket, the FBI jumped to the conclusion that the enemy were using THE ALMANAC to determine high and low tides! It was thought that they might be consulting it for their weather forecasts too. Robb Sagendorph, the editor of THE ALMANAC at that time, agreed to change the heading "Weather Forecasts" to "Weather Indications," which seemed to appease the government. With sales boosted by the publicity it received, THE ALMANAC was back on the newsstands the following year.

Owned since 1939 by Yankee, Inc.—publishers of *Yankee* magazine in Dublin, New Hampshire—contemporary editions of THE OLD FARMER'S ALMANAC, edited by Judson Hale, still contain astronomical data, weather predictions (historically, 80 percent accurate) and a handful of short articles focusing on such diverse topics as everyday uses for the lemon, autograph collecting as a hedge against inflation, and how to build a picnic table. As a gesture of respect for its practical New England tradition, each copy still has a hole punched through the upper left-hand corner so readers can hang it on a nail in their outhouses.

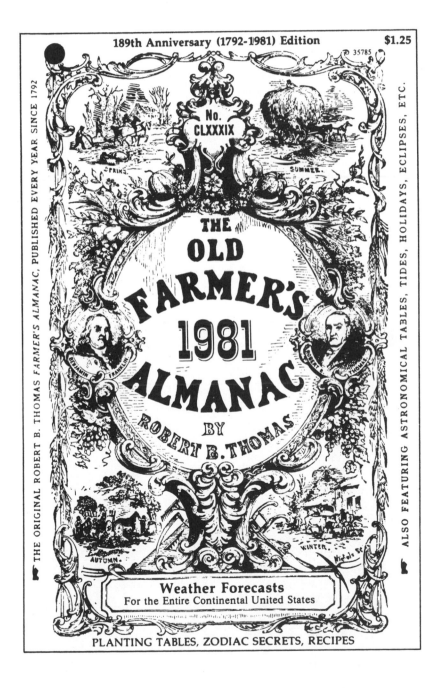

SMITH BROTHERS COUGH DROPS

IS THERE A TRADEMARK MORE classic than that of the SMITH BROTHERS, Trade and Mark, gazing thoughtfully at each other across the top of the well-known SMITH BROTHERS cough-drop box? Is it possible that the two bearded brothers actually existed?

The Smith Brothers were, in fact, named William and Andrew, sons of James Smith, a carpenter, restaurateur, businessman and candymaker. They lived in Poughkeepsie, New York, in the early part of the nineteenth century.

Knowing James Smith's interest in candy making, a visitor to his restaurant passed on to him a formula he knew for making a delicious and effective "cough candy." Smith immediately realized what a market there might be for

such a product in the cold, windswept Hudson Valley where people suffered one cold after another all winter long. He brewed up a batch of cough-candy mixture on his kitchen stove and dropped it out in small spoonfuls onto trays. When the candies were cool he gave them to everyone he knew.

The "drops" were an instant success! Demand for them spread fast along the Hudson Valley. The family was pressed to keep up with it. William and Andrew helped cook the candy mixture in the family kitchen, then packaged the drops crudely in plain envelopes. They sold them in the streets of Poughkeepsie and as far afield as they could manage to travel. The first ad for their product appeared in a Poughkeepsie newspaper in 1852,

inviting all "afflicted with hoarseness, coughs or colds" to test it.

As the success of the Smith product grew, a flurry of copies appeared, paying the original product the ultimate compliment of imitation. Soon there were "Schmitt Brothers," "Smythe Sisters" and, as patent laws were not strictly enforced, there were even other "Smith Brothers," all offering cough remedies. The real Smith Brothers, who had long flowing beards by this time, decided to have their pictures placed on the glass bowls and envelopes in which their cough drops were sold. By chance, the word "Trade" appeared under the picture of William and "Mark" under Andrew's. It has remained so ever since.

The glass bowl that stood on the pharmacist's counter and the envelopes inside containing cough drops had definite limitations as packaging. The Smiths had no way of being sure that only genuine SMITH BROTHERS cough drops would be sold in their envelopes. So in 1872 the brothers designed a box bearing their likenesses, which was filled under their personal supervision. This was one of the first "factory filled" packages ever developed.

After the Smith brothers died, the business stayed in the family until 1964 when they sold it to Warner-Lambert Company. F & F Laboratories in Chicago acquired SMITH BROTHERS in 1977 and are the present owners.

P A R T   T W O

1812–CIVIL WAR

"Tangible objects and ideas circulate throughout the Union. . . . Nothing checks the spirit of enterprise."

—Alexis de Tocqueville, 1831

Strained relations with Britain finally culminated in America's declaration of war against that country in 1812. Victory over the British, two and a half years later, was hardly decisive, but treaties that were drawn up at the conclusion of the war helped resolve many issues that had previously hindered British-American trade.

The ports of the East Coast began to hum with the activity of ships moving in and out. Fueled by the demand for more and better goods, industries grew and competition increased. It was a period of apparent prosperity and progress, until sectional differences divided the nation and the era of good feelings ended in civil war.

A.1.SAUCE

IT WAS WELL KNOWN IN THE court of England's George IV that the king was an epicure. He loved food and he enjoyed discovering new ways of serving it.

Master of the palace kitchen and master of his art was a chef named Brand. In search of a different gourmet experience to set before the king, he hit on a sauce that pleased his own fastidious tastes. That same day the new sauce went to the royal table. Legend has it that when the king tasted it, a pleased smile curled about his lips, his eyes rolled heavenward and Brand was summoned from the kitchen.

In his white apron and towering chef's cap, Brand bowed before his monarch and awaited the verdict. It must have seemed an eternity until George smiled approvingly and declared, "This sauce is A-1." Or so the story goes.

The new sauce quickly gained favor among the guests of the royal household. Before long, Brand resigned his position in the palace kitchen and began to manufacture the condiment privately.

Eventually the sauce became popular in America too, but at the start of the First World War shipments from England became increasingly sporadic. After making a mutually satisfactory arrangement with the Brand organization, Heublein began manufacture of the condiment in Hartford. That company reports that sales of A.1. helped it survive Prohibition, when there was virtually no market for fine liquors, wines and premixed cocktails. Today A.1. sauce is the top-selling bottled steak sauce in America—"The Dash That Makes the Dish."

STEINWAY PIANO

HEINRICH ENGELHARDT Steinweg built the first STEINWAY piano in his kitchen during a slow period in the cabinetmaking business. The year was 1836 in a small town called Seesen, in Germany.

A few years later, as the cabinetmaking business had not improved markedly and wasn't likely to with Europe in the throes of political upheaval, the Steinwegs emigrated to America where the Steinweg name was Anglicized to

Steinway. They moved into a tenement on New York's lower East Side, and the men in the family went out in search of piano-building jobs.

The Steinways' timing was fortunate. Jenny Lind was America's sweetheart in those days; her triumphant tour in 1850–51 had made everyone aware of the pleasures of singing and playing the piano. More and more families wanted one of their own, not only for its music-giving possibilities, but

as furniture, often the centerpiece of the entire living room.

In spite of being discouraged by various hardships during their early days in America, the Steinways were able to open their own business in a rented loft. Doretta Steinway, the eldest Steinway daughter, proved herself an excellent saleswoman and was, perhaps, the first to think of the clever gimmick of offering free lessons to clinch the sale of a piano.

The Steinways soon outgrew the rented loft on Varick Street. In 1860 they built their own factory, a city block in length, at what is now Park Avenue and Fifty-third Street in Manhattan. As writer Helen Epstein points out, this was an ideal location for advertising: "The Harlem and New Haven Railroad passed directly in front of the factory at the time, and passengers could not miss the logo STEINWAY & SONS just before their train pulled into Grand Central Station."[1]

The Steinways knew the value of good marketing techniques, even for a product as unique as theirs. Associating one's product with a celebrity was a tried-and-true strategy, but William Steinway, the firm's second president, demonstrated previously unimagined ways of using it: Not only did he sponsor artists and concerts and provide pianos at no cost for rehearsals and performances, he and the Steinway family had Steinway Hall built as the perfect setting for their pianos and the performers who used them. Steinway Hall opened its doors for the first time in 1866 and remained New York's leading concert hall for twenty-four years . . . until "that upstart steelmaker from Pittsburgh built Carnegie Hall," as Vice-President John Steinway used to say.

In 1896 the great Anton Rubinstein, heir to the virtuoso tradition established by Liszt, agreed to a tour of the United States sponsored by the Steinways. It was a major cultural breakthrough in this country, and Rubinstein was welcomed with overwhelming enthusiasm in small towns and cities alike. The effect of Rubinstein's

[1] Helen Epstein, "Steinway: When the Best Demand the Best," *Companion* magazine, May 1977 © East/West Network, Inc.

performance in some of the backwater towns is suggested in the following popular humorous essay, "How Ruby Played" by "Jud Browning," a fictitious contemporary of Josh Billings, Artemus Ward and Peck's Bad Boy:

Well, sir, he had the blamedest, biggest catty-corneredest pianner you ever laid your eyes on—something like a distracted billiard table on three legs. When he first sit down, he peered to care mightly little about playing, and

wished he hadn't come. He tweedled a little and twoodle-oodled some. I was about to git up and go home, being tired of that foolishness, when I heard a little bird waking up away off in the woods, and calling sleepy-like, and I looked up and see Ruby was beginning to take some interest in his business, and I sit down again. All of a sudden, old Ruby changed his tune. He ripped out and he rared, he pranced and charged like the grand entry at a circus. He set every joint in me a-going. I jumped spang on to my seat, and jest hollered—"Go to it, Rube!" With that, some several policemen run up, and I had to simmer down.[2]

Though the Steinway firm did not sponsor too many more artists' tours,

---

[2] Stuart Segal, "Pianomaker Henry Steinway," *Town and Country* magazine, December 1977.

it has always maintained its ties with current concepts of musical excellence by persuading performing artists to endorse its piano by stating that they use it, exclusively, and by choice. This endorsement of the STEINWAY has long been a feature of the company's considerable and often elaborate advertising.

One of the most valuable endorsements the STEINWAY ever

had was also one of the most cryptic. It came, in the early days, from a recognized authority on sound, Thomas Alva Edison. On his purchase order for a STEINWAY he wrote:

I have decided to keep your grand piano. For some reason unknown to me, it gives better results than any tried so far. Please send bill with lowest price.

ARROW SHIRT

THE HISTORY OF THE ARROW shirt dates back to the invention of the detached collar at Troy, New York, in 1820. The credit for it is given to Mrs. Orlando Montague, wife of a fastidious blacksmith who insisted on having a clean shirt every evening when he attended civic events and rehearsed with the local choral group. One day, in a fit of desperation brought on by countless hours of laundering her husband's shirts by hand, Mrs. Montague cut off all the collars, bound the edges and neckbands and attached narrow strips of fabric to hold them in place.

Though this innovation alarmed Mr. Montague at first, he accepted it soon enough and could not resist demonstrating the merits of his wife's detachable collar to his friends. The idea caught on quickly, and in a very short time other Troy housewives had liberated themselves from slavery to their laundry tubs by snipping the collars from their husbands' shirts.

As happened so frequently during

this remarkable period in American business history, there was a member of the community who recognized the commercial possibilities of the idea. This time it was a retired minister, Ebenezer Brown, who ran the general store in Troy. He realized that there was no special trick to making detachable collars and began manufacturing them in the back of his store. As demand for them increased, small shops and lofts all over Troy were converted into sewing rooms for making collars. The Cluett Company, predecessor of Cluett, Peabody & Co., manufacturers of ARROW shirts, started out from just such humble beginnings.

Originally Cluett made starched collars only, but of all the small companies making them in Troy at the time, Cluett's was one of the most successful. By 1899 Cluett was ready to merge with Coon & Company, which brought into the joint company the ARROW trademark registered by the Coon brothers some years before. The

merger also brought along an enterprising salesman, Frederick F. Peabody, who soon became a partner in the company, renamed Cluett, Peabody & Co., Inc.

Peabody collaborated with J. C. Leyendecker, a commercial artist, to create a manly figure to represent the ARROW look. The ARROW Collar Man began to appear in advertisements all over the country. A little like the MARLBORO Man, he changed progressively with the times and styles, and he always seemed to appeal to men and women equally. He had more than the desired effect on ARROW business: By the end of World War I, with six thousand people employed in its factories and sales exceeding $32 million, ARROW expanded the company's line of collars to include four hundred different styles.

Cluett, Peabody could not foresee that American soldiers returning from overseas would have grown accustomed to the soft collar-attached shirts they were introduced to in the service. They were not interested in going back to the stiff separate collars they had worn before they went away. To meet the new demand, in 1921 the company began making shirts with collars. The new ARROW shirt, designed to meet dozens of consumer specifications, was called the ARROW Trump. It was stylish and comfortable, but it had the same drawback shirts had always had: It shrank when it was washed.

The shrinkage problem was finally resolved in 1928 by Sanford Cluett, at that time vice-president in charge of research. He developed a process to compress cotton fabric under tension so that shrinkage was reduced to a minimum. The process, named after its inventor, was licensed, under the trademark "Sanforized," to cotton finishers all over the world. Today Cluett, Peabody makes some $9 million annually from these licensing arrangements.

Though Cluett, Peabody goes out of its way to keep up with changing fashions, it admits that the fashion market is one of the hardest to second-guess. After opening fifty-seven new retail stores in the late 1960's, it was forced to sell or close thirty of them. The flower children of that decade had left their mark on everyone's taste for casual, easygoing clothes. Even for relatively formal occasions, a proper shirt and tie could be dispensed with. As the fashion pendulum swings back to a middle position, ARROW plans to make more sports shirts, with heavy emphasis on those made of 100 percent cotton that can be spun wrinkle-free in the clothes dryer.

JELL-O

JELL-O IS ONE OF THE FEW TOP sellers around today that was not an instant winner when it first came on the market.

The predecessor of Jell-O gelatin was a dessert patented in 1845 by Peter Cooper, inventor of the "Tom Thumb" locomotive and patron of the arts and sciences. He described his gelatin confection scientifically as a "transparent, concentrated substance containing all the ingredients fitting it for table use . . ." but beyond that he did nothing to promote his product.

Forty years later Pearl B. Wait, a carpenter by trade in Le Roy, New York, became interested in the market possibilities of gelatin. Pearl Wait had another trade in addition to carpentry: He made patent medicines. He had developed a fairly successful cough remedy, also a laxative tea, and in 1895 he was anxious to extend his business in order to cash in on the new packaged-food trend that extended all the way from Hershey, Pennsylvania, to Battle Creek, Michigan. Wait soon figured out that patent medicines were not going to make him rich. He probably assumed that something that would make the housewife's life easier and that her children and husband would clamor for would certainly be the answer. He set himself to developing a tastier variation on Cooper's gelatin dessert. His wife, May Doris Wait, was more than supportive; she even coined a marvelous name for the new product, a name that distinguished her husband's concoction from all others like it and was remarkably easy to remember. But, except for Mrs.

Wait's flair for marketing, the couple had few resources to support the product. They lacked capital, sales experience and any concept of how to introduce it to the consumer. Wait's sales were so poor that by 1899 he was ready to unload the JELL-O name and product formula to the first person who showed any interest in it.

The man who presented himself, Orator Frank Woodward, had grown up in the Horatio Alger tradition. A school dropout at age twelve, he had gone to work at an assortment of jobs, always planning to seize the opportunity to make it big whenever such opportunity should come along. He had started his own business at the age of twenty, making balls used in target shooting (before the advent of clay pigeons). He went on to manufacturing cement nest eggs infused with some substance designed to kill lice on hens as they were laying or hatching eggs. In 1883 he diversified still further, proving that there was, in fact, money to be made in patent medicines: He bought the rights to manufacture and sell Kemp's Balsam for Throat and Lungs, Kemp's Laxative, Sherman's Headache Remedy, and Raccoon Corn Plasters (to name only a few).

Hoping, perhaps, to follow in the footsteps of C. W. Post and W. K. Kellogg, Woodward obtained a patent for Grain-O, a roasted cereal beverage "for those who could not drink tea or coffee." With his combined assets from sales of the other products, Woodward was able to properly advertise and promote his new coffee substitute. Its success made it possible for Woodward to found the Genesee Pure Food

Company and add JELL-O gelatin to the company roster as a companion product for Grain-O.

According to Dr. Burton Spiller, writing in the March 1972 issue of *Spinning Wheel:*

In the beginning Mr. Woodward had little more success with Jell-O than did his predecessor. Sales were so poor that on one occasion he offered to sell the company to his plant superintendent. The two men had been touring the plant and reached the storage section. In front of them lay cases upon cases of Jell-O piled high. Woodward surveyed the scene glumly and asked his companion, "Will you give me $35 for this entire Jell-O business?" The offer was refused.

Fortunately for Woodward the tide turned a very short time after he had thought he would have to give up on JELL-O. For whatever mysterious reasons, housewives who for years had served nothing but rich, filling pies, cakes and puddings for dessert suddenly became interested in JELL-O. Woodward's investment in advertising was finally paying dividends. Sales soared to $250,000 in 1902 and in 1906 came to nearly $1 million. Grain-O was discontinued so that the company could turn all its attention to JELL-O.

Woodward spared no expense in promoting JELL-O now. Pretty women dressed in tidy white aprons appeared in ads everywhere proclaiming JELL-O "America's Most Famous Dessert." Booklets were distributed with details of the countless different ways JELL-O could be prepared. The booklets also included favorite JELL-O recipes from the collections of such celebrated ladies as Ethel

Barrymore, opera singer Madame Ernestine Schumann-Heink and others. The booklets were illustrated with the work of some of America's most noted artists, including Maxfield Parrish, Norman Rockwell and, most notably, Rose O'Neill. Her Kewpie drawings and verses purveyed the JELL-O message to the housewife much as Campbell's "kids" sold soup. After 1908 Rose O'Neill's modernized version of the JELL-O girl was actually used on the JELL-O box.

Woodward supplemented his lavish ad campaigns with personal contacts made by his handpicked sales force. The men Woodward chose to represent JELL-O had to meet his high standards of good grooming and impeccable manners. He sent them forth in elegant horse-drawn rigs and later in vans emblazoned with the JELL-O name along the side. They would turn up at every sort of social event—picnics, church socials, banquets and fairs—bearing huge quantities of JELL-O to give away free. They would busy themselves with demonstrations of ways to prepare JELL-O gelatin and send their captivated audiences home with samples and molds, enough for themselves and plenty more to share with relatives and friends.

In 1923 the Genesee Pure Food Company was renamed Jell-O Company, Inc., in an attempt to protect the JELL-O trademark and prevent it from becoming a generic term. The matter of protecting the JELL-O trademark passed out of the hands of Woodward and his executives in Le Roy, New York, when the Jell-O Company was sold to and merged with the Postum Cereal Company of Battle Creek, Michigan, in 1925. The new joint company formed the nucleus of the present General Foods Corporation.

The business Woodward had been willing to sell in 1899 for $35 had appreciated in twenty-six years to a value estimated at $67 million. And it has not suffered any major setback since.

Potato Chips

George Crum, an American Indian, inadvertently invented the POTATO CHIP in 1853 when he was working as chef at an elegant resort in Saratoga Springs, New York. The french-fried potatoes he made kept being sent back to the kitchen by a disgruntled guest who claimed they were much too thick. In exasperation Crum cut slices so thin you could see through them and fried them to delicate crispness in boiling fat. The guest was finally satisfied and so were many other visitors at Moon's Lake Hotel where Crum's potatoes, known as Saratoga Chips, became the specialty of the house.

Though figures are not available to indicate today's best-selling brand of POTATO CHIPS, it is known that eleven percent of the U.S. potato crop goes to make America's Number One snack food.

SINGER SEWING MACHINE

THE SINGER SEWING MACHINE IS an invention that evolved in the hands of several people, but the person who added the ultimate, decisive refinement was able to claim credit for the whole concept.

The first patent for a sewing machine was issued in England in 1790, and others appeared after that. The most promising one, invented in 1846, was the work of an American, Elias Howe, Jr., and his wife, who had suggested the best position for the eye in the mechanically operated needle. But like the other machines invented before it, Howe's could sew only a few stitches at a time. When Isaac Merritt Singer came across one of these machines, cast aside in a repair shop in Boston, it seemed to him that if he could figure out how to make it sew a seam more than six inches long, he would make more

money than he ever had at any of his erstwhile occupations as a ditch-digger, sawmill worker or inventor.

Singer was thirty-nine years old in 1850 when he put the finishing touches on his machine and had it patented, incorporating all the features of its forerunners: the Howes' eye-pointed needle, a presser foot, lockstitching, a two-spool thread feeder and the capacity for straight or curved-line stitching. No sooner had word of this invention begun to travel than Singer found himself faced with lawsuits from Howe and two other manufacturers who claimed that parts of the SINGER machine infringed on their patents. At this point Singer decided to team up with a young lawyer, Edward Clark, who could defend him from all these legal entanglements in exchange for a share in the business.

As partners, Clark and Singer formed the I. M. Singer Company in 1851 and two years later opened their doors to the public on Centre Street, New York, with machines that sold for $100 apiece. (Some current models may be purchased for that price today.) Clark dealt with the accusations of patent infringement by retaliating with counter suits against his opponents, and when there seemed no possible end to "the infringement war," Clark calmly suggested that the companies pool their resources (including patents) to form the Sewing Machine Corporation. Singer and Howe agreed to take one third each of the price of any machine sold in the United States; the other two manufacturers involved at that point shared the remaining third.

Edward Clark was responsible for

Singer Sewing Machines

during the half-century of their evolution have been steadily progressing, constantly attaining higher excellence in design, construction and artistic finish. They are a little higher in price than some, but—the most satisfactory machine ever made to do

Sewing for the Whole Family

Compare these machines with any other. You can try them free in your own home upon application to any of our offices, *located in every city in the world.*

The best is always cheapest in the end.

They cannot be obtained through department stores or merchandise dealers.

Either Lock-Stitch or Chain-Stitch

Any Style of Cabinet-Work

AFTER FREE TRIAL, they are sold for cash or leased, old machines being taken in part payment. :: :: .: :: :: :: :: :: ::

THE SINGER MANUFACTURING COMPANY

---

many of the innovative policies that led to the early success of the Singer Company. He promoted the idea of a machine in every household, and by hiring comely girls to demonstrate the machine's many functions, proved that any woman could run one. He developed the concept of Singer sales agencies communicating directly with the consumer as they still do around the world today. Even in the early days, Clark was already organizing plants abroad that would ultimately provide the company with a cushion against ups and downs in the United States economy. He offered generous allowances for trade-ins; he

planned toward a time when volume in sales would permit dramatic price slashes.

But perhaps Clark's most inspired contribution was the "installment plan." He realized that in a family earning roughly $500 a year, a woman would rather pay $100 for a machine bought on monthly installments of $5 than spend $50 outright. He followed up with mercilessly aggressive marketing techniques: Newly arrived immigrants found SINGER sewing machines waiting for them to buy in their lodgings; victims of the great Chicago fire of 1870 were given huge discounts on new machines

whether they had lost one in the fire or not.

Meanwhile, in the midst of all this clever management of his company, Isaac Singer was making headlines almost daily in New York's scandal sheets with his outrageous antics. At the time of the formation of his partnership with Clark, Singer had already fathered eleven of his total number of offspring (twenty-four) by four different women, only one of whom he had the courtesy to marry. By virtue of extremely intricate planning he managed to keep each of his affairs secret from the other women until 1860, when he let his guard slip just long enough to be seen by one of the women while he was accompanying another. The offended lady promptly proclaimed the sordid details of her relationship with Singer for all New York to read and hear. The police became involved; terrible lawsuits were threatened. Edward Clark suffered desperate embarrassment for the sake of the company. And Singer? He persuaded the younger sister of one of his mistresses to flee with him to Europe.

Three years later Clark and Singer dissolved their partnership, each retaining some of their stock and selling the rest to employees. Singer died in 1875 while building a $500,000 palace that he called his "Wigwam" in Torquay, England. Clark continued a somewhat limited involvement with the Singer Company until his death seven years later in 1882.

In the years since Clark's death, SINGER has become as well-known as COCA-COLA in parts of the world as disparate as Labrador and Kuala Lumpur. (It is said that the South Pacific islanders once ranked the three basic essentials of life as food, shelter and a SINGER sewing machine.[1]) But the fortunes of the company have not followed a perfectly straight line over the years. The demand for machines tapered off after World War II, and the reduced market that existed was deeply affected by the influx of cheaper machines from abroad. Singer responded by expanding its overseas operations while diversifying into other businesses at home. But the basic problem from the fifties right through to the eighties was keeping profits ahead of the company's considerable costs and investments.

The closing of the company's 109-year-old plant in Elizabeth, New Jersey, was announced in February 1982 as a move toward a "marketing strategy of more cost-effective foreign production and diversification in aerospace products."[2] But for those who know something of Singer's history, it seems a sad fact of our changing economy that the manufacturing base of such a fundamentally American product can no longer be in America.

---

[1] *Everybody's Business.*

[2] *The New York Times,* February 19, 1982.

LEVI'S

I don't dude up in fancy clothes
Trimmed with frills and furbelows.
I'd feel silly in chinchilly furs.
And tho' I'd like to look enchantin'
Ranchin' keeps me gallivantin'
In Levi's, plaid shirt, and spurs.

This popular song published in 1949 is a good indication of how far LEVI'S had come in one hundred years. The implication of Stephens and Bibo's lyrics is, clearly, that the lady knows she looks terrific in her cowboy duds. . . . LEVI'S, first institutionalized for their practical features, were on their way to becoming a fashion classic as well.

Levi Strauss came to New York from Bavaria in 1847 at the age of seventeen. He managed to scratch a meager living as an itinerant peddler of clothing and household goods in the rural towns and villages of the New York area until 1850 when, lured by tales of gold-rush fortunes, Strauss traveled to San Francisco where he opened a retail dry-goods business supplied from New York by his two brothers. His primary stock-in-trade was canvas for tents and wagon covers, but he found there was more demand from the miners for a sturdy pair of pants. Strauss made a few pairs out of canvas and later switched to a tough cotton fabric loomed in France called *serge de Nimes,* soon contracted to *denims.* As an experiment, he dyed a few pairs indigo blue and borrowed the idea of a Russian-Jewish tailor in Nevada named Jacob Davis of adding copper rivets at the "stress" points. To Strauss's amazement, at a price of $30 per dozen or $3 a pair, retail, the pants with rivets rapidly became the uniform not only of miners but of cowboys, lumberjacks, railroad

workers, farmers and oil drillers. Within a few years the company was selling nearly six thousand dozen riveted pants, vests, coats, jumpers and blouses with gross sales of almost $150,000 for the year 1874 alone.

It was the pair of pants, described by the manufacturer as the "501 Double X blue denim waist overall," better known within the company as "the 501," that represented the ultimate, perfected blue jeans produced by Levi Strauss. Made with extra-strength denim, snug, low-hipped and tapering at the legs, the style and details of the basic 501 have remained unchanged since they first came on the market in the 1870's. But it was not until the late 1920's, when sales were running at about $4 million a year, that 501's became Levi Strauss's big money-maker . . . and not until the late thirties and forties did the public begin to think of blue jeans in terms of any style except Wild West. Things began to change after a story appeared in the *New York Herald Tribune* advising prospective dude ranchers to dress simply for a ranch vacation, "or buy in the West a pair of Levi overalls." A month after the story appeared in the *Herald*

Tribune, Levi Strauss took an ad in *Vogue* that showed two debonair, obviously eastern women of fashion wearing LEVI'S on a ranch vacation. "True Western chic was invented by cowboys," the copy read, "and the moment you veer from their tenets, you are lost. And so you have the newest outdoor vogue for women— Levi's—worn by the knowing not merely on dude ranches but at the more exclusive resorts, beaches, and camps throughout the country."

Whether LEVI'S ever became the accepted garb of holidaymakers at exclusive clubs and beaches in the thirties is questionable, but there is no doubt that they are seen everywhere today, worn by everyone—striding across Fifth Avenue, bouncing along the Ginza, slinking down the Via Veneto. Several pairs are part of a permanent display at the Smithsonian Institution's Americana collection. In the face of competition from manufacturers ranging from BLUE BELL to CALVIN KLEIN and GLORIA VANDERBILT, true LEVI'S still impudently bear the ironclad guarantee "to shrink, wrinkle and fade"—all features prized by the purists in the jean-wearing crowd.

Tradition and inventiveness continue to go hand in hand in the top management of the firm that Strauss founded. Old Levi, a bachelor, eventually turned over the company to a nephew who, when the time came, passed it on to his son-in-law, Walter Haas, Sr. Executive control stayed in the family as Haas senior left it to his two sons, Peter and Walter, still at the helm today.

The two brothers work in such close concert that, even between themselves, they quip occasionally about being interchangeable parts. Though the company went public in 1971, it remains essentially a family-and-employee-owned operation characterized by an appearance of informality lightly disguising total seriousness about the company's reputation for quality and workmanship.

A credit to the inventiveness of its founder, Levi Strauss has not missed opportunities to diversify and to expand its merchandising base. International sales amounted to $915.3 million in 1981—35 percent of the company's total sales. Nor has Levi Strauss failed to invest in the development of new fabrics, styles, finishes and fibers, partly as

34 protection against the day when the jeans may become less fashionable and the company may be forced to become its own best competition. Toward this end, Levi Strauss recently acquired Koracorp

Industries, Inc., a major apparel company with 1978 net income of $7.8 million. In late 1982, Koracorp, now known as Diversified Apparel Enterprises, Inc., helped to redress the balance for Levi Strauss

as the anticipated recession in jeans was marked by the closing of four jeans plants in eight months. Still, among all the jeans sold, whether they are in or out of fashion, every fourth pair is made by Levi Strauss.

STETSON HAT

WHEN JOHN B. STETSON STARTED from St. Joseph, Missouri, for Pike's Peak, his baggage consisted of the clothes on his back, a shotgun and a hatchet. His companions, a dozen or so in number, were similarly equipped.

Stetson, son of a New Jersey hat maker, had traveled west in the late 1850's for many of the same idealistic reasons as his adventure-seeking contemporaries. In addition, he suffered from consumption and his doctors had recommended the fresh air and wide open spaces of the West. Stetson succeeded in starting a promising brick-selling business, but a few weeks before the expedition to Pike's Peak, the floodwaters of the Missouri River had totally wiped it out.

On the way to Pike's Peak the plains and prairies were often windswept and stormy. Stetson and his friends had not brought anything with them to make a shelter. As muskrat, rabbits, beaver and coyote were plentiful, the young men became adept at trapping them and sewing the skins together as protection against the wind and

rain. But there are certain disadvantages to using untanned skins, particularly in midsummer. When the sun came out they smelled so bad the campers had to throw them away.

It was then that Stetson began to piece together his memories of the steps in the felt-making process he had learned in his father's hat shop. First, Stetson took some of the skins his friends had discarded, sharpened his hatchet and shaved off the fur. He then cut a branch from a hickory sapling, sliced a thong from one of the skins and made a hunter's bow. With this bow he agitated the fur, making a little cloud that hung in midair. Stetson kept the fur in the air until precisely the right moment, when he allowed it to fall gradually, distributing itself over a small area in front of him. As it fell, Stetson, with a mouthful of water, blew a fine spray of moisture through the fur. Soon there was a mat of the fur that could be lifted and rolled. It weighed about as much as a large sheet of wet paper. There was a campfire nearby and a pot of boiling water. Into this Stetson dipped his

sheet of matted fur. It began to shrink. By manipulating it with his hands—almost as one stretches pizza dough—and rapidly dipping it into hot water, he soon had a little blanket of soft, sturdy cloth.

Stetson had demonstrated the basic techniques of the felt-making process. Except that the fur is now manipulated by a machine fan and sprayed mechanically with water, the procedure for making felt is much the same today.

When the travelers finally made it to the top of Pike's Peak, properly equipped at last with protective headgear, Stetson began to think about returning to the East to build up a business based on the felt-making technique he had rediscovered.

Reaching Philadelphia with $100 in capital to start his business, Stetson bought the tools of his trade and rented a small room at Seventh and Callowhill streets. He started making hats and sold a good many just by modeling them for potential retailers and their customers. But Stetson was barely breaking even. He decided that instead of relying

John B. Stetson's "catalogue"—1872

mail could carry them.

Within two weeks the orders started pouring in. He sent out more samples as fast as he could make them and dispatched them with the suggestion that, if a man wanted his hats by return mail, he should send the money in advance.

From then on the reputation of the STETSON hat spread far and wide. The Boss of the Plains (B.O.P.) model had served its purpose by drawing attention to the company; it would become a classic symbol of the Wild West and the men who tamed it. But Stetson went on to make many other styles. In an age when men owned as many hats as women have pairs of shoes today, the name STETSON was considered synonomous with quality and style.

For over one hundred years STETSON hats enjoyed worldwide distribution and acclaim. Then in the 1950's, because of new trade restrictions and duty increases, it became economically impractical to export hats abroad. At this juncture, Stetson decided to license foreign hat manufacturers to make STETSON hats rather than build and maintain hat factories in foreign lands. In 1966 the company began to license hat manufacturing in the United States. Also in the 1960's, Stetson started a diversification program using the STETSON name in other fields of men's apparel. By the late 1970's and early 1980's, diversification extended to use of the name not only on hats but also on shirts, neckwear, belts, coats, shoes, even men's toiletries, and blankets.

So, if you want to own a true Boss-of-the-Plains hat, you can, and it will bear the STETSON label, though the company that made it may not be precisely the same as the one that made the original.

on the local trade of the Philadelphia hatters and haggling with them over prices, he would make a new kind of hat for the Cattle Kings of the West that would be so stunning they would all want to own one. He called this new hat "The Boss of the Plains," and his marketing technique was not to advertise (he had no money to spare for that) but to send each of the major clothing and hat dealers in every city and town of the Southwest a sample hat with an accompanying letter asking for an order of a dozen.

Stetson realized that his marketing strategy would either make or break him, but he was so convinced that it would work that he went into debt to the full extent of his credit. He made up as many of the big, natural-colored hats as he had materials for, then whipped them out to the West as fast as the

PART THREE

1865–1900

As the nation recovered from civil war, plentiful supplies and pent-up consumer demand led to vigorous retail trading. Hundreds of products as diverse as shoelaces and bunion plasters appeared on, and often soon disappeared from, the shelves of local general stores. The best-selling ones were frequently those presented in the most colorfully lithographed containers, an early form of advertising which sometimes cost more than the product itself.

In the last quarter of the nineteenth century, America entered an era of scientific breakthrough and technological advance unequaled before or since. The telephone, the telegraph, the radio, the phonograph, the electric light, the Bessemer converter for making steel, the linotype printing press—these were just a few of the inventions that changed American life forever.

"The sky's the limit" was the feeling that permeated American thinking in business and industry. Everywhere, astute entrepreneurs were rushing to get on the bandwagon.

FLEISCHMANN'S YEAST

CHARLES FLEISCHMANN, WHO first visited the United States while the Civil War was raging, found our bread almost as appalling as our political situation. Most American bread was, in fact, baked at home in the family kitchen with yeast made from fermented potato peelings. The result was unpredictable and often inedible. As soon as Fleischmann could afford to, he traveled back to Austria, collected samples of the yeast used in making Viennese bread and returned to the United States, this time accompanied by his brother, Maximilian. The brothers demonstrated the effectiveness of their yeast and proposed some ideas for selling it to James M. Gaff, a well-known Cincinnati distiller, and the three went into business as Gaff, Fleischmann & Company. In 1868 the company began making yeast in compressed cakes of a uniform size. It was a milestone in the history of American baked goods. From that day on, the guesswork was virtually removed from baking; the way was paved for WONDER bread, ENGLISH MUFFINS, TWINKIES and whatever treats and abominations entrepreneurs in this field succeeded in putting on the market.

Gaff, Fleischmann & Company knew very well the value of advertising, point-of-purchase displays and special promotions. They attended fairs and exhibitions where they demonstrated their yeast in a special "Vienna Bakery" booth. Visitors to the booth would sip hot coffee and savor warm, freshly baked bread made with yeast. The demand for yeast soared and Gaff, Fleischmann was obliged to seek more and larger production units.

Nor did the partners waste any time finding another valuable use for yeast. Through a subsidiary called the Fleischmann Distilling Company, they started producing America's first distilled gin. Both the distillery and the yeast-making company (known as the Fleischmann Company after the death of James Gaff) were part of the group of companies that consolidated in 1929 to form Standard Brands Incorporated. Since the 1981 merger with Nabisco, they are part of the gigantic Nabisco Brands, Inc., corporate family.

The most recent company history reports that, during Prohibition when there was no market for gin, Fleischmann concentrated its marketing efforts so effectively on selling yeast that by 1937 its one-pound cakes of baker's yeast were bringing in almost $20 million a year—more than any other product made by Standard Brands. The company relied heavily on ads to sell the smaller foil-wrapped packages of yeast for use at home. Armed with testimonials from medical authorities, it ran a "Yeast for Health" campaign that boosted annual consumer use of yeast by millions of dollars. As always, it followed up with personal contacts, including appearances at fairs where thousands of free cakes of yeast were given away along with information about the many wonders the product could perform.

A story that testifies to the high esteem people had for the Fleischmann name is still told around the company: Sometime in the early 1930's the owner of a small bakery outside of Pittsburgh was having terrible problems doing his accounting. He happened to ask advice of the Fleischmann sales representative who called on him that day.

"What you ought to do," suggested the salesman, "is put yourself on a salary. Say twenty dollars a week."

Several months later he got a call from the baker:

"My business is doing pretty good," said the baker. "Would it be all right if I gave myself a five-dollar raise?"

With the repeal of Prohibition in 1933 Fleischmann went back to producing gin at its Peekskill distillery. Whiskey, vodka, rum and an assortment of liqueurs have since been added to the roster of products from the distilling company, and there seems to be no major threat ahead to the market for FLEISCHMANN'S yeast.

In possession of the magic ingredient for bread baking and booze making, how could Fleischmann ever fail?

Fleischmann's® ACTIVE DRY Yeast

ARM & HAMMER BAKING SODA

ARM & HAMMER WAS FIRST SOLD for baking in 1867. That same year, James Church joined his father's baking-soda business, bringing with him from his own company, Vulcan Spice Mills, the famous trademark depicting the arm of Vulcan about to strike an anvil.

Mined in the Green River Basin in Wyoming, ARM & HAMMER baking soda is used today by millions of homemakers not only to get a rise out of baked goods but also to add a shine to dull surfaces and to freshen stale air. At fifty cents a pound, it's not expensive now compared to other household cleaners, but it's five times as much as it was in 1870.

ARM & HAMMER BAKING SODA
AND
COW BRAND BAKING SODA

are identically
the same product
and are

**PURE
BICARBONATE
OF SODA**

equally good for Medicinal
and Cooking purposes.

FOR SALE BY ALL GROCERS

The requirements
of the U. S.
Pharmacopoeia
are exceeded.

BALL JAR

DID YOU EVER CONTEMPLATE THE sensible, sturdy girth of a BALL jar and wonder how long it had been around? Even when they're brand-new, they look at least fifty years old.

The original sealed glass storage container was the MASON jar, named for John L. Mason, a tinsmith in Brooklyn. He designed and patented his jar in 1858.

Twenty-one years later, two enterprising brothers in Buffalo, New York, realized that the patents on both the MASON jar and the zinc cap necessary to seal it had expired. If one company were to make both the jar and the zinc cap, reasoned the brothers, the best possible fit for

a jar and cap could be controlled, thus assuring successful results for the canner.

The Buffalo team acted fast. By 1886 they had moved into the sealed-jar business and produced "Buffalo" jars with their own name and BUFFALO, N.Y. pressed into the glass lids or into the glass liner of the zinc cap. In that first year of their new business they produced 12,500 containers called fruit jars. Until then the fruit-jar business had been monopolized in the United States by the Hero Fruit Jar Company and the Consolidated Fruit Jar Company which controlled the MASON Improved jar and the porcelain-lined-cap patents. These two

companies fought their new competition by notifying the trade that the Ball brothers were infringing on their rights and they planned to sue the upstarts, and anyone handling BALL jars, to the limits of the law.

As usual, the Balls lost no time in reacting. They hired patent lawyers who soon confirmed that the MASON patents had moved into the public domain. They sent circulars to this effect to everyone in the trade, offering in addition to protect buyers and handlers of their jars against any damage or infringement suits.

No suits were brought. The Balls had won a clear-cut victory. Their

initial decision to make the jars, similar as they were to MASON containers, and to defend their right to do so are classic examples of the importance of moving quickly and confidently in the marketplace.

The well-known fruit jar became the backbone of the Ball Corporation for many decades to come. Unfortunately, because furnaces are such a major factor in glassmaking, the Ball company existed in constant danger of fire. More than once the plant was devastated and rebuilt, until methods and materials for fireproofing finally improved enough to give them adequate protection. Eventually headquartered in Muncie, Indiana, the business developed slowly until, in the post-World War II period, the company management finally began to diversify and expand—into glass, rubber and zinc production.

Few people who stock up on BALL jars each season know they are patronizing the aerospace industry. In the late 1950's, by way of Ball's

interest in acquiring a company called Control Cells in Boulder, Colorado, the Ball Corporation became involved with scientists doing pure research in the aerospace program. The involvement led to a series of contracts with the government to make advanced aerospace equipment, including NASA's Orbiting Solar Observatory to study radiation from the sun. Contracts for six more OSO satellites followed in rapid succession.

Other businesses expanded gradually in the fifties and sixties, acquiring companies that manufactured products related to their own. By comparison, Ball's leap into the twentieth century was dramatic. If anyone had predicted Ball's involvement in aerospace twenty years before, its executives would have been as surprised as anyone. But when the opportunity arose, Ball decision-makers were fortunate to be in a position to seize it.

CAMPBELL'S SOUP

JOSEPH CAMPBELL'S COMPANY IN Camden, New Jersey, was one of the businesses spawned by early nineteenth-century developments in canning and preserving food. Campbell, a fruit merchant, and his partner, Abram Anderson, an icebox maker, formed a partnership in 1869 to produce canned jellies, mincemeat, tomatoes and other vegetables. Anderson sold his interest in the company seven years

later and Campbell retired in 1894. At that point, Arthur Dorrance assumed management of the Campbell Company.

The credit for the first major breakthrough in the canned-food business belongs to Arthur Dorrance's nephew, Dr. John Thompson Dorrance, who joined the company in 1897. He had a particular interest in soup making and had spent several months after

he finished his studies visiting the kitchens of Parisian restaurants to observe their methods of preparing soup. He came home convinced that there was a big market for a new kind of soup, a condensed canned soup that would cost less to ship than other soup, would occupy less space in the store and in the kitchen and could be sold for less to the housewife.

Consumer reaction to the first

"*Campbell's* for dinner,
For supper, for lunch—
Eating this soup
Is what gives me the punch!"

You gain real vigor and energy from

Campbell's Vegetable Soup

You get the strengthening properties of the rich meaty stock made of selected beef. And combined with this you get the valuable tissue-building material which is supplied by choice vegetables, beside the vegetable salts which aid digestion and regulate the blood.

White potatoes, sweet potatoes, carrots, yellow turnips, tomatoes, and "baby" lima beans are among the thirteen different vegetables we use in this inviting soup.

We flavor it with celery, parsley and other delicate herbs. And we add a sprinkling of "alphabet" macaroni to increase the attractive appearance.

Have this tasty Campbell "kind" again today, and you will realize more than ever that it is as wholesome and nourishing as it is delicious.

21 kinds   **10c a can**

Campbell's SOUPS

LOOK FOR THE RED-AND-WHITE LABEL

condensed soup (tomato) Dorrance produced confirmed his opinion. People were mad for it. The company seized the opportunity to promote the new product by organizing an advertising campaign using trolley-car posters. Why trolley cars? Because women were frequent riders and they were the consumers Campbell's hoped to reach.

Another line of reasoning in Campbell's evolving advertising strategy was that "the best way to reach the housewife is through child appeal." During the time the advertising department was mulling this over, a Campbell's salesman brought in some sketches by his artist wife, Grace Gebbie Drayton, that he thought might be suitable for one of the trolley posters. Mrs. Drayton had a flair for drawing what she called "round roly-polies"—fat-cheeked cherublike children who soon became famous as the "Campbell Kids."

The roly-polies appeared in ads and posters from 1904 on, though they disappeared temporarily during the Depression and World War II when it was felt that their chubby, chucklesome appearance was inappropriate for the grim times. The appeal of the roly-polies led to a tremendous demand for Campbell Kids dolls, which helped finance Campbell's move into the West Coast market and national distribution.

Condensed tomato soup was followed in 1904 by Campbell's pork and beans and twenty condensed soups which sold for ten cents apiece in the classic red-and-white cans bearing the gold medallion. As Campbell's moved prosperously into the twentieth century, more new soups were added to the line, and in 1915 Campbell's acquired Franco-American, which had been the first company in America to make canned soups. The next purchase was made forty years later when Campbell's stepped into the frozen-foods business by affiliating with C. A. Swanson & Sons, originators of the "TV" dinner. Baked goods were added to the company larder with the acquisition in 1961 of Pepperidge Farm, the "home style" bakers whose sales now exceed $300 million.

Though Campbell's has moved via more acquisitions into pickle packing, candy making, dog food, restaurants and retail garden centers, they continue to be known mainly for their soups which now represent less than half their business. The company has a particularly strong professional interest in tomatoes, the main ingredient in their first and consistently best-selling soup. They announced in September 1981 that they planned to invest $10 million in a new company, DNA Plant Technologies, "to produce a tomato with better color, flavor and resistance to disease." Campbell also plans to establish laboratories in Brazil to research improvements in coffee, sugarcane and other crops—all to be able to offer still more ingenious answers to the perennial question, "What's for lunch today?"

LOUISVILLE SLUGGER

One warm spring afternoon in 1884, with the encouraging shouts of the fans ringing in his ears, Pete "The Old Gladiator" Browning, champion slugger of the Louisville Eclipses, swaggered up to home plate with his favorite bat in hand. He took his usual position next to the plate, pulled his bat back to his shoulder and looked the pitcher straight in the eye. At just the right moment, Browning swung confidently at the ball. But instead of the resounding thwack of the Old Gladiator's bat belting out another home run, the fans heard the crunch of the bat breaking.

While the game went on, as Browning grudgingly reached for another of the clumsily hewn short poles the team kept in reserve, a young sports fan in the crowd, John "Bud" Hillerich, decided to seek Browning out later. Hillerich persuaded the Gladiator to come along with him to his Dad's wood-turning shop where young Hillerich worked as an apprentice.

Ferreting around in the pile of wood where his father kept the rudiments of bedposts and handrails, eighteen-year-old Bud found a length of sturdy white ash, fastened it on a lathe and gradually honed it into a bat. Now and then Browning would take a few swings, then advise Bud that it needed "a smidgeon off here, a smidgeon there." By game time the following day Browning's custom-made bat—the first in the history of the sport—was ready for active duty. Its effectiveness was proved as Browning cracked three long hits in one game and credited his success to his new equipment. Within a few hours the rest of the Eclipse team was lining up at the

door to Hillerich's little shop demanding similar equipment for themselves.

Bud's father wanted no part of this new business. He had more orders than he could fill for butter churns, newel-posts, bowling balls and balustrades. He could see no future in producing what he regarded as toys. Ten years later, however, he began to come around to his son's point of view. Sales were falling off in butter churns and balustrades; more players from both minor and major leagues were demanding the LOUISVILLE SLUGGERS that Bud was turning out after hours. Hillerich senior made his son a partner in 1897, and when Frank Bradsby, who had been active in the sporting-goods field, agreed to join them, the name of the company was changed to Hillerich and Bradsby.

Part of the appeal of the LOUISVILLE SLUGGER was that, along with its trade name, the name of each athlete who bought a bat was branded onto it, replacing the players' traditional habit of notching their bats for identification. After 1894 the square letters of the names of Willie Keeler, Hugh Duffy and Cap Anson were burned onto all

bats made in the style preferred by that player. In 1905 Honus Wagner, "The Flying Dutchman," gave the company permission to use his signature on the bats—the first use of signature-endorsement advertising in the annals of American business. In subsequent years, the signatures of such baseball greats as Napoleon Lajoie, Ty Cobb, Babe Ruth and Frank "Home Run" Baker were similarly etched on LOUISVILLE SLUGGER bats.

It can be no surprise to baseball fans that idiosyncrasies have always abounded among the hitters themselves. The Hillerich and Bradsby Company keeps good files not only on the players' exact specifications for bats but also on their habits of caring for them. Some players oil their bats, some rub them with secret ointments or plain tobacco juice, others mutter mumbo jumbo over them before carrying them to the plate. Frank Frisch hung his sluggers in a barn to cure like sausages during the off-season. Ted Williams liked to blacken his bat handle with oil and resin, and if he was in the middle of a daily hitting streak he would give it an alcohol bath to cool it off. The

wood for Hugh Duffy's bats had to have a certain ring to it when bounced on a concrete floor. Ty Cobb, a creature of habit, never once changed the specifications for his bat in the course of his long career. Other players changed theirs with each passing mood.

Today the highest grade of ash, from dense thickets of trees protected from buffeting by wind, is used to make LOUISVILLE SLUGGERS for professionals. A specialized group of craftsmen turn the bats for their best customers by hand rather than trust them to the perils of automation. (Thus the bats offered for sale bearing the trademark of a particular slugger may vary somewhat from the one the player is actually using.)

Though Hillerich and Bradsby has diversified to the extent that it also manufactures golf clubs and other sporting goods related to baseball, and has even developed a line of aluminum bats for amateur use, the keystone of the company remains the product old man Hillerich originally felt had no future—the solid ash LOUISVILLE SLUGGER.

CRACKER JACK

WHAT WOULD A BASEBALL GAME be without a box of CRACKER JACK to nosh on? And who can imagine a trip to the zoo or the circus without it? The first centennial of the inimitable candy-coated popcorn-peanut confection, now owned by

the Borden Company, was celebrated in 1972.

CRACKER JACK is sold in fifty-three countries outside the United States. The name and logo are ranked among the top five in America by the Brand Rating Index

and their sales hit an all-time high in 1981.

The CRACKER JACK story began the day F. W. Rueckheim, a German immigrant who had saved $200 working on a farm near Chicago, came into the city to help clean up the debris from the great fire of 1871. Something about the Big City must have appealed to him for he lingered long after the debris was cleared and eventually went into business with a friend who had a small popcorn stand on Federal Street.

A true businessman, Rueckheim bought out his partner as soon as he could afford to and persuaded his brother Louis to leave Germany and join him. A sign went up outside the popcorn factory reading F. W. RUECKHEIM & BRO.; within two years the brothers had invested in some elaborate candy-making equipment and had added marshmallows and other confections to their line.

Between 1875 and 1884 the Rueckheims' business, like so many that burgeoned during that period, outgrew its space many times. In 1893 the brothers went to the Columbian Exposition where they had arranged to make and sell their popcorn-peanuts-molasses concoction on the site. That was CRACKER JACK'S introduction to the nation and the world. The ensuing challenge of keeping up with the increased demand became greater than ever.

The confection was now being shipped great distances in wooden tubs. The only flaw in the system was that the popcorn tended to stick together in large, less-than-appetizing lumps. Louis Rueckheim set himself to resolving this problem and finally did so in 1896 with no compromise to the gooey succulence of the candy. "That's a crackerjack," one of the salesman remarked after tasting the new, improved concoction. "So it is," said F. W. Rueckheim, and had the name trademarked, along with the

slogan passed on by a customer who said, "The more you eat, the more you want."

Shortly after that, the Rueckheims took on another partner and became Rueckheim Bros. and Eckstein. E. G. Eckstein was a packaging expert who added immeasurably to CRACKER JACK'S marketability by developing a wax-sealed package that protected crispness and flavor. It was the predecessor of an even more effective moisture-proof package introduced three years later.

CRACKER JACK did not always come with prizes in the box. Between 1910 and 1913 CRACKER JACK boxes carried coupons that

could be redeemed for premiums. After that, the coveted prizes were actually packed in the boxes. Today a Prize Committee evaluates prizes according to a formal prize selection procedure that determines their suitability to be placed in the same box with a food product, their safety and their appeal to children.

In 1916 a little sailor boy named Jack and his black and white dog, Bingo, began to appear in promotional brochures and ads. Three years later Jack and his dog became the CRACKER JACK logo. They were featured on the front of the box and have symbolized CRACKER JACK ever since.

NATHAN'S HOT DOGS

NATHAN DID NOT INVENT THE HOT dog, nor did he introduce it in America. Logically enough, the first sausage officially known as a frankfurter was made and sold in Frankfurt, Germany—in 1852. Two German immigrants both claim to have brought it with them when they traveled to this country.

Antoine Feuchtwanger, a Bavarian, is said to have sold the frankfurter served in a sandwich in St. Louis in the 1880's. His rival claimant, Charles Feltman, a pushcart peddler in New York City, offered frankfurters in toasted rolls to Coney Island boardwalkers for ten cents apiece in the 1890's.

Recently arrived from Poland, Nathan Handwerker was working at Feltman's Coney Island stand as an $11-a-week grill man when a pair of entertainers named Eddie Cantor and Jimmy Durante, both unknown at the time, suggested to Nathan that he open his own place and "sell a frankfurter at a price we can afford—a nickel." Nathan's response to the suggestion was the beginning of the most famous hot dog business in the world.

The secret of Nathan's success is probably nothing more complex than the superiority of his product. One of the few family-owned nationwide fast-food chains left in America, NATHAN'S still uses the recipe of Ida Handwerker, Nathan's wife, for seasoning the frankfurters. The meat is 100 percent beef with no fillers added; natural sheep-gut casings are used instead of synthetics. And NATHAN'S franks are grilled, not boiled, then served in a warm bun. The American public has shown its appreciation by eating over five hundred million of them in sixty-two years!

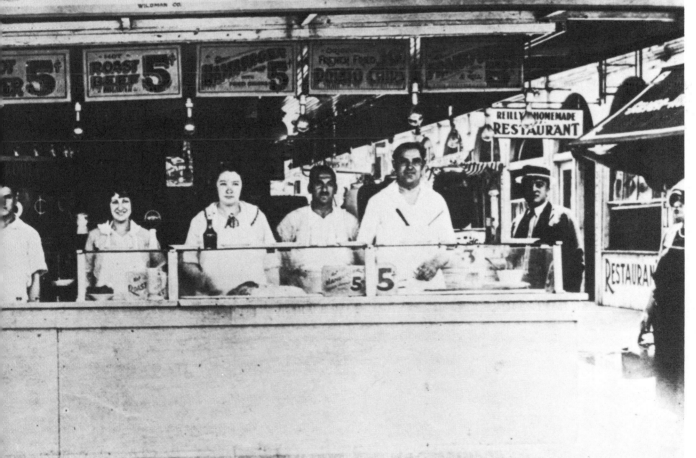

BACARDI RUM

ASKED TO NAME THE BEST-selling brand of distilled spirit in the United States today, people may say SEAGRAMS V.O. or J & B Scotch. Wrong. SMIRNOFF vodka? Close, that's Number Two, but BACARDI rum is Number One and has headed the list by hundreds of thousands of cases since 1979.[1]

Rum, of course, has been part of the American tradition longer than whiskey or vodka. The favored drink of Colonial Americans was rum, distilled in New England from West Indian molasses. That was the second stage of the famous three-way operation whereby rum was shipped from New England to Africa's Guinea coast as payment for slaves who were shipped to the West Indies to work on sugar plantations. Plantation owners paid for the slaves in molasses, which was sold in New England to make rum. Only when the British broke up the triangle with a blockade and a trade embargo did this system fail to work smoothly. Eventually, Congress's abolition of the slave trade put a stop to it for good.

But Americans didn't stay thirsty very long. Pennsylvania farmers were raising bumper crops of rye and converting much of it into whiskey, the most popular form of currency on the American frontier. Variations on the basic distilling process were developed all along the eastern seaboard as a form of barter for such vital necessities as gunpowder, building materials and manufactured goods of all kinds.

Not until America was one hundred years old did rum regain its rightful place on the barroom shelf. In 1876 BACARDI rum was awarded

a gold medal for excellence at the International Exposition at Philadelphia, celebrating the centennial of the United States.

Don Facundo Bacardi's special brand of rum was the result of several experiments made in an attempt to develop a spirited drink free of the harshness and bite that characterized most distilled-liquor drinks available in Cuba in the mid-nineteenth century. Señor Bacardi was a wine merchant with refined tastes; he had almost given up hope of finding any drink made from Cuba's native molasses that would please him. No one knows how long it took Bacardi to get the result he sought, but when he did he soon realized what a rare combination of mellowness and taste he had achieved. He began to serve his rum to friends and neighbors in Santiago de Cuba where he operated his wine shop and to think ahead of how he could produce it on a larger scale.

Using as a still an ancient cast-iron pot purchased for $3,500 and an odd assortment of fermenting tanks and barrels, Bacardi officially opened his rum distillery on February 4, 1862. News of Don Facundo's unusually delicious rum spread quickly among sugar planters of the Cuban provinces. Soon both planters and peasants were lining up with bottles, buckets and barrels to collect free samples. As always, giving away samples proved a fruitful marketing strategy, and reports of the new brand of rum were carried beyond eastern Cuba to Havana and the Straits of Florida and finally to the Exposition in Philadelphia where it won its international acclaim.

The prosperous future of

BACARDI rum was ensured in 1892, the year the future Spanish King Alfonso XIII became ill with the grippe at a country residence outside Madrid. The young prince had been restless and fitful for more than a week. Nothing seemed to soothe him or have any effect on his fever. Almost in desperation, the royal physician, who had spent some time in Cuba, prescribed some BACARDI rum to comfort the princeling. For the first time in days, Prince Alfonso fell into an easy, restful sleep and the fever passed. The Spanish court was so enthusiastic about the prince's recovery that a letter was immediately dispatched to the Bacardi Company, thanking them for producing an elixir "that saved His Majesty's life." As a token of the close relationship between the royal family and the Bacardi Company, the coat of arms of nineteenth-century Spain remains today on every label of BACARDI rum.

In 1896, the Bacardi Company fortunes received another boost when a young American mining engineer concocted a new rum drink to toast some visiting friends. The American, Jennings Cox, was working in the copper mines in the Sierra Maestra mountains outside Santiago near a hamlet called Daiquiri. When Cox's friends expressed their delight with his new drink and asked him what it was called, he decided, after a moment's thought, that "the Daiquiri" was a good name.

Two years later, intervention of the U.S. Army into Cuba's struggle for freedom, following the sinking of the battleship *Maine* in Havana harbor, sent legions of American soldiers to Cuba's shores. On hot

[1] *Business Week*, March 14, 1980.

afternoons during that August of 1898 a few adventurous GIs amused themselves by inventing a new drink made by mixing COCA-COLA and rum. The result was considered sensational, and they christened it a "Cuba Libre," in honor of Cuba's newly won freedom.

In 1919 Prohibition came to the United States. According to a *Fortune* article of 1933, "Havana became the unofficial United States saloon. People who had thought Bacardi was the Spanish word for bat (one of Bacardi's trademarks is a bat), sat in bars and drank Daiquiris by the dozen." So many Americans visited Havana and enjoyed Daiquiris during Prohibition that when Prohibition laws were repealed in 1934, BACARDI was already a household word. In the first year following repeal, Bacardi sold eighty thousand cases of rum.

By this time, another Bacardi rum company was flourishing in Mexico. Distribution rights in the United States had been set up and the company was anxious to begin manufacturing rum somewhere on U.S. territory in order to cut out the entry tariff of nearly one dollar a bottle. The company representative, José M. Bosch, known as "Pepin" Bosch, invested in some swampland in Puerto Rico that was known for

(Reg. U.S. Pat. and TM off.)

some time as "Pepin's Folly." Eventually, a handsome industrial complex rose there to make BACARDI, and the company was securely established on U.S. soil.

That security was not seriously shaken until 1960 when Fidel Castro's Communist government confiscated the physical properties of major companies operating in Cuba, including Bacardi's Santiago distillery and three Bacardi-owned breweries. But Bacardi survived under the guidance of Pepin Bosch.

The need for expansion into other markets was recognized, and the secret formula for BACARDI rum was soon being followed in Puerto Rico, Mexico and Spain. In 1961 a Bacardi company began bottling rum in Recife, Brazil. Their fortunes buoyed by a trend which continues today toward lighter, more subtly flavored alcoholic drinks, other Bacardi companies have since been started in the Bahamas, Venezuela, Martinique, Bermuda and Canada.

SEN-SEN

IN THE LATE NINETEENTH century, when a country swain went courting, he often carried in his shirt pocket an unobtrusive little envelope of SEN-SEN. When his

younger brother indulged in smoking behind the barn, he made sure he was equipped with the means of removing the evidence. The handy little SEN-SEN packets

were as easy to come by as a pack of cigarettes. They were displayed prominently on the counter of every country store worth its salt.

The flavor of SEN-SEN is unique

50 and its formula is a carefully guarded secret. The ingredients are gathered from many lands— Bulgaria, France, Turkey, Greece, Italy and some almost inaccessible regions of Asia. The list of sources reads like a perfume manufacturer's bill of lading. In fact, for many years pharmacies listed it as a cosmetic.

The formula was developed by a man named Kerschner who worked as superintendent of the T. B. Dunn & Company chewing-gum plant. By 1909, when T. B. Dunn merged with four large gum manufacturers to become Sen-Sen-Chiclet Company, SEN-SEN had become a household word. Before long, it was marketed internationally.

Today foil is used in place of the

small paper envelopes that originally wrapped the product. The formula remains unchanged, as SEN-SEN

continues to be a steady seller in restaurants, tobacco shops and drugstores around the world.

CRAYOLA CRAYONS

"An artist's crayon at a scholar's price."—1903

"It's fun to create with Crayola."—1981

LAMPBLACK WAS THE FIRST product of Binney & Smith, the company that makes CRAYOLA Crayons in a rainbow of colors today. It was used to darken printing inks, rubber boots, stove polish and, eventually, carbon paper and typewriter ribbons.

It was common knowledge in the nineteenth century that lampblack could be derived from almost anything that would produce smoke, but until 1879 no one realized that burning natural gas produced a very high quality, durable carbon black. Joseph W. Binney, a veteran of the

Crimean War who had manufactured lampblack in Peekskill, New York, since 1864, was aware of the carbon-producing properties of natural gas and therefore observed with great interest the boom in petroleum from the gas deposits discovered in 1880 in the fields of Pennsylvania.

The oil drillers manning the rigs in the Pennsylvania fields considered natural gas a nuisance. Their business was to produce petroleum and they allowed the "waste gas" to blow off into the air. But one oil-rig operator, a man

named Drew, recognized the value of the waste substance and built a small "smut mine" to convert it into carbon.

It was only a few months until Joseph Binney's son Edwin and his new partner, C. Harold Smith, a cousin recently arrived from England, heard about Drew's smut mine and got together with him to use his equipment to produce carbon that was truly black as night.

The operation became more streamlined once it was discovered that the pent-up pressure of the gas itself could be used to operate the carbon-producing machinery. It was expensive to make the new carbon black, but it sold well and won prizes in the numerous competitions that Binney & Smith entered around the turn of the century.

Finally, in 1912, came the breakthrough Binney & Smith had been waiting for. Edwin Binney's son-in-law, Allan Kitchel, who would later become chairman of the board and chief executive officer of the company, sold a large quantity of carbon black to an enterprising tire manufacturer looking for a way to make his tires more distinctive by darkening the outsides. When it was discovered that the tires colored with carbon not only looked better than the usual zinc-white tires of the day

but also wore longer, Binney & Smith knew they really had something. Lab tests confirmed that carbon black could prolong tread life by as much as four or five times. Tire manufacturers have been using it ever since.

During the years when Binney & Smith was busy perfecting the ultimate inky black, C. Harold Smith returned from a visit to England with the American rights to a new line of red iron oxides. Edwin Binney, who was as captivated by color as his elders were with black, was convinced that the oxides had great possibilities. He found that a deep earthy shade of red paint could be made from them, and on his frequent expeditions into the

countryside, he managed to persuade a good many farmers to paint their barns with it. The "old red barn" and the "little red schoolhouse" became symbols of rural America for which Binney & Smith claims its share of credit.

Not long after that, on a train trip in the South, Edwin Binney met a man named John Ketchum who had a talc mine in North Carolina and was looking for a place with cheap waterpower where he could grind talc. Binney knew just the spot, a gristmill near Easton, Pennsylvania. His mind raced ahead to how he could work with Ketchum to use an old slate quarry ten miles up the river from the mill. He remembered tons of unused waste slate at the

51

quarry and soon thought of a way of combining slate with cement and Ketchum's talc to make Binney & Smith's first finished school product: a high-quality slate pencil that could be mass-produced and sold for use in schools and offices all over the country.

One day a man came to the Easton plant on the site of the old gristmill and asked the company to make him several thousand slate pencils half as long as the ones they had been making, which were just under six inches long. With the existing machinery, it was impossible; the pencils were cut off at a certain length and that was that. But the Binney & Smith people figured out a way to make everyone happy. They turned a load of their sharpened pencils around, sharpened the other end and cut them in two for the new customer. He was delighted.

In the same spirit, Binney & Smith began to call on schools to sell the new slate pencil and the first white "dustless" chalk stick which followed soon after. As the salesmen talked to teachers, they noticed that the wax crayons the children were using were brittle, not uniform in color and priced too high to be affordable by all the "scholars." Binney & Smith set itself the task of finding a solution to this problem.

B & S technicians felt sure that the methods they had been using for mixing pigments with wax to produce a black marking pencil could easily be adapted to a variety of colors. It seemed a simple enough progression, but they found that to equal the color uniformity of fine imported crayons, time-consuming procedures such as hand-mixing of small batches were required.

The company struggled through the first year of producing the new crayons. Mrs. Allan Kitchel, daughter of co-founder Edwin Binney, now in her nineties, recalls how all the children in the family became involved in turning out promotion pieces for the crayons. They colored in by hand the "artist's palettes" that showed the range and quality of the new crayon colors. These were then packed into envelopes and sent out to potential customers.

It was Mrs. Kitchel's mother, Alice Stead Binney, who coined the name CRAYOLA for the product, joining the French word *craie*, "chalk," with *oil*. Another member of the Binney & Smith extended family who became involved with promoting the new product was Marie C. Falco, originally Mr. Binney's secretary and eventually general manager of the crayon department. Her talent for marketing, combined with her understanding of teachers' needs, prompted her to persuade the company to recruit art consultants who worked with her to develop new methods of teaching art. These ideas were conveyed to classroom teachers through a newsletter, published monthly, and by visits from the consultants themselves.

By the mid-sixties, the original eight CRAYOLA colors had increased to sixty-four and Binney & Smith had expanded its line to include other products related to creative art and education. SILLY PUTTY, another happily-named product, was acquired in 1977 from the company that converted an aircraft cockpit sealant (because it was impervious to radical change in temperature) into a popular toy.

One might assume that the arrival of MAGIC MARKERS on the art-supply scene shook the market for CRAYOLA crayons somewhat. Actually, Binney & Smith had introduced its own felt-tipped pen, called FEATHERMARK, in 1953. It came in large and small sizes with a refill system. That same year saw the arrival of MAGIC MARKERS—an instant success for two reasons: They had one of the best trade names in business history . . . and they were disposable. (In the late fifties, post-wartime consumers relished the recklessness of throwing away lighters, ball-point pens, toothbrushes.) MAGIC MARKERS briefly enjoyed the distinction of having its trademark become synonomous with the product itself. But as a result of poor management and strong competition from Bic and Gillette as well as Binney & Smith, the MAGIC MARKERS company was compelled to file for bankruptcy in 1980. The trademark was recently bought by Doral Industries, another company in the school-supply business. From now on, all their products will bear the MAGIC MARKERS name.

A by-product of the CRAYOLA line has been the graphic design of CRAYOLA packaging. The original box was a good example of pleasing traditional motifs; the more familiar contemporary-style CRAYOLA box, designed by Eric Pasquini in the early 1960's and modified slightly in recent years, has consistently lured customers away from any other crayon-type product. Binney & Smith now makes licensing agreements for the design to be adapted by manufacturers of everything from sleeping bags to lunch boxes—another marketing strategy from a company that has never shown any lack of imagination.

VASELINE

CHESEBROUGH-PONDS IS A company that can claim top-selling products in categories as diverse as cold cream and spaghetti sauce. In the field of petroleum jelly, it has never had much competition, perhaps because VASELINE is unique.

In 1850 Robert A. Chesebrough, was a twenty-two-year-old chemist with a kerosene business in Brooklyn. He eagerly followed reports of the oil boom in Pennsylvania and one day decided to go there himself.

What interested Chesebrough most in the oil fields of Titusville was not the oil itself or the natural gas that had so fascinated other entrepreneurs but the paraffinlike residue called rod wax that collected on the rods of the oil pumps. The workers in the oil fields drew his attention to it, saying that it had healing properties and there was nothing like it for treating cuts and burns.

In his laboratory in Brooklyn, Chesebrough refined a small sample of the waxy substance and applied it to a few of his own abrasions. To his amazement he found it as effective as the oil workers said it was. He then spent months working out a means of extracting the residue from the petroleum without actually installing an oil pump in the lab.

By 1870 Chesebrough was able to turn out his balm in quantity. He called it VASELINE Petroleum Jelly (from the German *wasser*, meaning "water," and the Greek *elaion*, "olive oil").

Chesebrough did not initially invest great sums of money advertising his new product. He preferred to promote it personally, traveling the roads of upper New York State with horse and wagon, handing out thousands of jars of VASELINE to everyone who was willing to try it. But the response to Chesebrough's new product was so great that within months he had a team of twelve horse-and-buggy salesmen to peddle VASELINE at a penny per ounce through New Jersey and Connecticut. Chesebrough incorporated his growing business in 1880. The

Vaseline

As the Chesebrough Manufacturing Company grew from horse-and-buggy enterprise into corporate giant, letters sent to the company by VASELINE users revealed that Chesebrough's translucent jelly possessed a versatility beyond its discoverer's wildest dreams. Gobs of VASELINE have, inexplicably, lured trout to fishermen's hooks. Dabs of it on the famous faces of movie stars have simulated tears of cinematic grief. Commander Peary's intrepid Arctic explorers took it with them because it resists freezing even at 40 degrees below zero. Reports reaching the Chesebrough company from remote jungle regions indicated that natives used jars of VASELINE as money after finding that not even blazing tropical suns would turn it rancid.

Still, a novice Chesebrough employee cringed when the company got a report that people in India were using VASELINE to butter their bread. Chesebrough assured the young man that it could do them only good; he himself ate a spoonful every day as a general panacea.

When, in his late fifties, Chesebrough was seriously ill with pleurisy, he prevailed upon his nurse to rub him from head to foot with VASELINE. He recovered, surviving to the age of ninety-six. On his deathbed, in 1933, he attributed his longevity to VASELINE.

SOOTHES MINOR SCRAPES

Vaseline TRADE MARK ®
PURE PETROLEUM JELLY

following year Standard Oil, Chesebrough's source of supply for petroleum, offered to buy the company. Thinking he was unlikely ever to have a better offer, Chesebrough agreed. In 1911 when the Standard Oil Trust was dissolved, Chesebrough once again became an independent company. Not until 1955 did Chesebrough merge with Ponds, best known at the time as the manufacturer of the skin cream advertised by socialites and European royalty. Since then Chesebrough-Ponds has added several strings to its bow, including PERTUSSIN cough syrup, PRINCE MATCHABELLI perfume, RAGU sauce, HEALTH-TEX and BASS loafers.

WEEJUNS

1876: THE YEAR CUSTER MADE HIS last stand, George Henry Bass made his first pair of shoes, designed to meet the requirements of his customers—farmers, lumberjacks and the river drivers who rode the logs down the rivers of Maine to pulp mills farther south. According to Bass company legend, George Bass delivered in person the shoes he made, seizing the opportunity to talk to his customers and find out more about their needs in shoes. From this kind of informal market research, the No. 50, "Bass Best" shoe evolved and became the most popular shoe of the lumbering industry, a position it enjoyed for more than half a century.

What also evolved was a major shoe-manufacturing plant that went on to produce the boots for both of Admiral Byrd's successful Antarctic expeditions. And when Charles A. Lindbergh guided the *Spirit of St. Louis* down the runway for his transatlantic flight to Paris . . . he

Bass ®
Since 1876

was wearing BASS flying boots.

In 1936 Bass came across a Norwegian shoe (thus the name WEEJUN, a spelling variation of the last two syllables of *Norwegian)* made in a moccasin style. Bass secured permission from the Norwegian manufacturer to interpret the shoe design for the American market and sell it in the United States.

For more than twenty years the WEEJUN was simply one style in the distinguished line of BASS shoes. Then in 1960 a writer for the student newspaper at the University of North Carolina at Chapel Hill declared BASS WEEJUNS an indisputable status symbol for "with it" people. His proclamation was evidently accepted without question. BASS WEEJUNS became the most popular hand-sewn moccasin ever made. For that style, they are still considered the standard of the industry.

WEEJUNS ®

BUDWEISER

THE BUSCH FAMILY AND THEIR representatives in the Anheuser-Busch company like to attribute the success of BUDWEISER to the superior quality of the product—made from the costliest ingredients, aged longer than other beers by a unique process—but all the evidence indicates that it has been the combination of a high-quality product with ingenious marketing that has made BUDWEISER King of Beers today.

"Our business," young Adolphus Busch used to tell his father-in-law, "is not just making beer. No. Making *friends* is our business."

If Eberhard Anheuser ever had twinges of apprehension about the ability of Adolphus to run the faltering brewery he had put young Busch in charge of, his doubts proved totally unfounded. Busch had a talent for marketing which each subsequent generation of the family seems to have inherited. One of the first indications of Adolphus Busch's extraordinary knack for winning friends and influencing people was his habit of giving people he met something to remember him by—a pocketknife, for example, or a corkscrew with the company name emblazoned on the outside and a little peephole at one end. A peek through the peephole revealed the image of Adolphus Busch himself.

In a land of locally brewed beers, German-born Adolphus Busch dreamed of being able to offer the beer market a national beer that would appeal to virtually everyone's taste. Toward this end, Busch collaborated with his friend Carl Conrad, a St. Louis restaurateur, to create a new beer similar to the light beer brewed in Budweis,

BUDWEISER GIRL

56 Czechoslovakia. The partners chose to use the traditional European "Kraeusening" process, calling for a time-consuming second fermentation period with beechwood chips. The results were of such high quality that neither the basic recipe nor the process has ever been radically changed.

Right from the start Busch thought in terms of far-flung markets for his new beer, but he realized that was only possible if he could find ways of protecting it from flavor-destroying heat and oxidation. He experimented by applying relatively new pasteurization processes to his beer and by setting up a network of railside icehouses to cool cars of beer awaiting shipment. A year later, in 1877, he launched the nation's first fleet of refrigerated freight cars.

Having given the new product every possible technological support, Busch knew the time had come to make sure people knew about this beer and would buy it. In 1877 everyone was still talking about the savage fight between the doomed 7th Cavalry and the Indians at Little Big Horn. Busch lost no time in capitalizing on this fascination by ordering thousands of reproductions of a copy of Cassily Adams's painting *Custer's Last Fight* for display in taverns across the country. Busch favored striking graphics, including posters of "BUDWEISER Girls" for both indoor and outdoor advertising. He would have been proud to see, years later in 1952, the "electric spectacular" the company ignited above Times Square. One hundred feet long and eighty-five feet high atop the Brill Building at Forty-ninth and Broadway, it dramatically touted the excellence of BUDWEISER and celebrated the

"Best beer" medallions won by BUDWEISER between 1876 and 1904

company trademark, the "A & eagle," with flashing lights to simulate a real bird in flight across the mammoth display.

Adolphus Busch's talents as a brewer and his flair for marketing lifted company sales first to 105,234 barrels in 1879, then to the million-barrel mark (1,006,494) in 1901. The company continued to thrive until 1920 when the Volstead Act closed all breweries at the beginning of Prohibition.

In a series of desperate attempts to keep the company alive, August Busch, the founder's son, converted the company's facilities to produce corn products, baker's yeast, ice cream, refrigeration cabinets, bus and truck bodies, malt syrups, soft drinks. All the while, Busch lobbied steadfastly to have Prohibition repealed. When Repeal was finally announced he was standing ready to send a team of the company's spectacular Clydesdale horses to parade up Fifth Avenue in New York City to the Empire State Building. There, one of the first post-Prohibition cases of BUDWEISER was presented to former New York governor Al Smith, a tireless supporter of Repeal.

Unfortunately, the effort to keep the company going during those difficult years had taken its toll on August Busch. In poor health, he shot himself to death in 1934.

In recent years BUDWEISER has taken some marketing cues from its biggest competitor, Miller Brewing. It was Miller that, with the support of its new owner, Philip Morris, introduced the first low-calorie beer, LITE, in 1971. Promoted by TV ads featuring former athletes, the beer sold extremely well. Anheuser-Busch was not far behind in bringing out NATURAL LITE, which Miller alleged contained unnatural ingredients. Anheuser-Busch countered by persuading some of the athletes in the MILLER commercials to join the BUD promotion team. The matter was never totally resolved but it is doubtful whether either company suffered from the publicity that the issue generated.

In 1976, Anheuser-Busch endured a damaging three-month strike in St. Louis, and it seemed there might be some real danger of BUDWEISER's losing its crown to MILLER. But BUD remained King, partly because, after the strike, the company took a good look at itself, hired more salespeople, increased marketing spending at all levels and substantially revamped the whole organization. The company management decided that, although BUDWEISER was selling about twenty-six million barrels a year, there was room for further growth. They followed Miller's lead into heavy sports promotion, initiated an ad campaign (not unlike Miller's) that stressed BUD as the beer for the workingman and -woman and announced in February 1982 that Anheuser-Busch, already a heavy advertiser in cable television, had signed a "multi-year, multi-million dollar" contract to become the exclusive brewer on the Black Entertainment Network which would soon be broadcasting seven days a week.

In the spring of 1982, as Pabst and Schlitz struggled to resist takeover bids from other brewers, the giant BUDWEISER sign that had recently replaced the one for SCHLITZ in downtown Milwaukee said it all: Other brewers might wrangle and brawl to secure third place in the Big League of Beer, and Miller could pride itself on being runner-up, but for the foreseeable future BUDWEISER is Number One, even in Milwaukee!

IVORY SOAP

OCTOBER 1879. IN THAT MONTH, Thomas Edison successfully tested the first incandescent light bulb and, some distance away in Ohio, Proctor & Gamble's first bar of IVORY soap floated upon the American scene. Whereas Edison, a former employee of Proctor & Gamble, had toiled for months to create the electric light, the floating soap was the result of a company operator's negligence in letting the soap-mixing machine run during his lunch hour. The machine beat the mixture to a froth so light that the cakes bobbed around in the kettle like apples in a tub of water. The operator's foreman was ready to

order the floating soap dumped back in the pot for reboiling, but someone with more imagination said, "Let's see. Maybe the customers will like it."

The customers did. From up and down the Ohio River they wrote, "Give us more floating soap." White Soap was its prosaic name at first, until one Sunday morning in church Harley Proctor, son of the co-founder of Proctor & Gamble, thought of a better one. The reading that morning was the forty-fifth psalm: "All thy garments smell of myrrh, and aloes, and cassia, out of the ivory palaces, whereby they have made thee glad." Proctor liked the connotation of ivory as a name for soap.

Harley Proctor wisely foresaw that Edison's electric light was destined to snuff out the company's profitable candle business and make it imperative to build up a market for a basic, household necessity like IVORY. As cleverly as a modern Madison Avenue advertising executive, he organized his campaign.

By 1879 Proctor & Gamble had had many years of experience in making and selling soap. As suppliers of soap and candles to the Union armies of the West during the Civil War, the company was set up to turn out these products on a very large scale. When IVORY came on the market, P & G plant production was up to two hundred thousand cakes of soap a day. The company directors realized that IVORY had to expand its market steadily if sales were going to keep step with that kind of production. They voted to spend almost $11,000 on IVORY soap advertising in 1882–1883—a huge investment in those days and a major marketing decision for P & G.

It was Harley Proctor's idea to carve a groove in the middle of each laundry-size bar of IVORY so that the thrifty housewife could break it into two toilet-size cakes if she chose to, and it was Proctor who decided that advertisements for IVORY must be lavish, full-page and compelling. He fastened on a phrase from the unusually fervid reports of chemists about the quality of the new soap, "We find this soap 99 $^{44}/_{100}$% pure," and incorporated it in the opening sentence of the first advertisement for IVORY: "The Ivory is a Laundry Soap with all of the fine qualities of a choice Toilet Soap, and is 99 $^{44}/_{100}$% pure." The ad has been called one of the most effective in American advertising history.

Proctor was soon urging consumers to buy a dozen bars of IVORY at a time and to keep a cake handy in every room of the house.

To dramatize the mildness of IVORY, he introduced "The IVORY Baby," and supplied shopkeepers with life-size cardboard posters for display. He sent graphic designers to Europe to study color printing and had the full-color ads that they made for IVORY preprinted and sent to magazines that previously had used color only on their covers. He commissioned well-known artists to paint babies and children for his ads, then offered reproductions suitable for framing. He called upon aspiring poets to enter a contest with prizes awarded for the best verses about IVORY soap for use in IVORY ads.

Having provided a marketing base for IVORY soap that would support it and related IVORY products for many years thereafter, Harley Proctor kept the resolution he had made as a young man to retire from business by age forty-five. Actually, he was only forty-four when he left Cincinnati to take up residence in his wife's home state of Massachusetts. Proctor had proved beyond any doubt the power of advertising and clever marketing. One can't help but wonder what might have happened if he had turned his talent and energy to other products, like tiddledeywinks, maybe, or jelly beans.

Bon Ami

The world's oldest chick still decorates the red and yellow BON AMI package with the slogan "Hasn't scratched yet." BON AMI, invented in 1886, has had its ups and downs in the face of competition from boldly advertised cleansers like MR. CLEAN and FANTASTICK, but BON AMI is enjoying a resurgence of popularity now as a gentle cleaner for surfaces like stainless steel, ceramic tile and porcelain.

Tide

If IVORY soap is an example of a Proctor & Gamble product that enjoyed a natural progression toward success, TIDE is one that came on the market only after the company had virtually guaranteed that it could not fail.

TIDE was made to be the answer to the prayer of everyone who dreamed of a detergent that would work in hard water and wouldn't leave a residue of curdlike foam in the washtub. After twenty years of research, P & G's experiments culminated in a combination of chemicals that literally dissolved dirt and grease in the wash water, truly getting clothes cleaner than any soap previously invented. The company's timing was particularly fortunate; the new product first appeared in 1946, just when every housewife in America was deciding she could not live without an automatic washing machine. TIDE was the forerunner of all the heavy-duty detergents that would compete for that market, a market that did not begin to decline until the late fifties when people began to be concerned about nonbiodegradable substances.

LYDIA PINKHAM

There's a face that haunts me ever,
There are eyes mine always meet
As I read the morning paper,
As I walk the crowded street.

Ah! She knows not how I suffer!
Hers is now a world-wide fame,
But 'til death that face shall greet me.
Lydia Pinkham is her name.

PERSONIFICATION THAT SHE WAS of nineteenth-century virtues, Lydia Pinkham would still have felt right at home in a gathering of modern

60

businesswomen. She might be something of a feminist today, for her belief that women suffered needlessly at the hands of doctors was the crux of the philosophy behind her product. She had a penchant for reform that led her from antislavery through a labyrinth of movements from temperance to the Greenback party, but none of these involvements distracted her from her commitment first to her family and, when her four children were old enough to look after themselves, to her business.

In Lynn, Massachusetts, where Lydia Pinkham lived, the story is told that during one of the few periods when her husband, Isaac Pinkham, was enjoying good financial credit, he endorsed a note for a machinist named George Clarkson Todd. When Todd defaulted, Pinkham paid twenty-five dollars on the note. As a token of his appreciation, Todd gave Pinkham the formula for a medicine purported to cure "female complaints" ranging from painful menstruation to prolapsed uterus.

Such remedies were not unusual in the mid-nineteenth century. Public distrust in orthodox medical practices had given rise to a wave of patent medicines including Oman's Boneset Pills, Vegetine and Hole's Honey of Horehound and Tar. Mrs. Pinkham was herself an advocate of the Sylvester Graham diet so highly revered by Dr. John Harvey Kellogg and Mother Ellen Harmon White, co-founders of the Battle Creek Health Sanitarium.

But it wasn't until the Pinkhams fell on severely hard times in 1875 that anyone seriously thought of capitalizing on the formula they'd been given for female complaints. Lydia had always kept a few bottles

of the mixture on hand. She gave some away to friends and occasionally, when pressed, would sell a small quantity. The day a party of ladies from Salem drove up to the house unannounced and asked for half a dozen bottles for which they were willing to pay five dollars, the Pinkhams began to realize the marketing possibilities for the cure.

LYDIA E. PINKHAM VEGETABLE COMPOUND

It was a family venture right from the start. Dan Pinkham, the most enterprising of the Pinkham children, became business manager. Lydia brewed the mixture on a stove in the cellar. Young Charles and Aroline Pinkham turned over their wages from other jobs to help pay for the alcohol and herbs. (The original formula called for life root, unicorn root, black cohosh, pleurisy root and fenugreek seed macerated and suspended in approximately 19

percent alcohol.) Lydia and another son, Will, worked up advertising copy and compiled a pamphlet called "Guide for Women." Even Isaac, patriarch of the Pinkham family, now enfeebled by illness and old age, contributed from his rocker. He folded and bundled the pamphlets for Dan to distribute.

Sarah Stage, in her book *Female Complaints*, tells how Dan and Will Pinkham went about drumming up trade:

Dan, who worked as a mail carrier, distributed the pamphlet on his rounds. Will joined him and together they covered the towns surrounding Lynn. Finally they tackled Boston. Riding into town on the ten-cent workingmen's train, they carried a few thousand circulars a day in knapsacks slung over their shoulders and worked door to door. Slowly their efforts began to pay off . . . but for a long time the Pinkhams counted themselves lucky if they could sell a bottle a day.

Dan Pinkham began to think in much broader marketing terms. In the spring of 1876 he packed a goatskin trunk full of circulars and set off for Brooklyn to sell the COMPOUND. He rented a two-dollar room on Willoughby Street, borrowed a pen and ink from the local post office to save money and set himself the task of planning a detailed marketing strategy. One of his ideas was to change the copy on the front page of the "Guide" to include the claim that PINKHAM'S remedy was good for kidney complaints. "About half the people out here are either troubled with Kidney Complaints or else they think they are," wrote Dan to his family back in Lynn. He wanted to be able to offer the pamphlet to men as well as women because, he shrewdly noted, "men have more money to spare these times than women." Brother Will followed his suggestion and soon copy headed "Weak and Diseased Kidneys" appeared alongside claims that the VEGETABLE COMPOUND cured uterine complaints.

Dan's imagination when it came to marketing was boundless, but most of his ideas, like the one to run a Pinkham poster the full length of the Brooklyn Bridge, cost more than the struggling company could afford. Not until Dan came up with the truly inspired idea of putting his mother's picture on playing cards to advertise the COMPOUND did any of his schemes really pay off. The picture was a stroke of genius. To look at Lydia herself, sagacious and composed in her best black silk and white lace fichu was to feel confidence. Her image in the ads seemed to confirm the credibility of the product. About six months after the cards began to appear, the

family refused an offer of $100,000 for the business and the new trademark.

Lydia Pinkham became a national figure. Her face was truly everywhere, in newspapers, magazines, drugstore displays. The Dartmouth Glee Club was the first, in the 1880's, to parody Lydia in song. Other college singing groups followed suit, embellishing the original lyrics with infinite ribald verses. The free advertising boosted sales of the product still further. By 1881 the COMPOUND was selling millions of bottles a year; profits for the Pinkhams amounted to almost $200,000 annually.

Unfortunately, Dan Pinkham did not live to enjoy the fruits of his labors on behalf of the family product. He died an untimely death of pneumonia in 1881. Will Pinkham died of consumption less than two months after his brother, at the age of twenty-eight. Their mother lived barely two years

longer, dying after a paralytic stroke at the age of sixty-four.

Lydia and her sons would never know of the countless investigations and tests done on the COMPOUND to determine its true efficacy or lack of it. By 1949 it was decided that the COMPOUND did indeed contain estrogenic material in appreciable quantities, though it was never clearly determined to which of the ingredients these properties could be attributed. (There was never any doubt about the "sedative effect," caused by the alcohol.) Folklore and ballad, meanwhile, served to keep alive the notion that, no matter what the scientists might say, the COMPOUND possessed mysterious potencies of inestimable value:

OH-H-H, we'll sing of Lydia Pinkham,
And her love of the Human Race.
How she sells her Vegetable
  Compound,
And the papers, the papers they publish,
  they publish, HER FACE!

AVON LADY/FULLER BRUSH MAN

AVON AND THE FULLER BRUSH Company both capitalized on the tradition of the Yankee peddler to stake their claims to fame and fortune. FULLER BRUSH, once a dyed-in-the-wool American institution, suffered a decline in profits when it lost the Number Two spot in in-home sales to TUPPERWARE during the 1960's. But today, under the aegis of Consolidated Foods, sales are up.

Avon is Number One in cosmetic sales nationwide and owns sixteen factories outside the United States. (It also owns Tiffany's on New York's Fifth Avenue.) There are about 440,000 AVON Ladies ringing doorbells from coast to coast (more than a million worldwide), selling not only cosmetics but also costume jewelry, perfumes, skin- and hand-care products, grooming preparations for men, lotions, soaps

and powder for babies, clothing for men and women and more!

The AVON story began during the 1880's when David H. McConnell was working as a door-to-door book salesman in upstate New York. It occurred to him that a housewife might be more inclined to open her door to him if he presented her with a free flacon of perfume before displaying his line of books. This strategy worked so well that many

AVON

doors were indeed opened to McConnell, and he soon figured out that he'd be better off selling the perfume rather than the books.

McConnell theorized that the housewives who so warmly welcomed the little gifts of scent did so partly because they were shy about buying perfume and cosmetics at the local pharmacy where it was considered unladylike to make such purchases for oneself. In 1886 McConnell, then twenty-eight years old, founded the California Perfume Company and put in an early plug for the feminist movement by staffing the sales force of the company solely with women.

The first AVON Lady hired by McConnell (though the company did not change its name to Avon until 1939) was Mrs. P.F.E. Albee, a widow from Winchester, New Hampshire, who started her chime-ringing career selling McConnell's Little Dot Perfume Set and recruited other women whom she trained as salespeople. She is credited with developing for McConnell's

company both the selling network that is the keystone of Avon today and the public image of the AVON Lady as a friendly neighbor.

The AVON Lady's counterpart in the door-to-door business, the FULLER BRUSH Man, originally fared very well. The first FULLER BRUSH Man was Alfred Carl Fuller who came to the United States from Nova Scotia in 1903 with combined assets of $75, a Bible, a needle and thread. In a rented room in Hartford, Connecticut, he stayed up late at night making small wire-and-bristle brushes that were exceedingly well suited to cleaning the nooks and crannies of late-nineteenth-century houses. In the daytime he sold the brushes door-to-door for fifty cents apiece. In 1909 his four-line want ad in the local paper brought such good response from prospective salesmen that Fuller was inspired to broaden the scope of his operation even more than he had originally planned.

In seventy-five years the business grew to include thousands of FULLER BRUSH Men operating independently across the country. The original line of twelve household brushes was expanded to

include a complete artillery of household cleaners and related products.

In the 1960's when record numbers of women hung up their brooms to enter or return to the marketplace, both Avon and Fuller Brush felt the impact on their sales figures. Avon responded by revising its product line, limiting territory size for more intensive selling and tripling its advertising. Lacking the capital to revitalize its marketing program, in 1968 Fuller Brush joined several other companies, including SARA LEE frozen foods and SHASTA beverages, under the wing of Consolidated Foods. Fuller Brush headquarters moved to Great Bend, Kansas, where three manufacturing plants were incorporated into one in a centralized location with greater access to all areas of the United States. Len Dunlap, president of the Fuller Brush Company in 1982, feels that the company is now well on its way to "regaining the Number One position in the direct-selling industry."

Facts About Avon Ladies in 1982

To join the ranks of AVON Ladies (more than one million strong internationally) a woman must pay a one-time franchise fee of $20, for which she receives a starter kit and an exclusive territory of some one hundred households. She sells within her territory from catalogs and samples, writes up orders and sends them to an AVON distribution center. When the saleswoman receives the order from AVON, she delivers it to the customer and collects payment. The AVON Lady receives a commission of approximately 40 percent on what she sells. It is estimated that most AVON Ladies take home about $1,900 a year.[1]

[1]Everybody's Business.

LISTERINE

INVENTED IN A SMALL laboratory in St. Louis by Dr. Joseph Lawrence, and named after Sir Joseph Lister who developed the first antiseptic, LISTERINE has been the world's best selling mouthwash for over one hundred years. LISTERINE was originally manufactured by the Lambert Pharmacal Company in St. Louis which later joined forces with the Warner Company to become Warner-Lambert.

During the 1940's and 1950's Lambert Pharmacal spared no expense on full-page ads in major magazines, usually offering a glimpse into a soap-operalike scenario. "Here comes Herb! For Pete's sake, duck!" is the hooker on one ad with an illustration showing two people lurking behind the living-room curtains as another one drops to the floor next to the window. The ad copy tells us that the schemers wait it out while unsuspecting Herb rings the doorbell furiously, then gives up and retreats to his car. Ann is obliged to explain to Chick that Herb "is an awfully nice fellow, a bachelor with some money, and, incidentally, he plays a swell game of bridge, but

he's 'that way.'" Eventually Chick gets the point as he watches Herb drive off, a social pariah with bad breath who has lost all hope of social acceptance. LISTERINE is the only possible solution to his problem.

At the time Warner and Lambert came together in the late fifties Elmer Holmes Bobst, an inventive executive of the Warner Company, decided to try something new in advertising LISTERINE. He capitalized on a widespread warning of a flu epidemic to advise the American public via full-page ads in *Life* to "see your doctor for flu shots, avoid crowds, and gargle twice a day with LISTERINE." The ad agency for Warner-Lambert made fun of Bobst's idea but ran it anyway. LISTERINE grossed an extra $26 million that year—and more in subsequent years. Though the company was ultimately compelled to spend $10 million in advertising the disclaimer that LISTERINE "will not prevent colds or sore throats or lessen their severity," the accompanying publicity and the effectiveness of the anticold-germ ads may have been worth the expense.

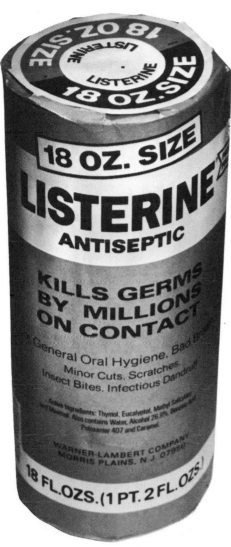

LISTERINE and its companion product LISTERMINT, on the market since 1976, account for more breath-freshener sales in the United States than any other single product.

EBERHARD FABER PENCILS

A NATIVE OF BAVARIA WHO CAME to New York as sales agent for a European pencil company, Eberhard Faber left his mark throughout the United States.

A few years of working for the European pencil company made it sharply clear to Faber that what America needed was its own pencil factory to free consumers from

dependence on Europe for their supply. In 1861 he opened his own mass-production pencil factory at Forty-second Street and the East River where the United Nations building now stands. With the help of Faber's brothers, whom he persuaded to leave Germany to join him, and later of his two sons, the new American pencil business prospered.

In 1900 Eberhard Faber introduced the pencil that represented the culmination of his commitment to quality materials and style. It was bright yellow and he called it THE MONGOL. It is said, somewhat apocryphally, that the name was inspired by the fondness of one of the Faber brothers for the soup *purée Mongol*. More likely, the name was chosen to suggest Siberian graphite, the highest-quality graphite for pencil leads at the time.

Though Eberhard Faber now makes pencils to match any office, home or school decor, only THE MONGOL is considered a classic.

WOODCLINCHED   U.S.A.   EF EBERHARD FABER   MONGOL 482   ②

LIPTON TEA

THOMAS JOHNSTONE LIPTON, son of a Scottish grocer, believed that "the more you sell, the more you make." Lipton became a millionaire at an early age by opening one grocery shop after another in Scotland, always pouring the money he made from each successful venture into the next enterprise. By the time he was forty years old he had made enough money to buy several tea plantations in Ceylon where, in 1890, they were for sale at bargain prices during a grave economic depression.

Lipton recovered his investment by wholesaling tea, first through his own shops in Britain, then in the United States where he soon captured most of the market with his convenient half-pound and quarter-pound boxes.

The tea bag was a strictly American idea, the ingenious invention not of Lipton but of a New York merchant named Sullivan who sent samples of his teas to his favorite customers in bags made of silk (not so expensive in 1909). Sullivan's customers in the restaurant trade demanded more bags, but not as samples. They realized the extraordinary convenience of the little porous packages for making a single cup of tea.

In 1920 Thomas Lipton began to compete with Sullivan for a piece of the tea-bag business. At first he made and sold them only to hotels and other institutions. But demand for them increased rapidly as homemakers who had discovered the tea bags in restaurants clamored for them to use in their own homes. In 1929 Lipton, who was now *Sir Thomas*, introduced in retail grocery stores a lithographed "gold" tin containing fifteen hand-tied gauze tea bags. The tin remained a popular item in the Lipton line even when a wider variety of package sizes diffused the demand for this more expensive container.

Six years after Sir Thomas Lipton's death in 1937, Lipton's American company enlarged its international connections by becoming part of the Anglo-Dutch–owned Unilever group of companies based in London. The American company remains headquartered in New Jersey, however, where it has diversified into marketing not only tea but also SUNKIST orange juice, soups, noodles and condiments "to make almost anything taste better."

COCA-COLA

THOUGH COCA-COLA IS THE world's best-known trademarked product, no one really knows what its creator, pharmacist John Styth Pemberton, hoped to accomplish when he invented it. Evidence is conflicting as to whether his goal was strictly a soft drink to be dispensed at soda fountains, a palatable tonic for headaches or a combination of the two.

According to Coca-Cola Company sources, Pemberton's utensils for making his concoction were a brass or iron kettle and a boat oar. When, during the month of May 1886, he decided he had enough of it ready for market, he decanted a few jugsful from his kettle and, at the suggestion of his bookkeeper, Frank Robinson, who designed a label for the jugs, the new brew was named COCA-COLA.

Pemberton took the first jug of COCA-COLA syrup along to the most centrally located of four new soda fountains in Atlanta. He offered it to Willis E. Venable who operated the fountain in the pharmacy of Dr. Joseph Jacobs at the corner of Peachtree and Marietta streets. Venable sampled the mixture and approved. He agreed to sell it mixed with plain water for five cents a glass as an alternative to ginger ale and root beer. One day, probably in early 1887, Willis mistakenly added carbonated instead of plain water on a call for COCA-COLA. The customer was delighted. Word of the zesty new combination spread quickly and increased sales soon reflected the drink's rise in popularity.

John Pemberton was enough of a businessman to know the value of advertising. He invested his limited assets in point-of-sales signs, ads in the Atlanta newspapers and dozens of complimentary drinks offered upon presentation of a "sampling" ticket. At the end of COCA-COLA's first year, Pemberton noted that with modest help from a handful of investors, he had spent $73.96 on advertising but had sold only fifty gallons of syrup at a dollar a gallon. He had no inkling of the future that awaited his product and two years later, in failing health, he sold shares of interest in COCA-COLA to business acquaintances in Atlanta.

Over a three-year period the Pemberton business changed hands quickly until it was in the possession of another Atlanta pharmacist, Asa Briggs Candler. From personal experience, Candler thought highly of COCA-COLA as a cure for headaches and dyspepsia. He also had good instincts about the syrup's other possibilities. Candler lost no time in forming the Coca-Cola Company as a Georgia corporation and by 1893 he had registered COCA-COLA as a trademark. His manufacturing facilities were limited to a fifteen-hundred-gallon wooden tank and a one-hundred-gallon copper kettle set up in a rambling old mansion not far from the birthplace of COCA-COLA. The formula and precise ingredients of the mixture were known only to Candler and his associate, the bookkeeper Frank Robinson. Though some part of the coca plant

may once have been part of the magic recipe, the facts about this are shrouded in mystery. The formula for COCA-COLA is passed on from one management to the next in the company by word of mouth. Even today it is one of the most closely guarded secrets in American industry.

Candler dispatched teams of men across the country to show druggists what to do with a keg of COCA-COLA. And he did not stint on advertising. Signs appeared on barns from coast to coast. Souvenir fans, serving trays, calendars, clocks and countless other merchandising items turned up everywhere to remind people to drink COKE. By 1895 COCA-COLA was on sale in every state and territory in the Union and, by 1898, in Canada, Hawaii and Mexico as well.

Though other people were beginning to contemplate broader sales for COCA-COLA through bottling, Candler remained convinced that the future of COCA-COLA would continue to be at the soda fountain. When in 1899 Benjamin Franklin Thomas and Joseph B. Whitehead came from Chattanooga with the goal of persuading Candler to give them the rights to bottle COCA-COLA on a large scale, Candler remained skeptical but granted the two lawyers the rights they sought. Thomas and Whitehead went back to Chattanooga elated. The agreement they had reached with Candler entitled them to bottle COCA-COLA syrup and carbonated water and to ship it to distributors all over the United States. It was a unique marketing concept, but one for which the country was ready in 1899, with its improved systems of communication and transportation. The next step was the actual franchising of COKE through the sale of rights to additional bottlers in every part of America in return for the bottler's agreement to make the investment in resources and effort necessary to carry out his share of the bargain. In the following decade, 379 bottling plants came into operation and throve.

As COCA-COLA moved into the twentieth century, virtually everyone agreed that it needed a distinctive bottle design, one that, as Ben Thomas used to say, "a person could recognize as a COCA-COLA bottle when he feels it in the dark." There was too much variation in the current COKE bottles. They came in different colors and shapes from different parts of the country. By 1915 the company had found a solution: a classic contour design conceived by Alexander Samuelson, a Swedish glassblower who had emigrated to Terre Haute, Indiana. Many years later the graceful bottle design itself would be registered as a trademark of the Coca-Cola Company—the second package in America to be given this distinction. (The HEINZ ketchup bottle was the first.)

About the time the new bottle appeared, in 1916, Asa Candler had become so involved in the affairs of the city of Atlanta that he decided to step down as president of Coca-Cola to serve as mayor. Three years later, Candler family members who had received shares of Asa's stock when he retired decided, without consulting him, to sell to a group headed by Georgia financier Ernest Woodruff. The price was $25 million. It was the largest financial transaction ever to take place in the South.

Ernest Woodruff was well qualified to lead the Coca-Cola Company into the future, but he was unfortunate in entering the picture just as postwar inflation pushed the price of sugar up 400 percent. Battles ensued with bottlers over the fixed prices in their contracts while a deteriorating sales force caused sales to drop drastically. Ernest Woodruff decided the time had come to bring in a younger man at the helm of the Coca-Cola Company. He chose his son, Robert, then thirty-three years old. In a variety of ways, mostly based on his personal concept of Coca-Cola's obligation to cater to the needs of COCA-COLA's customers and through massive advertising efforts, Woodruff pulled the company out of its temporary slough and set it back on the road to even greater triumphs.

COCA-COLA's place in American life was ensured forever during World War II. Woodruff himself declared immediately after the Japanese attack on Pearl Harbor, "We will see that every man in uniform gets a bottle of Coca-Cola for 5¢ wherever he is and whatever it costs." General Dwight D. Eisenhower backed him up with a telegram dated June 29, 1943, requesting sufficient machinery to operate COCA-COLA bottling plants as close as possible to ten major battlefronts. These became the forerunners of sixty-four others set up in Europe and the Pacific during World War II.

Until the mid-fifties COCA-COLA was the company's one product, available in the six-and-a-half-ounce bottle or in a glass at the fountain. Since 1955 COKE has been sold in several larger bottles, in plastic bottles and cans and from every conceivable type of vending machine.

In the 1960's and 1970's the Coca-Cola Company spread out still further to produce more soft drinks, including TAB, FRESCA, MR. PIBB and MELLO YELLO. Through its acquisitions, Coca-Cola has ventured into the areas of citrus drinks, wine, water-pollution-control equipment, seawater desalters, disposable plastic items, bottled water and, most recently, the entertainment business (Columbia Pictures). Its closest competitor in soft drinks, PEPSI, actually owns more bottling plants than Coca-Cola (and more fast-food outlets than McDONALD'S) but, in spite of a variety of aggressive marketing techniques, has never managed to nudge COCA-COLA out of the Number One spot as America's favorite soft drink.

Unwilling to admit that even the sky is the limit, Coca-Cola has begun to think about bottling franchises on the moon. It was, after all, this indomitable organization that greeted the astronauts returning from their moon flight with a sign in Times Square flashing WELCOME BACK TO EARTH, HOME OF COCA-COLA. When the first billboard goes up in outer space, it's not hard to imagine what the message will be.

1880-1905   1889-1894   1887-1895   1889-1910   1906-1910   1910-1916   1916-1920

HEINZ KETCHUP

WE TEND TO THINK OF KETCHUP as a relatively recent American invention, associated perhaps with fast food. In fact, ketchup is neither recent nor American in origin, except as it is known to most of us in the familiar narrow-necked bottle designed for Henry J. Heinz's particular version of an age-old recipe.

In *Foods of the Western World*, Theodora Fitzgibbons likens ketchup to a Roman relish called *garum* or *liquamen* made from a brine of pickled fish flavored with vinegar, oil or pepper: "Several towns were famous for their factory-made *garum* and in the ruins of Pompeii a small jar was found bearing the inscription, 'Best strained *liquamen*. From the factory of Umbricus Agathopus.'"

The Oxford English Dictionary bears out Mrs. Fitzgibbons's contention that ketchup has been around longer than we realize. The *Dictionary* notes a reference to *koe-chiap* or *ke-tsiap* in China as early as 1690. There is further evidence that late in the seventeenth century English seamen discovered natives

of Singapore using a tangy sauce of this name to enhance the flavor of fish and fowl. Back in their homeland, the English tried to imitate the subtle blend of fish brine, herbs and spices they had enjoyed in the Orient. In the absence of many of the Eastern ingredients, they substituted mushrooms, walnuts, cucumbers and tomatoes. The results must have been satisfying because in her *Housekeeper's Pocketbook* published in 1748, the Julia Child of that era, a lady known as Mrs. Harrison, counseled homemakers never to be without the pungent condiment.

Sometime around the middle of the nineteenth century ketchup made with a tomato base became a staple of the English kitchen. In 1841 Charles Dickens in *Barnaby Rudge* smacked his lips over "lamb chops breaded with plenty of ketchup," and Lord Byron sang the praises of the rich, red sauce in his poem "Beppo," published about the same time.

By this time American seafarers who had traveled to the Far East or England had developed a taste for

the condiment too. Like the English, American cooks experimented with the ingredients. Cookbooks of this period list recipes for as many as a dozen different kinds of ketchup, some featuring oysters, others gooseberries or grapes and, quite infrequently, tomatoes. (Writer Florence Fabricant points out in an article about ketchup in *Americana* magazine that before the 1820's tomatoes were cultivated strictly for ornamental purposes because they were thought to be poisonous.)

Mariners from Maine who had been to Mexico or the West Indies were, apparently, the first to know the flavor value of a zesty tomato. It was they who ventured to plant tomato seeds in the rocky soil of the Northeast so they could make ketchup to enjoy on their codfish cakes, baked beans and meat.

But making ketchup at home required long hours of stirring over a hot fire, with careful attention not to let it stick or burn. Henry J. Heinz, who had set up a company to make a horseradish condiment in 1869, recognized an opportunity to expand

1920–1939   1939   1940–1944   1944–

his market and save the American housewife hours of labor by manufacturing a product for which there was a growing demand.

The recipe Heinz devised, now generally considered the standard by which good ketchup is judged, calls for fresh ripe tomatoes (grown especially for Heinz), natural sweetener, salt, onion powder, spices and natural flavorings—all boiled to a dense, slow-pouring thickness. Originally Heinz probably used sugar instead of natural sweetener and onions instead of onion powder. Otherwise the recipe is the same today as it was in 1876. The Heinz people take pride in reporting that their ketchup is sold all over the world and nowhere is the recipe altered in any way to appeal to the taste of a particular country.

Like COKE and CRAYOLA crayons, HEINZ ketchup had the good fortune to meet the American consumer in a container so well designed that it has become a classic. In the late 1800's, a package's usefulness was more important than its appearance. Shapes of containers were frequently determined by the use for which they were intended. Because ketchup is a pourable substance, Heinz packed it in clear-glass, long-necked bottles with "shoulders" you could get a good grip on to shake the ketchup out. Virtually the only changes that have been made in the basic bottle design are the addition of screw caps in the 1890's to replace corks and wax and, during the same period, the alteration of the shape of the bottle to make it almost imperceptibly octagonal. The Heinz Company felt this design was less ornate and easier to handle than the sharply ridged design of the earlier HEINZ bottle.

Today the H. J. Heinz Company makes many more than the fifty-seven varieties of products it was famous for at the turn of the century. WEIGHT WATCHERS, STAR-KIST and 9 LIVES are all Heinz brands, but ketchup sells better than any of them: three hundred million bottles each year. That's almost one and a half bottles per U.S. citizen!

MR.
PEANUT
®

PLANTERS PEANUTS

No one seems to know why or by whom Amedeo Obici was sent by ship to New York City at the age of twelve, penniless, ignorant of the English language and with no one to meet him when he arrived. He knew that somewhere in the United States he had an uncle, but no arrangement had been made to bring the two together. Only by persistent effort and ingenuity did Amedeo finally manage to reach his relative in Scranton, Pennsylvania.

The uncle agreed to let his nephew stay with him in exchange for a certain number of hours of service at the family fruit stand: unloading and carrying crates, selling and delivering merchandise. It was hard work, especially in combination with going to school and struggling with a new language.

After a year, Amedeo decided to simplify his life. "I quit school," he told an interviewer some years later. "I quit because it was dull and I was bored. All I could understand was arithmetic and I understood more arithmetic than they were teaching."

He continued to work for his uncle for a while, then moved on to work for bigger fruit merchants in nearby Pittston and Wilkes Barre.

In 1896, at the age of nineteen, he started his own business. In Wilkes Barre he opened a fruit stand, the major feature of which was not the fruit but a peanut roaster, representing an investment by Obici of $4.50.

"The trouble with that roaster and all the other roasters of that time," Obici later said, "was that you had to keep turning them by hand so the peanuts wouldn't burn. So I spent about a year developing a device with pulleys that would turn the roaster automatically."

Obici also experimented with salting the nuts to perk up their flavor and adding a chocolate

coating to occasional batches. He soon had the automatic roaster working perfectly and was ready to advertise his product. He put up a sign saying OBICI, THE PEANUT SPECIALIST. Customers came from all over Pennsylvania to sample the unscorched, salted peanuts and to see the equipment used to produce them.

Amedeo Obici devoted increasingly more time to peanuts and less to fruit until, in 1906, he abandoned fruits entirely and, in partnership with another immigrant from Italy, Mario Peruzzi, formed the Planters Nut and Chocolate Company which eventually became

part of Standard Brands, now merged with Nabisco to form Nabisco Brands, Inc.

Right from the beginning, the Planters Nut and Chocolate Company prospered far beyond its founders' wildest dreams. Part of the reason dated back to the Civil War. Although the peanut had been available in America since the early eighteenth century, for many years it was well known only in Virginia where most peanuts were grown. When Union and Confederate forces converged on Virginia in the 1860's, thousands of soldiers from all over the nation tasted peanuts for the first time.

Showman P. T. Barnum also played a role in the peanut boom. He sold peanuts in glassine bags for a nickel apiece at each performance of his circus. As the circus

flourished in the 1880's and 1890's, so did PLANTERS peanuts.

By the time Planters made its peanuts available in the marketplace, consumers were waiting for them eagerly. The first Planters office/factory was a two-story loft rented for twenty-five dollars a month in Wilkes Barre. There were eight employees including the two partners. In less than a year the new business outgrew its quarters and had to be moved to a four-story building. The Planters product line had expanded to include peanut bars, chocolate nut bars, peanut rolls and walnut bars. Business continued to improve so fast that soon the company was compelled to move again, right into the heart of peanut country. A processing plant for raw peanuts was established in Suffolk, Virginia,

where eventually it was enlarged to cover seventy-six acres.

During the busy early days of PLANTERS peanuts, partners Obici and Peruzzi were eager to find new ways to promote their product and burnish the PLANTERS image. In 1916 they offered a prize for the best piece of art suitable for use as the company trademark. The winning design, by a schoolboy, was an animated peanut. Later a commercial artist took the peanut figure, added a top hat, monocle and cane, and Mr. Peanut was born.

The debonair gentleman, usually depicted leaning on his cane with legs crossed nonchalantly, has remained for the years since 1916 the universal emblem for PLANTERS products—and one of the most successful commercial symbols ever designed.

SHREDDED WHEAT

JUST ABOUT THE TIME AMEDEO Obici was arriving at his uncle's farm in Scranton, a Denver lawyer named Henry Perky was en route by train to Watertown, New York, to enlist a friend, William Ford, in a new undertaking.

Perky, who had always preferred inventing to pleading cases in court, was, at the age of forty-seven, in search of a method for processing corn so it would remain edible after being dehydrated. During his Watertown experiments he developed a machine that could press wheat into shredlike strips.

When baked, these strips became delicious biscuits.

After naming the biscuits SHREDDED WHEAT, Perky returned to Denver where he plunged into the SHREDDED WHEAT business with an enthusiasm he had never displayed for law.

The initial batch of SHREDDED WHEAT biscuits had emerged from the Watertown oven in late 1892. By the autumn of 1893 Perky was operating a small bakery in Denver to make them, a restaurant to serve them in various shapes and sizes—there was even a mashed-potato

version—and a fleet of wagons from which to sell them door to door.

One employee, taking note of the rapid and sustained increase in sales, told Perky one day, "This looks as if the business is growing."

"Sir," Perky replied with a characteristically expansive gesture, "this is but a playhouse compared to what this business will be in the future!"

His faith in the new product turned out to be justified. As Perky moved quickly into regional, then national distribution, he was compelled to move into ever larger

Mainstay of the Family

Men of responsibility seldom realize that their own health is their first responsibility to their wives, their children, and their dependents.

In guiding your husband's diet you are guarding his health. Fortunately there is a food that combines every needed element that the human system must have to work at its fullest efficiency. That food is Shredded Wheat.

Delightfully combines the *bran, vitamines, proteins, carbohydrates and mineral salts* of the Whole Wheat Grain in little loaves of nut-brown crispness.

Ready to eat and easy to serve, covered with milk and sweetened to taste, or smothered in cream and your favorite fruit. Provide your provider with the food for success.

Make It a Daily Habit

SHREDDED WHEAT

THE SHREDDED WHEAT COMPANY, NIAGARA FALLS,

and larger facilities. Finally, faced with the question of whether to have many small manufacturing centers or one large one, he decided to consolidate all his operations on a ten-acre site in Niagara Falls, New York. He put up a $2 million "air-conditioned" plant there, decked it out in marble, tile and glass and called it, not entirely without justification, the "Palace of Light." In May of 1901 the plant began turning out biscuits within sound of the mighty falls.

The plant proved to be a Perky stroke of genius. So magnificent was it by turn-of-the-century standards that each year it was visited by more than a thousand wide-eyed tourists, many of whom were instantly converted into SHREDDED WHEAT customers. In the plant's guest book a visitor from Philadelphia praised the factory as one that "considers the comfort and welfare of the employees as well as dividends to the stockholders." Industrialist-politician Mark Hanna wrote: "A

model establishment and worthy of imitation."

The acquisition in 1928 of the Shredded Wheat Company by the National Biscuit Company turned out to be a precedent-setting event. It marked National Biscuit's entry into the ready-to-eat cereal business and signaled a move toward diversification that few other companies were prepared at that time to make.

From *The History of Nabisco Brands, Inc.* by Melvin J. Grayson.

QUAKER OATS

THERE IS AMUSING IRONY IN THE fact that Quaker Oats, giant of the hot-cereal business, baker of cookies for the Girl Scouts and well known today for its commitment to Quaker traditions of peace and harmony, was, in its early days, a company nearly torn asunder by disagreement and plays for power. The problem was not only an unfortunate combination of personalities but a conflict of nineteenth- and twentieth-century concepts of business objectives.

Ferdinand Schumacher, a native of Hanover, Germany, who had followed a wave of his countrymen to America in 1850, had by 1875 made a sizable fortune as a miller in Ohio. He was the first to market a brand of oats for human use and he soon developed a method of extending his business beyond his own doorstep. He sold oats by mail order, and as demand for his product increased with each influx

of German, Scottish and Irish immigrants, Schumacher filled larger and larger orders from grocery wholesalers on tight credit terms of thirty to ninety days. Schumacher liked to have a full year of orders booked by September so he would know how much of the new oat crop to buy and when to schedule grinding and deliveries.

Eighteen eighty-six was a milestone year for Schumacher. At the beginning of that year, his mill in Akron, Ohio, was producing 360,000 pounds of oatmeal a day. Only a few months later, fire destroyed Schumacher's empire, leaving him uninsured and crippled with debts. He vowed he "would live on as best he could," from the output of two small mills in other locations, but even Schumacher must have realized that times had changed too much for that. An era of mergers had begun: Schumacher was up against the growing trend

1877

toward monopoly, pooling of resources, national marketing and technological advance which would mark the early years of the twentieth century and generate the fortunes of America's great industrialists.

Henry Parsons Crowell, Schumacher's nearest and most energetic competitor, was the first to try to capitalize on Schumacher's disaster. He and his product, QUAKER OATS, were familiar to Schumacher by virtue of an aggressive marketing campaign of Crowell's which led to very successful sales of Crowell's oats, put up in two-pound measures and sealed in cardboard boxes with explicit cooking directions on the side. The QUAKER package displayed a picture of a lean, solemn-looking gentleman holding in his hand a scroll that proclaimed the word "Pure." Crowell, who was a genius in the annals of American marketing, had already done a good job of trading on all the implications of the Quaker religion in association with his product and had advertised QUAKER OATS in every major newspaper sold in cities where there were large populations of German, Scottish and Irish immigrants. Crowell's marketing talent and Schumacher's experience may have seemed like the keys to a great partnership, but the two men were worlds apart in outlook.

In the year preceding Schumacher's fire, Crowell and another miller, Robert Stuart of Cedar Rapids, Iowa, and Chicago, had organized a voluntary association of grain processors—which had failed because Schumacher, alone, refused to support it. With Schumacher now unable to dominate the industry, Crowell and Stuart undertook

1946

1957

QUAKER

1970

another merging of milling interests. What eventually evolved was the American Cereal Company, an operating company with seven component members. The lion's share of the stock, and voting control, went to Schumacher, who was not about to let himself be dethroned by men who, he maintained, knew less about the business than he did. He immediately exercised his authority by installing himself as president. Crowell became vice-president and general manager. Stuart was the secretary-treasurer. Schumacher was on top, and there he stubbornly stayed through the next seven years as the company changed and grew—almost in spite of him— until, when he was seventy-three, Stuart and Crowell and their supporters finally succeeded in buying him out.

One can imagine how blustery old Schumacher rumbled and roared against what he believed to be the total foolishness of Crowell's marketing schemes. As Crowell's goal became that of keeping the QUAKER name constantly before the public by means of billboards, ads, booths at fairs, gold letters spelling QUAKER Rolled White Oats glued to grocery-store windows and doors, Schumacher deplored every penny in cost to the company.

Every device of the advertiser's art was used by American Cereal Company between 1890 and 1896. Techniques later men claim to have innovated were tested by Crowell as early as 1893. In his ads he appealed to love, pride, cosmetic satisfactions, sex, marriage, good health, cleanliness, safety, labor-saving, and status-seeking. His boldness, at the height of prudish Victorianism, reached its peak in 1898 in an advertisement in *Birds* magazine

76 and several other periodicals of the day. The illustration was a voluptuous, bare-breasted girl, her torso draped in Roman style, sitting on a Quaker Oats box. The caption under this display—respectable by reason of its classic tone—

Ceres, fair goddess of the harvest fields, Now to the world her choicest treasure yields.[1]

Before and after Schumacher's time with Quaker Oats, Crowell kept coming up with "firsts." Not only was he the first food processor to present his product in a distinctive, four-color printed package, he also offered miniature reproductions of the carton for house-to-house sampling. Crowell was the first to think of using the space on packages to tell the housewife how best to deal with the product she had just purchased and how else to use it, if she'd run out of ideas herself. As a result, each time the clever housewife invested in a box of oatmeal she received a free complement of recipes not only for breakfast porridge but also for fried pudding, pancakes, Quaker bread and other homely treats.

Another of Crowell's innovative "firsts" was the buying of "blind" ads in newspapers—paid space which he devoted to engaging stories thinly disguised as news, in which Quaker Oats saved the day. Nor was Crowell above using bits of doggerel in his newspaper promotions, always with the hope of engaging the attention of some curious reader:

[1] Arthur F. Marquette, "The Story of The Quaker Oats Company," from *Brands, Trademarks and Good Will* (New York: McGraw-Hill, 1967).

When breakfast's called
    In cheery notes
I eat my dish
    of Quaker Oats.

Crowell's ingenuity soon extended to introducing the packaged premium in a box of Quaker Oats. The earliest lure was one piece in a set of dishes. Repeated purchases were required, and much swapping among friends, to collect the entire series. This ploy was so successful that the supplier of the chinaware had to build twelve new kilns to keep up with the Quaker orders. Other premiums, including spoons, kitchen gadgets, coupons redeemable for double boilers, or cash reductions on the purchase price of other Quaker products all led toward the ultimate Crowell goal—making Quaker Oats a national institution.

One of the most ingenious marketing schemes from Quaker Oats was the brainchild, in 1955, of professional ad man Bruce Baker who had been given the assignment of thinking up an appealing premium that would attract customers without costing the company too much. Baker came up with a scheme for capitalizing on every 1950's kid's fascination with Sergeant Preston and his dog, Yukon King. Why not, mused Baker, offer a miniature deed in every box of Puffed Wheat or Puffed Rice, entitling the bearer to one square inch of land in Sergeant Preston's own Yukon Territory? The company loved the idea. Baker, a Quaker representative and an attorney flew to the Yukon to check out the real-estate possibilities. They selected a 19.11-acre plot on the Yukon River that was mostly ice and bought it for

$10,000. After risking their lives to survey their newly acquired property, they laboriously found their way home and made their report. Quaker's marketing committee approved the Big Inch promotion and eventually 21 million deeds were dispatched in Puffed Wheat and Puffed Rice boxes. A persistent collector later wrote to the company claiming he had collected 10,800 deeds which he reckoned represented a piece of land seventy-five-feet square. He wished to consolidate his holdings into one piece. The company lawyers were compelled to explain to him that it was unlikely that even two of the inch bits were contiguous and it would be difficult to find any that were because names and addresses of the other owners were not known to the company!

In the years between 1918 and 1968 Quaker's sales had advanced only just past the $500 million mark, indicating to Quaker management that it was time to follow the example of other companies that had gone on acquisition sprees during the 1960's. In 1969 Quaker bought Fisher-Price, the nation's largest maker of preschool toys; Magic Pan, a San Francisco-based restaurant chain specializing in crêpes, and Celeste, a small frozen-pizza company. In 1972 they acquired Needlecraft Corporation of America, maker of yarns and needlecraft kits.

Quaker has another top seller, called furfural. It's a chemical by-product of oats, made from the hulls. Furfural and its derivatives have many uses, the most notable one being that of a solvent in oil refining. Furfural makes more money for Quaker than oatmeal.

During the seventies the Quaker

Company symbol had become a stylized, abstract rendering of the QUAKER Man trademark. In 1982, for a few months, QUAKER OATS boxes once again featured the solemn little QUAKER Man with the scroll that says "Pure," framed by sprigs of golden oats and other graphic touches more evocative of the turn-of-the-century than of modern times. It seemed that the corporation's image makers were trying during this short period of commemoration to reestablish some connection with those years of inventiveness that captured everyone's interest in QUAKER OATS and led millions of Americans, if not to a taste for hot cereal, at least to an affectionate regard for the company that makes it.

AUNT JEMIMA PANCAKES

EVEN TODAY, NEARLY ONE hundred years after her first appearance as the personification of southern hospitality, there must be thousands of people who believe that an ageless black woman named Jemima still travels the countryside, telling stories of her childhood as a slave in the South, smiling warmly and flipping pancakes all the while.

Several black women have thus demonstrated pancake mix, but they weren't named Jemima. Nancy Green was the first one. She was hired in 1893 on a lifetime contract by R. T. Davis, a flour miller in St. Joseph, Missouri, to promote ready-mix pancake flour made by a small company he had recently bought. But the story of AUNT JEMIMA goes back before that.

It was a former newspaperman named Chris Rutt and his partner, Charles Underwood, who first had the idea for a ready-mix pancake flour. In an attempt to improve their financial situation, Rutt and Underwood had bought a small mill called the Pearl Milling Company in St. Joseph. They soon realized that in order for their business venture to pay off, they'd have to come up with a product the local competition didn't offer. What, they pondered, does almost everyone like to eat that would consume a lot of flour? Pancakes. But they're tricky to make, one of the partners mused, and it's hard to get two batches to turn out the same. Then it dawned on them that they would make a fortune if they could produce self-rising flour that would yield perfect pancakes every time. After weeks of trial and error, the young entrepreneurs hit on a combination of ingredients that worked.

The first commercial batch of packaged pancake flour was put up in paper sacks with no trade name. One evening months later, Rutt went along to the local vaudeville house and watched a pair of blackface comedians, Baker & Farrell, perform a jazzy, rhythmic New Orleans-style cakewalk to a tune called "Aunt Jemima." Baker performed in the apron and red bandanna headcover that was the official uniform of the traditional southern cook.

Here was the image Rutt wanted his product to suggest! He appropriated the name of the cakewalk number for his pancake flour, as well as the likeness of the southern "mammy" on the lithographed posters advertising the Baker & Farrell act.

Though their product was now ready for the marketplace, Rutt and his partner lacked the capital to advertise it properly. Eventually Rutt was obliged to go back to his newspaper job, and Underwood went to work for the R. T. Davis Milling Company, the largest flour miller in town. After meeting Underwood, R. T. Davis took an interest in the AUNT JEMIMA product and decided to add the small company to his chain of milling investments.

The first thing he did as owner of the company was to improve the flavor and texture of the product. Then he simplified the ready-mix principle by adding powdered milk. Now all the housewife had to add was water. Davis had perfected the first packaged ready-mix. It was a huge breakthrough. He knew it, and he had the funds and the talent to put behind it. Davis was a master promoter. It was he who envisioned a living AUNT JEMIMA to advertise his product. He asked all his food-broker friends to help him find a black woman who would exemplify the good southern cook and could demonstrate with winning poise and charm all the best features of the incredible package mix. This was a dynamic concept: to bring a trademark to life! Scores of advertisers have used it ever since.

The search for a living AUNT JEMIMA led Davis to Nancy Green, an attractive and personable woman who happened to be a fine cook. Davis presented her for the first time at the Chicago World's Fair of 1893. According to Arthur P. Marquette, historian for the Quaker Oats Company, which would later acquire the Aunt Jemima business, Miss Green's pancake demonstration proved almost as gala as the Midway's flamboyant belly dancer, Little Egypt.

Purd Wright, who had personally tested and approved the first AUNT JEMIMA pancake ever made, was appointed AUNT J's ad manager. He devised a souvenir lapel button to pass out to visitors who came to see her. It bore the likeness of AUNT JEMIMA with the caption I'SE IN TOWN, HONEY. The phrase became a catchline wherever AUNT J traveled.

After the fair, Davis published a souvenir booklet entitled *The Life of Aunt Jemima, the Most Famous Colored Woman in the World.* There were demonstrations in grocery stores from coast to coast and boxtop premium campaigns offering AUNT JEMIMA rag dolls in exchange for one trademark off the carton and twenty-five cents. This promotion was so successful that soon almost every city child in America had an AUNT JEMIMA doll. Eventually a whole family of dolls emerged, featuring Uncle Mose and twin moppets, Diana and Wade.

After the death of R. T. Davis in 1900, the AUNT JEMIMA business had its ups and downs. During World War I, the government restricted the domestic use of wheat flour and the AUNT J management was obliged to sell a blend of flours that turned out to be unacceptable to the public. A new advertising campaign was mounted by James Webb Young, manager of the J.

From the collection of Marguerite Ross Barnett

An example of a series of advertisements that presented Aunt Jemima as a jolly servant beaming with pleasure as she basked in compliments on her wonderful pancakes, this ad appeared in *The Ladies' Home Journal* in 1910. Aunt Jemima's male counterpart in product promotion via stereotypic images of blacks was Rastus, who appeared cheerfully obsequious in hundreds of CREAM OF WHEAT ads.

Walter Thompson Company in Chicago. This new series of ads featured episodes from the life of AUNT JEMIMA. One ad, handsomely illustrated by N. C. Wyeth and reproduced in four colors, carried the heading "The Night the Emily Dunstand Burned." It showed AUNT JEMIMA looking dismayed as she watched a Mississippi riverboat burn to the level of the water. The text of the ad told how grateful passengers found their way ashore to her cabin where AUNT J greeted them with platefuls of pancakes. Another ad, entitled "The Visitors from the North," showed four enterprising gentlemen making their way to AUNT JEMIMA's door to negotiate with her for her famous pancake recipe.

Young's imaginative ads pulled the company away from the brink of disaster on which the business often seemed to hover after Davis's death. Then in 1920, when the commodity market collapsed, the trade refused delivery on commitments made at

higher price levels. The company had to write off millions in losses, draining off all its working capital. Six years later the Quaker Oats Company stepped into the breach. With Quaker's marketing resources behind it, the annual volume of AUNT JEMIMA business soon exceeded that of any year before.

Though the AUNT JEMIMA brand name fared well under Quaker ownership, sales of pancake flour, like all foods of marginal necessity, suffered during the Depression. Quaker decided that the way to revive public interest was to bring AUNT J back to life in an exciting contemporary background. Want ads in the Chicago newspapers brought hundreds of hopefuls. One stood out among the rest. Her name was Anna Robinson. She weighed 350 pounds and had the face of an angel. Quaker signed her up, and like her predecessor, she stayed on the company payroll until her death, which occurred in 1951.

As Quaker ventured further into the packaged-food field with the AUNT JEMIMA brand name they met with qualified success. AUNT JEMIMA's magic made no dent on the cake-mix market, but she led the company into the frozen-food business with crisp, brown waffles ready to eat after a minute in the toaster. Frozen corn sticks followed in the 1960's, then cinnamon twists, more toaster products and hot breads. By the late 1960's Quaker's investment in AUNT JEMIMA had paid off many times over.

Though there is no longer an official AUNT JEMIMA authorized by the Quaker Oats Company, various clones of her exist—in commercials and, as waitresses, in the restaurants that make up the AUNT JEMIMA franchise. In most cases there is scant resemblance to the earlier AUNT JEMIMAs, but the spirit of the jolly black woman somehow endures, in all its various incarnations.

JOHNSON'S WAX

"IF ALL THE PASTE WAX PRODUCED by Johnson's every year were filled in one-pound cans and the cans placed side by side, you could walk on a row of wax cans from the city of Racine, Wisconsin, to Cleveland, Ohio."

That staggering piece of information appeared in the September 1952 edition of the Johnson in-house journal. Today a walk on a row of wax cans from

Racine might take you somewhat closer to Toledo.

Times and flooring materials have changed since 1952 and, as the Johnson Wax Company knows very well, the American woman does not worry as much about "waxy yellow buildup" as she did thirty years ago. Though the company is known as Johnson Wax, it has, since the early seventies, moved in directions as diverse as sports equipment and

personal-care products—an area in which they have experienced both failure (CRAZY LEGS shaving gel for women, US deodorant) and success (AGREE, "Helps stop the greasies").

Still, as its advertising used to stress, there are at least one hundred uses for paste wax, and whenever there's a good mahogany bar top to shine up, a fine wood carving or an antique picture frame to polish, who would think of using anything but

JOHNSON'S PASTE WAX, known in the company as "the grandfather of all Johnson products."

Samuel C. Johnson custom-mixed his own paste wax to sell to people who bought the parquet flooring he manufactured. The first batch was mixed sometime in the year 1889, probably in the basement of the home of George McDougall, who worked in the furniture-finishing room of the Racine Hardware Company. The earliest cans of this wax contained a combination of different waxes dissolved in turpentine and naphtha. The exact formula, a secret even today, was calculated to keep wood surfaces of all kinds at their optimum shine.

Sensing the sales potential of the wax, Johnson began advertising the product in national magazines. He followed up with a promotional campaign giving away a half-pound can of JOHNSON'S PREPARED WAX free to anyone with a floor. Johnson's salesmanship paid off to the extent that he decided to give up floor making and concentrate on polishes. The business was moved out of McDougall's basement to a two-story frame house in downtown Racine where the wax was blended and mixed in twenty-five-gallon kettles. The long rows of cans, lined up on low tables, were filled by a man using a large sprinkling can with the sprinkling head removed. Three separate operations were required to fill each can. When the wax was cooled and solidified, lids were placed on the cans by one man while another climbed on the table and tromped on the containers to snap the covers tightly shut.

As business improved, wax-making operations became mechanized and Johnson added more waxes and polishes to the company line. At no point did Johnson underestimate the value of advertising. For many years the company sponsored *Fibber McGee & Molly*, and during the heyday of radio became one of the biggest buyers of commercial time in the industry. Today advertising for their products is handled by four different agencies, sharing a budget of nearly $66 million, making Johnson Wax, according to *Advertising Age*, seventy-ninth largest advertiser in the nation.

Chantilly Silver

Since 1895 the top-selling silver pattern in the world has been CHANTILLY by Gorham. Their adaptation of the Louis XV style of interlocking curves appeals to a variety of tastes, including Lynda Johnson Robb's and actress Kaye Ballard's. Our grandmothers could have had a dozen CHANTILLY teaspoons for $7.00 in 1906. In 1983 they cost $54.50 *each*!

GILLETTE RAZOR

It is a little-known fact of history that Alexander the Great ordered his soldiers to shave regularly so their beards could not be seized by the enemy in combat. The fact is remarkable only when you consider that "self-shaving" was a tedious and time-consuming process, not only during the time of Alexander the Great but for many centuries after, until King C. Gillette patented the original three-piece safety razor in 1904.

As a young man, Gillette had a flair for inventing things, and while working as a traveling salesman for the Baltimore Seal Company, he had been given a piece of good advice by his friend William Painter, who invented the bottle cap. Said Painter, "Try to think of something like the Crown Cork [bottle cap], which, when once used, is thrown away, and the customer keeps coming back for more."

The idea intrigued Gillette. He would go through the alphabet doggedly, considering all the things people used frequently, searching for an inspiration. Nothing clicked until one summer morning in 1895 at his home in Brookline, Massachusetts. As Gillette started to shave, he found his razor edge so dull he couldn't use it. His irritation grew as he realized the razor would have to be taken to a barber or a cutler for professional sharpening. He stopped himself from flinging it to the floor and looked at it more closely. In Gillette's words, "As I stood there with the razor in my hand, my eyes resting on it as lightly as a bird settling down on its nest, the Gillette razor and disposable blade were born."

He visualized a combination of parts: a very thin piece of steel with an edge on both sides and a clamp to center the blade over the handle. It seemed a simple enough concept but the task of finding a satisfactory holder for the blade took five years. The razor became a standing joke among his friends. "Well, Gillette," they would say, "how's the razor?" But no one took a serious interest in it nor were they willing to help

subsidize it. Even more discouraging, experienced toolmakers and scientists at the Massachusetts Institute of Technology to whom he went for help advised him to drop the idea as totally impractical.

But in the course of his search for an effective blade holder, Gillette met William E. Nickerson, an instructor at MIT. Eventually, after some badgering, Nickerson agreed to collaborate with Gillette. While Gillette tried to sell stock, Nickerson set up his first machines in a friend's shop over a fish market on Atlantic Avenue in Boston. When a factory was finally built in Boston, Nickerson became the mechanical genius who created machines and processes that were as novel as the safety razor itself.

Not until 1903 was an attempt made to place the GILLETTE safety razor on the market. Only fifty-one of these razors were sold the first year (at five dollars apiece), but as word of the razor's convenience spread, sales did increase. By the latter part of 1905, a driver with horse and wagon was working full-time to make deliveries to and from local suppliers, railroads and wharves. By 1906 production had grown to 300,000 razor sets and nearly 500,000 blades, each package bearing the portrait and signature of the handsome inventor, as they still do in many areas of the world today.

Between 1911 and 1914 Gillette production capacity and employment increased sharply with Nickerson's invention of fully

automatic sharpening machines to replace the "merry-go-round" type of apparatus in use since the company was formed. The new machines reduced costs and improved blade quality at just the right time.

With the entry of American soldiers into the war in April 1917, U.S. military commanders were worried about the unsanitary conditions of trench warfare. They learned that French soldiers who had already spent three years in the trenches relied on the GILLETTE safety razor to stay clean-shaven. The U.S. government decided to follow the example of the French; they ordered 3.5 million razors and 36 million blades to keep the entire American armed forces beardless. By the end of World War I the men returning from the battlefields had acquired the habit of self-shaving and were equipped with razors . . . that would always need more blades.

Gillette marketing executives have always recognized the value of offering free samples. Throughout the twenties they gave away razors with everything from chewing gum

to pairs of overalls. When the extravagant spirit of the twenties eventually tailed into the Depression and the thirties, Gillette was not spared. The company foundered temporarily, then reorganized under a new president (Gillette retired in 1931 and died fourteen months later). A "new and better *blue* blade" was introduced and Gillette went on to broaden its line by offering new products and acquiring companies such as TONI ("Which twin has it?") and PAPERMATE and the makers of CRICKET disposable lighters.

Though Gillette has branched out in new directions with acquisitions and improved shaving products, where beards are concerned, Gillette remains committed to the "wet shave" and to King Gillette's idea, borrowed from William Painter, of design for disposability. With more than a billion consumers in more than two hundred nations, and with annual sales of $1.5 billion, the razor and blade developed by Nickerson and Gillette, changed and refined over the years, are still the mainstays of the Gillette Company today.

Electric Razors

The famous electric razor, designed by Max Braun, was introduced at a trade fair in Frankfurt immediately after the Second World War. Its technology was copied by other razor manufacturers in Europe and America, but not until 1953 when Remington introduced the SUPER 60 did any company produce an electric razor that looked like a good example of contemporary design. After the SUPER 60 appeared, Braun improved the style of its product and in 1954 made a licensing arrangement with the American Ronson Corporation which ensured the sharing of both companies' technological expertise here and in Europe.

TALON ZIPPER

On April 29, 1913, a patent was issued to Swedish-born Dr. Gideon Sundback, an electrical engineer, for the Plako slide fastener—forerunner of the modern zipper. This somewhat unreliable fastener was soon succeeded by a more trustworthy device known as the

GOODRICH

MYSTIK BOOT

Goodrich again leads as it did in 1922

The great success of our PAVLOVO BOOT inspired Goodrich to do something even better for the coming season—Result—the

MYSTIK BOOT

with the patented Hookless Fastener

Opens with a pull   Closes with a pull

Hookless 2, made by the Hookless Fastener Company, which met with considerable success as a closure for money belts and tobacco pouches. Not until 1923, however, were such fasteners used in clothing, by which time they were known as "zippers"—the name coined by B. F. Goodrich because of the sound they made *z-z-z-zipping* up the rubber rain boots he put them in.

The Hookless fastener became a Talon fastener in 1928, the year the company executives decided it was time their product had a new trademark. (The word *zipper* was identified with the Goodrich boots. Although the public had begun to insist that any quick-fastening device was a zipper, Goodrich owned, and still owns, the trademark for the fasteners used in galoshes.)

As an incentive to creativity, the Hookless Fastener Company offered to a group of friends a prize of one share of stock for a winning name for their product. A long list of possibilities was drawn up, including the words *Utilok* and *Bobolink*. Little progress was made until William McCoy, a young lawyer in the company, discovered a code book with a long index of words easy to pronounce and understand. The book pointed out that five-letter code words are said to have the most pleasant and memorable effect on the ear. It was a short step from that line of reasoning to the selection of Talon as the perfect verbal symbol: Everything about it seemed right. The elements of the fastener were surely like the claws of the eagle, gripping with firmness. And the five letters comprising the word not only sounded right together but looked impressive graphically.

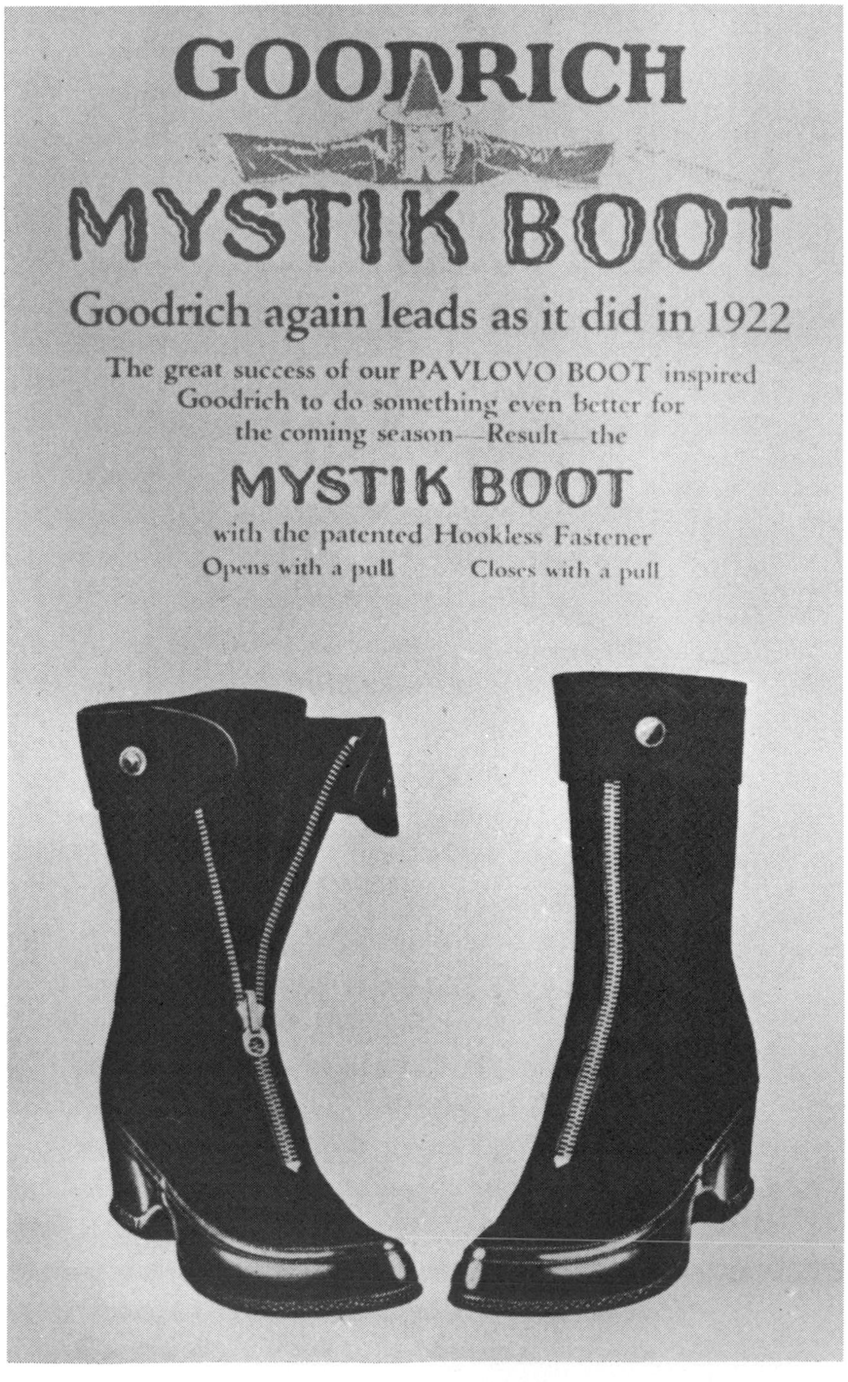

The Hookless Fastener Company changed its name to Talon in 1937, the year the zipper was given the ultimate endorsement by Parisian fashion designer Madame Elsa Schiaparelli whose 1938 spring collection arrived in New York—as an article in *The New Yorker* reported—"dripping with zippers." As Schiaparelli's prestige increased, so did that of the zipper.

The modern slide fastener remained relatively unchanged until 1960 when zippers were first made with nylon, rendering them both light and strong, good-looking and disaster-proof. Since then zippers (mostly TALON) have been zipping up everything from pencil cases to space suits, with new uses coming along every day.

MAXWELL HOUSE COFFEE

IN THE LATE NINETEENTH century, when Joel Owsley Cheek was a young man, coffee was almost as much a part of the American way of life as it is now. People had been drinking it for years in coffee houses—known as "penny universities" because of the wit and wisdom they engendered—and by 1892 when the MAXWELL HOUSE brand first appeared, coffee was routinely served in hotels and restaurants.

Cheek, a salesman for a grocery house in Nashville, Tennessee, was fascinated by coffee. In his spare time between calls, Cheek roasted various coffee beans and blended them, seeking "the perfect blend of matchless flavor." It took years of painstaking research over copper kettles, but when he finally had the result he wanted he resigned from the grocery firm and devoted himself to promotion of his own product.

With a true businessman's instinct for getting the kind of

86

The Old Maxwell House Hotel

promotion he needed, Cheek
approached the management of an
elegant southern hotel, the Maxwell
House in Nashville, hoping to

persuade them to serve his brew to
their distinguished guests. The hotel
management agreed, and Cheek's
coffee was so enthusiastically

received that he decided to name
the blend after the hotel.

In 1896 Joel Cheek joined forces
with John Neal to organize the

Cheek-Neal Coffee Company, which in 1928 became part of the Postum Company, now owned by General Foods. The MAXWELL HOUSE coffee cup-and-slogan trademark had been registered two years before, in 1926.

General Foods gives Theodore Roosevelt credit for originating the MAXWELL HOUSE slogan. It seems that sometime around the turn of the century, Mr. Roosevelt was an honored guest at The Hermitage in Nashville, home of Andrew Jackson. The hostess asked him if he would have another cup of MAXWELL HOUSE coffee. "Will I have another? Delighted!" he exclaimed. "It's good to the last drop!"

Sanka

Finding a way to remove caffeine from coffee without harming its flavor or aroma was the goal of Dr. Ludwig Roselius, head of the Café Haag company in Bremen, Germany. After years of experimenting, he developed the basis of the process in use today which removes 97 percent of the caffeine with almost imperceptible damage to the coffee's flavor.

When the product was introduced in France, Dr. Roselius named it SANKA, a contraction of the French phrase *sans caffeine*, "without caffeine." The SANKA trademark, now owned by General Foods, was registered in the United States in 1923.

KODAK BROWNIE

EVERYONE WHO HAS EVER USED A camera has a favorite KODAK product. For the professional and the serious amateur it may be KODACHROME film—consistently high in quality, reasonable in price. The less experienced amateur may cite the cartridge-loaded INSTAMATIC or the automatic DISC 4000, introduced in 1982, designed to take the last iota of guesswork out of amateur photography with a camera not much bigger than a cigarette case.

For years the KODAK BROWNIE was America's best-known everyday camera. While it never offered the superior results rendered by the INSTAMATIC or the DISC 4000, it could be used by any member of the family to document all manner of events. The BROWNIE sold for one dollar in 1900, the year it was

introduced. Film cost fifteen cents a roll. In addition to introducing millions of people to photography, the BROWNIE led the way to giant sales in film and processing—the ultimate goal, then and now, of Kodak's marketing strategy.

In 1899 George Eastman mentioned in a letter to his partner, Henry A. Strong, his plan to develop a truly simple, affordable camera. "Heretofore our cheap cameras have been rather too complicated," he wrote. "I am working on one at Brownell's which

I hope will fill the bill. It is a film camera, pure and simple."

In February of the following year the BROWNIE camera was presented. It was made of heavy cardboard, reinforced with wood and covered with black imitation leather. Each roll of film produced 2¼ × 2¼ inch pictures.

One might assume that the camera was named after Frank Brownell who, in collaboration with his staff of camera makers, manufactured it. However, it is also possible that the name is a tip-of-

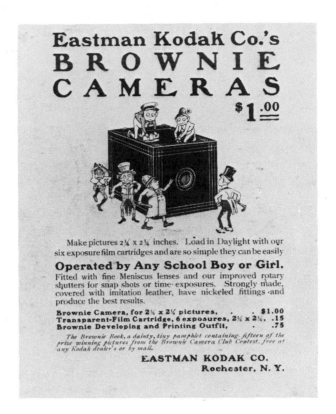

the-hat to artist Palmer Cox, whose popular "brownie" characters appeared in ads for the camera and on the camera package.

The simplicity of the BROWNIE was its major selling point. A child could operate it, or an adult beginner. Its one dollar price was irresistible, and the power it offered—to virtually anyone—was akin to magic. Kodak did not come up with another camera that was comparable until 1963 when it introduced the INSTAMATIC.

BUSTER BROWN SHOES

I'm Buster Brown; I live in a shoe.
  (WOOF! WOOF!)
That's my dog Tige: he lives there too.

THAT'S HOW THE ACT ALWAYS began, with Buster Brown dressed up in his scarlet jacket and breeches, fancy collar and bow tie, and crowned with the classic flat, broad-rimmed hat. The routine that followed was improvised, always including lots of chatter with the children and the ceremonial display of the label in Buster Brown's shoes. It concluded with the awarding of modest prizes for the children to take home.

The idea for this unique promotion for BUSTER BROWN children's shoes may be credited to John A. Bush, who was a young executive in the Brown Shoe Company in 1902—the year New York City newspaper readers were

introduced to America's first full-page, four-color comic strip, featuring Buster Brown and his little dog, Tige. The strip related the mischievous adventures of Buster and Tige, frequently in collaboration with Buster's sister, Mary Jane. Bush saw the trio, and particularly Buster Brown himself, as naturals to represent the company's new line of shoes for boys and girls.

He had little trouble persuading the company management to accept the idea, and artist Richard Outcault was eager to see his strip characters

brought to life. (As Bush never contracted for exclusive rights to Buster Brown, Outcault later had the pleasure of seeing his characters used to sell everything from chewing gum to horseshoes, waffle irons, cigars and bourbon). The official introduction of the Buster Brown "act" at the St. Louis World's Fair of 1904 was so successful that the company won the only Double Grand Prize awarded to a shoe exhibitor that year.

In *Great American Brands* David Powers Cleary describes how the Brown Company followed up on the

introductory promotion by hiring a midget to tour the country and appear—complete with Lord Fauntleroy suit, Dutch-boy wig and trained dog—in department stores, shoe stores and rented theaters from coast to coast. "In time," says Cleary, "there would be a succession of six Buster Brown midgets—and four-foot, two-inch

Ed Ansley, the most famous one of all, would devote twenty-eight years of his life traveling fifty thousand miles a year, ultimately visiting every county in the United States, drawing crowds as vast as twenty-five thousand. . . . Along the way he 'wore out' five dogs."

Buster Brown went on to radio and television in the forties and

fifties; Bush became president of the Brown Shoe Company and chairman of the board. Today Brown Shoe Company is a member company of Brown Group, Inc. Buster Brown makes 6 percent of all shoes manufactured in the United States (not all with the BUSTER BROWN label) and in 1980 showed profits of $41.8 million.

TEDDY BEAR

DESPITE THE PLETHORA OF TOY bears around today with names like Shakesbear, Zsa Zsa Gabear and Bear Mitzvah, earlier generations of American children were more than likely to call theirs TEDDY.

Morris Michtom was a Russian immigrant who owned a candy shop in Brooklyn. He was inspired to make a stuffed bear by a cartoon that appeared in *The Washington Star* in 1902. The illustration by Clifford Berryman showed Theodore Roosevelt, rifle in hand, standing with his back turned to a cowering bear cub. The caption read, DRAWING THE LINE IN MISSISSIPPI, referring to a trip Roosevelt had taken to the South in the hope of resolving a border dispute between Louisiana and Mississippi and doing a little hunting in between. The ever-gracious southerners whom Roosevelt was visiting wanted to make sure the President returned to Washington with a suitable hunting trophy. They trapped a young bear cub for the President to shoot. Once he was aware of the arrangement, Roosevelt refused to shoot the bear.

Berryman's cartoon depicting the situation was seen in newspapers everywhere.

Michtom must have reckoned that a small replica of the bear in the cartoon, placed in the window of his candy store with a small sign reading TEDDY'S BEAR would attract the attention of passersby. In fact, he was besieged by customers who wanted similar bears of their own. Michtom wrote to Roosevelt asking permission to use his name on the stuffed bears. The President granted permission but confessed that he "couldn't see what use my name would be in the stuffed animal trade."

Making stuffed bears proved so profitable for Michtom that in 1903 he sold his candy shop and started the Ideal Toy Company which makes millions of TEDDY BEARS today.

Reeves International is Ideal's biggest competition in the toy bear department. It claims its bear was the first, made by Margaret Steiff, a polio victim confined to a wheelchair, who began sewing felt animal toys in Germany in the 1880's. Bears and many other STEIFF toys sold by Reeves are today ongoing top sellers in the stuffed-animal kingdom.

HERSHEY'S CHOCOLATE

"CARAMELS ARE ONLY A FAD," proclaimed young Milton Hershey in 1892. "Chocolate is a permanent thing," he said, and he set out to make it and sell it at a price everyone could afford.

Hershey had considerable authority for his opinion about the future of caramels. At the age of thirty-five he was already something of a candy mogul. From an inauspicious beginning making caramels in the back room of a house in Lancaster, Pennsylvania, and selling them from a pushcart, Hershey had gone on to follow his father's advice: "If you want to make money, you have to do things in a *big* way." Even before venturing into chocolate, Hershey was what people in Lancaster called "a substantial citizen."

In 1884 Milton Hershey had met an Englishman named Decies, a candy importer, who was enthusiastic about Hershey's "homemade" caramels. He offered to introduce them in England if Hershey could manufacture them in

sufficient quantity to make it worthwhile. At first Hershey listened with a kind of desperation. Where could he possibly get the capital he needed to convert his back-room operation into a real business? He had already imposed on every relative he knew to support his modest existing setup. Convinced that his whole future depended on raising the capital he needed, Hershey began to make the rounds of local banks. He wanted a loan of just $700 to get started. The first banks he tried refused outright to give him a penny. Finally a bank officer named Brenneman, at the Lancaster National Bank, found something so persuasive about Hershey that he agreed to make the loan for ninety days. But when the note came due, Hershey could not pay it.

"I can't pay," he told Brenneman. "I want to renew the note. Come up to my place and see the materials and equipment I have. Let me show them to you."

Brenneman was not much

impressed with what Milton showed him. There was little in the way of machinery and equipment. The place was shabby and the wagonmaker's shop next door made a terrible din while Milton's only employees, his mother and aunt Mattie, sat wrapping candies.

Milton went back to Brenneman to the bank. "I need to have the note renewed," he pleaded. "I must have a thousand dollars to buy more equipment."

Brenneman later said that he lay awake all night worrying and the next day signed the note with his personal signature because otherwise

he was sure the bank officers would turn it down. "I didn't know where I was going," he said, "but it turned out all right."

Hershey's caramel pots were soon bubbling with caramels to send to England. Just ten days before the loan came due again, Hershey received a £500 note from the Bank of England. "In payment of goods shipped," the accompanying slip read. Hershey's caramel business was free and clear; the cornerstone of the Hershey empire was laid.

Future loans for Hershey's business were not made in Lancaster; the banks were too small to keep up with Hershey's burgeoning fortune. In 1894 Hershey was doing over a million dollars worth of business, selling caramels to all parts of the world, but he was not satisfied. He realized that the United States was importing twenty-four million pounds of cacao beans. At the Chicago Exposition in 1892 he had seen an exhibition of chocolate-making machinery from Dresden, Germany. Milton Hershey watched it hulling, grinding, mixing and molding and was fascinated by what he saw.

"Frank," he said to his cousin Frank Snavely, as they watched the machines together, "I'm going to make chocolate."

It did not take Hershey long to buy the machinery, all of it, and arrange to have it shipped to Lancaster as soon as the fair was dismantled. Hershey hired two expert chocolate makers and began to produce chocolate—enough to coat the famous HERSHEY caramels and produce a wealth of "novelties" that sold for two cents and three cents apiece.

By now Hershey could see that his prediction had been true. The future, his future, lay in chocolate. The caramel business was sold in 1900 for $1 million and Hershey centered his attention on making a single item, producing it in great quantity and pricing it so everyone could afford to buy it. That was a new marketing concept in 1900; Henry Ford adopted it in making automobiles a few years later.

The object on which Milton

Hershey concentrated his efforts was a simple chocolate bar. The chocolate would be milk chocolate made with fresh milk from Pennsylvania cows. By trial and error Hershey finally hit upon a formula using skimmed milk that produced the taste and texture of chocolate that he wanted. Milton was ready to start making HERSHEY BARS.

He built a factory to make them in huge quantities. He built a trolley line to carry his workers to and from their jobs. He had houses built for them to live in along streets named Chocolate and Cocoa avenues, Java Street, Granada Road. Schools were set up for Hershey factory-workers' children. Then an inn, a bank, a cooperative store. Soon there were an amusement park, golf courses, a football field, a dancing pavilion, and an outdoor theater where visiting vaudeville troupes performed.

Hershey went on to build other empires in Cuba, where he first constructed a sugar mill to supply his Pennsylvania factory, then a town and a railroad to serve it. He bought property in other sugar districts and built more mills giving work to thousands.

In 1920 the company suffered a temporary setback when Hershey's need for sugar exceeded the supply from all his mills. As sugar prices skyrocketed, Hershey frantically continued to buy against his future needs. He was confident that the market for his chocolate would hold up. It did, the company weathered the storm and Hershey went on to a new phase of development.

The outstanding lesson of the "bad year" in 1920 was that the Hershey Chocolate Company had grown too big and important to be administered by one man. Milton

Hershey agreed to dissolve the Hershey Chocolate Company and allow three separate companies to take its place. These were the Hershey Chocolate Corporation which acquired all the chocolate properties; the Hershey Corporation which acquired the sugar interests in Cuba; and the Hershey Estates which conducted the various businesses of the town and its public services.

The nickel HERSHEY BAR— symbol of Milton Hershey's belief that there was something better than caramels and that the world was waiting for it—now costs forty cents. Its size and price have changed over the years but only in relation to the cost of raw materials—in keeping with Hershey's original idea that chocolate is one of the good things in life that should be accessible to everyone.

WRIGLEY'S CHEWING GUM

WILLIAM WRIGLEY JR. (HE NEVER used a comma in his name), future monarch of the multimillion-dollar-a-year chewing-gum industry, attracted attention as a child by cutting up in school. His biographers estimate that he was expelled almost every third week of the school year. At age eleven Wrigley ran away from his home in Philadelphia to New York City's Park Row where he joined the local "newsies," selling newspapers to put some change in his pocket.

Eventually the boy returned to

Philadelphia, only to get into more trouble at school. His soap-manufacturer father was compelled to issue an ultimatum: "Your school life has not been a success," declared Wrigley senior in a classic example of understatement. "We'll see how work strikes you." A place for him was found in the soap factory.

At thirteen Wrigley persuaded his father to let him go on the road as a soap salesman. He rode from town to town in Pennsylvania on a horse-drawn wagon, selling his father's soap to retailers, always offering a box of baking soda as a bonus. (Wrigley never underestimated the persuasive power of premiums. Toward the end of his life he purchased twenty-nine carloads of GEM razors and fifty carloads of electric clocks—1 million—to give away.) When the baking powder drew more enthusiastic response than the soap, he started selling *it* and offered chewing gum as a premium. When people clamored for more gum, he sold that instead.

By this time—the year was 1892—Wrigley had moved to Chicago and the demand for chewing gum was growing daily. The first two kinds of gum he offerd were LOTTA GUM and VASSAR, soon followed by JUICY FRUIT and WRIGLEY'S SPEARMINT, which by 1910 became America's top-selling gum. Meanwhile, Wrigley was setting up companies to sell his gum abroad—in Canada, Australia and Great Britain.

No one believed more deeply in the power of advertising than William Wrigley Jr. He spent his first $100,000 on it, saw no return on that, raised $100,000 more and found the second investment as fruitless as the first. In 1907, year of

financial panic, Wrigley announced to his associates, "I'm going to pick up that two hundred thousand dollars I dropped in the big town." This time he put up $250,000 but with it he was able to buy, at panic rates, well over $1.5 million worth of advertising space. A bright future for the company was ensured.

For almost eighty years, selling only four kinds of gum, Wrigley's dominated the gum market. Then in the 1970's Wrigley's began to feel the heat of keen competition, mainly from Squibb's BUBBLE YUM and CARE-FREE sugarless gum (now owned by Nabisco Brands) and Warner-Lambert's TRIDENT and FRESHEN-UP. Wrigley's market share declined to about 33 percent.

But the Wrigley company, operating from the lofty eminence of its famous Renaissance-style Chicago skyscraper, soon rebounded

by introducing a series of "special interest" chewing gums: FREEDENT for denture wearers, BIG RED, a cinnamon-flavored gum, and, in 1979, its first sugar-free gum. In 1979 the company introduced HUBBA BUBBA to compete with Squibb's soft bubble gum.

At the same time Wrigley revamped its sales and marketing departments, replacing pre-World War II techniques with more up-to-date methods. The revisions paid off and Wrigley's reclaimed the top spot in the gum market, with a 44 percent market share. In early 1982, Wrigley's was Number One in standard chewing gum; Number Two in bubble gum, behind Nabisco Brands; and Number Two in sugarless. Plans for a new liquid-center chewing gum were being made to further confirm their lead in the industry.

Chewing Gum

The first makers of chewing gun in America were the Indians. They used the resin from freshly cut spruce bark. But not until the late 1860's did chewing gum become a commercial success, after Staten Island inventor Thomas Adams noticed that his visiting neighbor from Mexico seemed to derive a lot of satisfaction from chewing on what turned out to be lumps of gum from the sapodilla plant, now known as chicle. The visiting Mexican had every right to feel tension: He was deposed dictator Antonio López de Santa Anna, best remembered as the hated target of the Texas battle cry, "Remember the Alamo!"

Inventor Adams decided chicle was better than the limp paraffin sometimes chewed in those days and went to market with "Adams New York Gum—Snapping and Stretching." Later he tried adding flavors, found that licorice lasted best and still later invented a gum-making machine.

From *Great American Brands* by David Powers Cleary

Fig Newtons

In 1895, in Cambridgeport, Massachusetts, the Kennedy Biscuit Works was expanded to accommodate a spectacular new machine invented by a Philadelphian, James Henry Mitchell. One of the many feats the machine was able to perform was to extrude dough in firm little wraparound sandwiches which could be filled with jam.

Because the first jam the company used was made from figs, and because the plant manager liked to name new products after nearby towns, the jam sandwiches were called FIG NEWTONS.

TOOTSIE ROLLS

AS LEO HIRSCHFIELD hand-rolled some chocolates for his daughter Tootsie one afternoon in 1896, he never dreamed that eighty-four years later ten million TOOTSIE ROLLS would be made every day.

Young Hirschfield, recently arrived from Austria, expected to keep a single, small candy shop in New York, but the success of his chocolatey confections among the children of his neighborhood led him to think there might be a broader market. He began modestly, wrapping each little roll in paper to keep it clean and sanitary and pricing it at a penny. The pennies poured in, but Hirschfield soon realized he would need more than pennies to promote and expand his business. After a year he merged it with a local candy manufacturer, Stern & Saalberg. The new company was so successful that it soon outgrew its existing quarters, as

it continued to do through the First World War and the Depression. During World War II, TOOTSIE ROLL was one of the few candies that remained in production. Because of its propensity to stay fresh for long periods of time, TOOTSIE ROLL went overseas in the GI rations and was valued by American soldiers as a quick-energy giver.

The Tootsie Roll Industries company history does not indicate that TOOTSIE ROLLS ever had a really bad year. As the company grew, marketing programs expanded. The product was widely advertised on television, in newspapers, in magazines, on radio.

In 1949 a plant was opened in California to meet the growing demand for TOOTSIE products on the West Coast; then in 1970 this plant was consolidated with the company's main plant, which eventually found in Chicago space it was not likely to outgrow.

The company reports that since moving to Chicago its gross sales have increased by $40 million. Plans for diversification are being considered, but the company expects its best seller will continue to be the five-cent candy roll, remarkably similar to the penny roll first handmade and wrapped by Leo Hirschfield.

LIONEL TRAINS/ EVEREADY FLASHLIGHTS

FORTUNATELY FOR GENERATIONS of children, Joshua Lionel Cowen did not stop inventing things when his instructor at the Peter Cooper Institute told him that there would be no market for such an impractical thing as a doorbell. He didn't persevere with the doorbell but turned his attention to perfecting a tiny electric motor. He used it first in a fan, which Cowen himself praised in later years for its flawless design, admitting to only one fault. "It was the only draftless fan ever made. You could sit right in front of it and feel no breeze whatsoever."

In the search for a marketable product Joshua Cowen also developed a slender battery in a tube with a lightbulb on one end. This lighted tube could be concealed in a flower pot so that the light would illuminate the plant. A restaurant owner named Conrad Hubert became so enthusiastic about it that he gave up running restaurants and went on the road selling illuminated flower pots. Cowen was too busy tinkering with his miniature motor to care much about the market possibilities of the plant illuminator. He turned it over completely to Hubert, who came up with a new use for the gadget and started the Eveready Flashlight Company. Hubert fared well enough with that venture to leave $6 million to charity when he died.

Remembering fondly the hours of his childhood spent carving toy locomotives, Cowen decided that a miniature train powered by a minute motor might have considerable appeal. He designed a small flatcar with a tiny-battery operated motor, then constructed a thirty-foot circle of brass track to run the train around on. A small novelty shop offered to display one set. It was an immediate success at six dollars retail and the shop ordered six more. The real bonanza came for Cowen when a Providence shop ordered twenty-five sets. As a gesture of appreciation Cowen gave them exclusive rights to sell his trains in New England and set himself to finding a larger work space and more workers.

Increasing use of electricity in homes around America brought greater demand for Cowen's little trains. In 1903 Cowen invested in a marketing device that was not yet common in America: He issued his first catalog, a prized collector's item today. Complete with pictures of a derrick car, suspension bridge and electric trolley car with Lilliputian reversible seats, it stirred a million fantasies for model-train enthusiasts. The official history of LIONEL trains recounts that Cowen was as good a pitchman as he was an inventor and included in his catalog feature stories about his company and bombastic sales pitches to accompany the pictures and descriptions of his wares.

Each subsequent Lionel catalog showed more items—a cattle car, boxcar, oil tank car, day coach, coal car. With the addition of every tantalizing miniature, company revenues multiplied. Cowen redesigned his track system and had the new one patented. This three-rail innovation, LIONEL Standard, was adopted by other companies and contributed immensely to the success of all model railroading.

At the beginning of World War I most of Lionel's energy went into filling government contracts for compasses, periscopes, Signal Corps apparatus and navigation instruments. But Lionel had no trouble reverting to its prewar production schedule after 1918. The 1920's, in fact, saw a milestone in model railroading—the development of the sequence switch which permitted trains to be reversed by remote control, adding a new dimension to the fun of playing with trains for aspiring railroaders.

Lionel weathered the Depression better than many companies, but inevitably the hard times did affect business. To boost sales, Lionel offered to sell new train sets for 40 percent below the regular price if an already owned set was brought in for trade. The campaign was a flop. Who could expect boys to give up their old trains, even in exchange for new ones?

The company was desperate for a low-priced item to hold sales in 1933 and 1934. To the rescue came Mickey Mouse, known and loved by everyone at the time. Mickey Mouse's handcar was the Number One toy in the country in 1934. Designed by Joshua Cowen and his general sales manager, Arthur Raphael, it showed small figures of Mickey and Minnie Mouse poised on tiny platforms at each end of the

Advertising, promotion, packaging have long been the not-so-secret keys to the success of many of America's most popular products. Others have become classic top sellers on the strength of their quality, durability, or some mysterious combination of characteristics that makes them unique. However top sellers achieved their fame, some of the graphic images generated in their promotion became as famous as the products themselves.

The famous UNEEDA *Biscuit Slicker Boy demonstrated that the biscuits' package was moistureproof, even in the rain.*

Left above: The STEINWAY *piano,* "Instrument of the Immortals," *sets the standard for pianos all over the world.*

Top: The earliest known bill of sale for HUDSON'S BAY POINT BLANKETS *is dated 1779.*

Above: ARM & HAMMER *soda was first sold for baking in 1867.*

Left: In 100 years only one bar of IVORY *soap, made in 1944, ever failed to float.*

Opposite: The name of the product in this ad painted by Norman Rockwell appears with a discretion few advertisers would accept today.

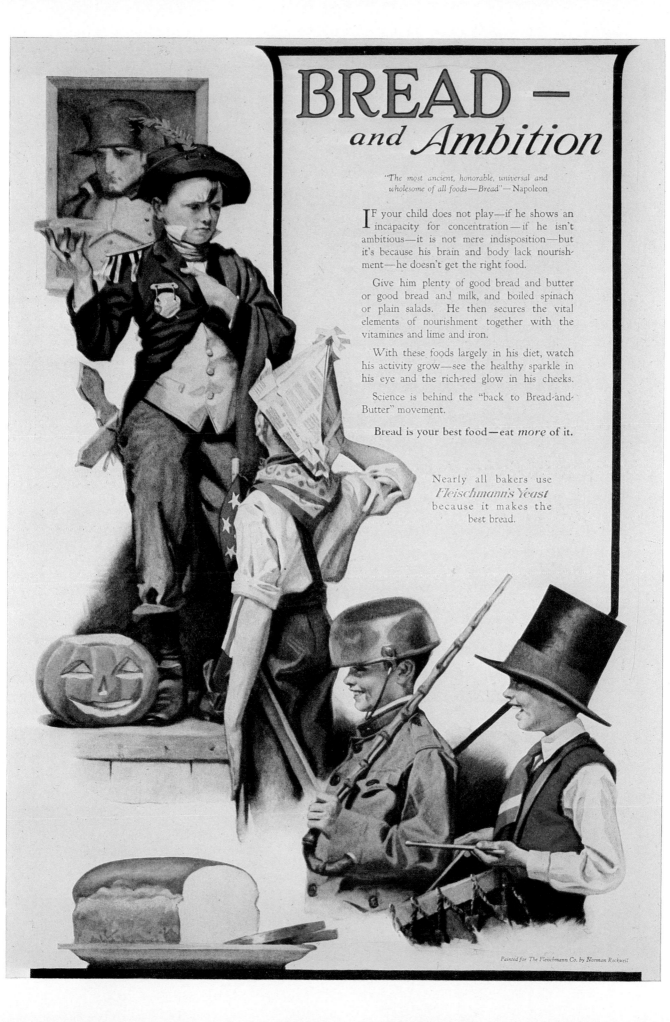

BREAD —
and *Ambition*

"The most ancient, honorable, universal and wholesome of all foods—Bread"—Napoleon

IF your child does not play—if he shows an incapacity for concentration—if he isn't ambitious—it is not mere indisposition—but it's because his brain and body lack nourishment—he doesn't get the right food.

Give him plenty of good bread and butter or good bread and milk, and boiled spinach or plain salads. He then secures the vital elements of nourishment together with the vitamines and lime and iron.

With these foods largely in his diet, watch his activity grow—see the healthy sparkle in his eye and the rich-red glow in his cheeks.

Science is behind the "back to Bread-and-Butter" movement.

Bread is your best food—eat *more* of it.

Nearly all bakers use *Fleischmann's Yeast* because it makes the best bread.

Above: The MONGOL, the world's best-known business pencil.

Left: Ads like this one paved the way for KELLOGG'S distinction in the cereal field.

Below: CRACKER JACK, "candy-coated popcorn, peanuts and a prize," was born in Chicago more than one hundred years ago.

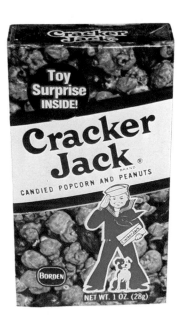

Below: OREOS were introduced at thirty cents per pound in 1912, along with two other cookies that never caught on.

ANIMAL CRACKERS *appeared on the market in 1902, thirty-three years before Shirley Temple helped make them famous by singing about "Animal Crackers in my soup."*

Above: BABY RUTH *candy bar was named not for the famous baseball player but in honor of President Grover Cleveland's daughter, who was the nation's pet as an infant.*

Below: *Symbol of the* APPLE *computer, so named because its creator wanted to project a friendly, nonthreatening image of his product.*

Below right: CRAYOLA *crayons—"An artist's crayon at a scholar's price."*

La Belle Chocolatière *captivated the original manufacturer of* BAKER'S *chocolate. Then and now, she represents the product.*

FORMICA® BRAND

products

Left: A strong graphic symbol for FORMICA has helped the product become a top seller.

Right: BUDWEISER, the "King of Beers" made by Anheuser-Busch, still leads the beer industry in sales.

Above: WRIGLEY'S chewing gum, from the company founded by William Wrigley Jr., whose first business was selling soap.

Left: SMIRNOFF, preferred vodka of the Imperial Russian courts, first advertised in America as "Smirnoff's White Whiskey. No taste. No smell."

Below: Forty million RITZ crackers are sold each day, ten billion a year in the United States alone.

Right: Around the turn of the century, the CREAM OF WHEAT Company made both advertising and art history by employing some of America's finest illustrators to design its ads. James Montgomery Flagg, Jessie Willcox Smith, and Philip R. Goodwin were among the artists whose work appeared as full-page advertisements almost every month in such magazines as Collier's, The Saturday Evening Post and The Delineator.

In 1907, N. C. Wyeth, just out of art school, was paid $250 for this painting called "Rural Delivery."

WHERE THE MAIL GOES CREAM of WHEAT GOES

Above: "Invent something people use and throw away." Inspired by this advice, King Gillette had the idea for GILLETTE Blue Blades in 1895.

Right: Pioneer of packaged bread, WONDER bread in its colorful wrapper still outsells all other brands of commercially baked bread.

car. As the handbar moved up and down the rubber legs on the mice flexed realistically. Company historians conjecture that without the handcar Lionel might not have survived the Depression.

As America headed into the late thirties Lionel kept up with new developments like the streamliners by hiring designers to do models of some of the famous locomotives, including the New York Central's Commodore Vanderbilt; the Pennsylvania's K-4 Pacifics which were designed by the well-known industrial designer Raymond Loewy; and the Milwaukee Road line's Hiawatha. By 1939 nearly four hundred different pieces of railroad equipment were being produced by Lionel.

Just when Lionel business was really booming, Pearl Harbor brought all peacetime work to a halt. Once again the company became committed to producing equipment for the armed forces. It manufactured more than one hundred different items, including an oil-filled compass, considered by many experts the best in the world. Production of the compass led to a resourceful solution to an unusual

problem for Lionel: After much experimentation it was decided that day-old egg whites seemed to be the best binder for the paint used in the compass bowl, but eggs were in short supply at the time. The company was compelled to set up its own egg-production operation. Lionel became one of the largest chicken-raising, egg-producing companies in the East. Disposing of the unneeded egg yolks was easy— omelets were added to the menu in the company cafeteria!

After the war, in 1948, Joshua Cowen was faced with a difficult decision. A devotee of steam locomotives, Cowen had to reconcile himself to the "diesel age." Realism and authenticity were Cowen's dual goals, and by the end of the decade Lionel's main production was switched, reluctantly, from steam to diesel models. Cowen's unhappiness was tempered by the success of his first diesel, the SANTA FE F-3, the top-selling model engine in the company's history.

During the early fifties Lionel's New York showroom had an authentic train-station atmosphere. A twelve-foot-high model of a

Pennsylvania Railroad steam turbine mounted at the entrance gave visitors the distinct impression that they were about to be run down by the *Broadway Limited*. Lionel salesmen amused themselves racing the dozen trains on the office's elaborate layout to various crossover points, resulting in several major wrecks a day. But Joshua Cowen didn't mind. He wanted to encourage adults to play with trains. "Why shouldn't a man run a train?" he used to ask rhetorically. "Operating a good train layout is one of the greatest challenges I know."

The market for model-railroad equipment in the 1950's was divided into two main segments: for the general consumer and for the die-hard hobbyist who scrimped and saved in order to purchase every possible item. But there were also peripheral markets for LIONEL trains. They were used to transport radioactive material in laboratories both for the armed forces and for clinics treating cancer. The military found them indispensable for teaching personnel the fundamentals of railroading. Even luncheonettes across the country

sent hamburgers from kitchen to counter via the LIONEL lines.

Yet the road was not always smooth for Lionel. In 1957 the company stumbled and began to lose money. The low period was triggered by an episode that seems almost ridiculous in retrospect. In response to a number of letters from girls asking why there were no trains for them, Lionel introduced a train set with the following components: a "robin's-egg blue" boxcar, a lilac hopper, a "buttercup yellow" boxcar and a "sky blue" caboose. Girls didn't like it, nobody liked it and it was out of the catalog by 1959.

There were other examples of Lionel's failure to judge its market in the late fifties. Retailing was undergoing a change and discount stores were popping up everywhere. Because they bought merchandise in great volume, they could sell at a lower price than small hobby shops. Many of these stores were forced to close down in the face of the discount-store onslaught. Lionel had to decide whether to refuse to sell to discount stores out of loyalty to the small operators or to take advantage of the great volume of business that the discounters could guarantee. Lionel decided to stay with the small merchants. Unfortunately, its competitors did not and their share of the market began to grow at Lionel's expense.

The company also failed to perceive the importance of new hobbies that were drawing attention away from electric trains. Slot cars and model airplanes began seriously to cut into the electric-train

business. And, more significantly perhaps, television had entered people's lives. From then on, all hobbies suffered.

In an attempt to recover its losses, Lionel diversified, first into fishing tackle, then into cameras and remote-control television switches. Later, led by a syndicate of investors headed by New York attorney Roy Cohn, the company moved into microwave equipment and radiation-detection equipment. But Lionel's problems continued. With rising U.S. labor and material costs further aggravating Lionel's problems, the company was compelled to move its train-manufacturing operations to Japan, resulting in a serious drop in quality of the products.

By 1968 the once-bountiful LIONEL catalog had shrunk to an eight-page brochure, offering only one complete outfit and a paltry selection of rolling stock and accessories. Lionel's financial

situation was so grave that the company began auctioning off its machinery and equipment. During the course of seven months numerous manufacturing companies descended upon the beleaguered factory, bidding for tools, moldings, die-casting equipment and presses, as the few remaining Lionel employees looked on, unwilling to believe that the age of model railroading had come to an end. Some of these Lionel veterans began hiding away files and records on the manufacture of trains, feeling certain that they would one day be needed again.

Their foresight proved correct. A survey conducted by General Mills in 1969 indicated that despite its

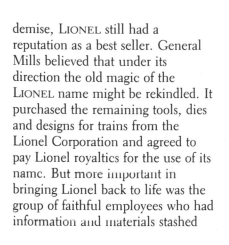

demise, LIONEL still had a reputation as a best seller. General Mills believed that under its direction the old magic of the LIONEL name might be rekindled. It purchased the remaining tools, dies and designs for trains from the Lionel Corporation and agreed to pay Lionel royalties for the use of its name. But more important in bringing Lionel back to life was the group of faithful employees who had information and materials stashed

away and wanted to participate in Lionel's resurrection. Once they heard the news, train buffs everywhere volunteered their help, recommending models that they thought ought to be revived, indicating their enduring interest in the product and its future.

By the end of 1970 Lionel was out of the woods, or the ashes, and had begun to rise again. Under the auspices of General Mills Fundimensions, a new catalog, proud heir to the tradition of the old ones, had appeared, and the

company had begun to direct the product's advertising campaign to the young fathers who had grown up during Lionel's heyday in the forties and fifties and wanted to share the LIONEL trains of their youth with their own children.

The new pitch worked, even though children of the seventies and eighties have scant familiarity with actual railroads and the giant locomotives that fascinated their parents as rocket ships captivate children nowadays. With each passing year Lionel's future is further ensured as Lionel now makes and sells enough equipment to construct a toy train nearly 150 miles long. If those engines and cars were real, they would form a train over 7,000 miles long!

PART FOUR

1900–WORLD WAR I

Amalgamation and consolidation were key words in turn-of-the-century American business. As manufacturers and sales outlets were drawn closer together by improved railroads and the Fords and Studebakers that studded the roads after 1909, companies pooled their resources to keep up the supply of goods in the rapidly expanding marketplace.

Workers had begun to organize into unions to claim their rights from industry. There were strikes and a Depression, and a few hard-earned gains for the labor movement. Businessmen who thought they had mastered the formulas for success were challenged to find ways to keep order in their ranks and at the same time meet ever-increasing consumer demands for new and better products.

UNEEDA BISCUITS

WHEN ADOLPHUS GREEN TOOK over the chairmanship of the conglomerate of companies that formed the National Biscuit Company in 1898, he longed to introduce a new product that would attract everyone's attention. He wanted it to represent a major improvement in the way baked goods were made and marketed.

Though there is no evidence to prove it, Green must have challenged each of the merged companies—all with a long tradition in baking—to present him with their best efforts. Whatever it was they showed him, we know that he opted for the universally popular soda cracker baked according to a recipe that would make it exceptionally light and flaky. He suggested clipping the corners off to give it a unique, octagonal appearance.

In naming the new product, Green sought the advice of N. W. Ayer & Son, the Philadelphia-based advertising agency that had helped R. J. Reynolds promote PRINCE ALBERT tobacco. The agency submitted a long list of possibilities: TakaCracker, HavaCracker, WantaCracker and, buried unobtrusively somewhere among the others, Uneeda Cracker.

Green liked the *Uneeda* part but felt that the word *cracker* had been associated too long with stale and soggy products. *Biscuit*, he felt, would be a better choice. The words UNEEDA Biscuit were duly registered with the U.S. Patent Office.

The outstanding feature of the UNEEDA Biscuit product may not have been the biscuit itself but the package it came in. Green solicited advice from dozens of packaging experts and eventually selected a design submitted by his law partner, a young man named Frank Peters who was devoting more and more of his time to the baking industry and less to legal affairs.

Peters's design consisted of interfolded layers of waxed paper and cardboard—a package that was so ingenious that it was given its own trade name, "In-er-seal." Now, at last, it was possible to buy biscuits that would retain their freshness and flavor for longer than a few hours.

Green thought there should be a symbol that would suggest the qualities of the new product, both on the package itself and in paid advertisements. Joseph Geisinger, a copywriter with the N. W. Ayer Agency, had a five-year-old nephew who embodied many of the characteristics then considered appealing in children: clear-eyed, chubby-cheeked, demure— everyone agreed he would make the perfect model. For the photography session the boy was dressed in boots, rain hat and oilskin slicker and given a box of UNEEDA Biscuits to hold, thereby demonstrating the moisture-proof quality of the package, even in the rain. Displayed everywhere an ad could appear, the UNEEDA Biscuit Slicker Boy soon became a well-known figure in America's cast of commercial characters.

Green continued to search for another symbol, one that would signify the entire National Biscuit Company. He found it late one night while leafing through a book of medieval Italian printer's marks. The one that caught his eye was an oval surmounted by a cross with two horizontal lines through it. It was said to represent the triumph of the moral and spiritual over the evil and worldly.

Both the simplicity of the symbol and its implications appealed to Green's classical mind, and the company adopted it, first to enclose the word In-er-Seal, later to set off the initials N.B.C. Still later, when the company name was changed, the word Nabisco appeared in it.

Having made such an enormous leap ahead in terms of packaging, N.B.C. capitalized on the success of UNEEDA Biscuits by introducing many new crackers and cookies in rapid succession: JINJER Wafers, OYSTERETTES Crackers, SOCIAL Tea Biscuits, GRAHAM Crackers, PREMIUM Saltines, NABISCO Sugar Wafers and BARNUM'S ANIMAL CRACKERS. They all came on the market in the first ten years of the twentieth century, marking the beginning of a new era when standardized, reliable, well-packaged merchandise became the rule rather than the exception.

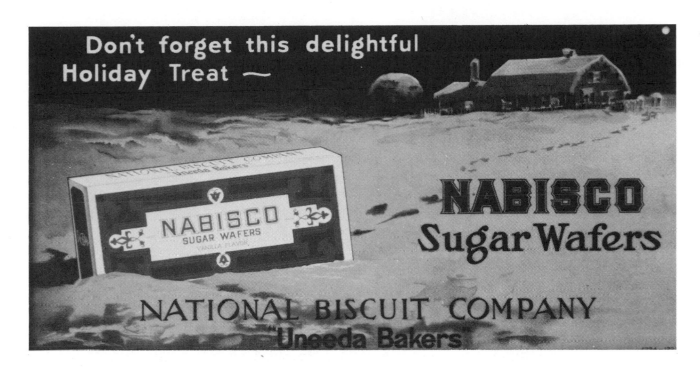

HOOVER VACUUM CLEANER

CONSIDERING THAT THE HOOVER vacuum cleaner was not patented until 1908, one wonders what standards of housekeeping prevailed in the parlors and boudoirs of our great-grandparents.

An Englishman named H. C. Booth is credited with the idea for the vacuum cleaner, which he once demonstrated by sucking vigorously on the plush upholstery of his seat in a Victoria Street restaurant to show how much dust could be pulled out of it. That, allegedly, occurred in 1901. But apart from building a single giant device powered by a heavy motor and fan, Booth did not pursue his idea of a

The Model "O," 1908

To Every Lover Of Cleanliness:

Note the evident satisfaction of the possessor of this **Hoover Electric Suction Sweeper**. You too, would enthusiastically recommend it to your friends when you had proven our claims as to its being the means of thoroughly cleaning your home and **keeping it clean** in the simple, sanitary and inexpensive "Hoover Way."

We'll be glad indeed to answer your request for a free demonstration. You will be surprised at results.

Very respectfully,

The Hoover Suction Sweeper Co.

vacuum cleaner much further.

Two Americans had similar ideas for vacuum cleaners in that same year. Corrine Dufour invented an electrically powered gadget that sucked dust into a wet sponge, and David E. Kenney designed a monstrously large suction cleaner that could be connected by a pipeline to outlets in a room one wanted to clean. Neither of these inventions caught on either.

A few years later, in 1907, J. Murray Spangler, an inventor who also worked as a janitor in a Canton, Ohio, department store, constructed a device that was more effective in cleaning the carpet of the store where he worked than the sweeper he had been told to use. His invention was made up of an old motor from an electric fan, placed on top of a soap box connected to a broom handle with staples. A pillowcase was attached to the fan outlet to catch the accumulated dust. Spangler was so pleased with his gadget that he refined it slightly and took it along to show his cousin, whose husband, W. H. Hoover, was

in the saddlery business. Hoover and his sons were impressed with the contraption which they thought might have a brighter future than saddles in an age that promised to be increasingly dominated by automobiles. The Hoovers mustered their considerable resources to form the Electric Suction Sweeper Company and began manufacturing a more sophisticated model of Spangler's vacuum cleaner in 1908.

At first the new machines were sold in hardware stores, where sales were spotty, to say the least. But on the occasions when young H. W. Hoover, one of the Hoover sons, would visit a store and demonstrate the machine to housewives, everything changed. The ladies couldn't wait to take a cleaner home to try it. The company was pleased to offer ten-day free home trials, finding that the experience turned many doubters into believers.

The company passed a major milestone when, later in 1908, the first of what was to become a large staff of salesmen was hired. At about the same time the company ran its

first national advertisement, which brought inquiries from hundreds of readers. The letters would be answered with an offer of a free demonstration of the machine in the reader's home. The demonstration almost always resulted in a sale, leading to the formulation of "the demonstration principle," still a key factor in Hoover's sales today.

After World War I the over-the-counter market for vacuum cleaners broadened and rival companies were soon turning out machines that modified the basic concept of the upright. In 1924 a sausage-shaped vacuum arrived in the United States with a salesman named Gustaf Sahlin. A product of the Swedish company Aktieblaget Elektrolux, it was the first canister, or tank-type, vacuum to be sold in the United States. Learning well from the early success of the Electric Suction Sweeper Company in selling cleaners via demonstration in the home, ELECTROLUX, marketed mainly door to door, has rivaled the sales of its upright American cousins ever since.

FANNIE FARMER

CONSIDERING THE ARRAY OF cookbooks that come and go on the shelves of bookstores, it seems remarkable that any of them could possibly be a steady best seller. But even experts who specialize in one thousand and one creative ways to stretch your food budget with peanuts, or who know everything there is to know about cooking

kosher-Creole, *all* had to start somewhere. For millions of Americans who cook, it has traditionally been with FANNIE FARMER.

Though Fannie Merritt Farmer was probably never accused of being a feminist, she struck a firm blow for women's liberation when she wrote a cookbook that brought order and

accuracy to American cooking. Often called "the mother of level measurement," she virtually eliminated guesswork from cooking by codifying measurements in teaspoons, tablespoons and cups and by specifying quantities in these terms rather than blithely suggesting "a pinch of salt," or "a walnut of butter," as her predecessors in the

field were wont to do.

When Fannie Farmer was seventeen a paralytic stroke put an end to her plans to finish high school and go to college. After her stroke Fannie spent most of her time at home, helping her mother in whatever ways her limited strength and agile mind would permit. She developed an avid interest in cooking, and as she regained her energy she was able to study at The Boston Cooking School. She then taught there and finally served as its director.

In 1902 Fannie Farmer opened her own school of cookery in Boston with five assistant teachers and five full-time maids. Several days a week she lectured to audiences of aspiring and skilled cooks and culinary professionals. (Her long-time editor Wilma Lord Perkins once noted that Fannie "was too impatient to cook a whole meal. Even when she lectured, someone else on stage did the actual cooking.") Detailed reports of the lectures were made in the Boston *Evening Transcript* and copied by newspapers all over the country.

When Miss Farmer approached the venerable firm of Little, Brown and Company with the idea of publishing her cookbook, she was told it was not interested in her manuscript. Apparently it seemed unlikely to Little, Brown that the American housewife could possibly be persuaded to buy *another* collection of recipes, especially one that proffered no advice on how to kill rats, cure diseases or make beautifying potions and creams, as most nineteenth-century books of that type did. Nevertheless, Fannie managed to persuade Little, Brown to publish three thousand copies with the understanding that she would pay the printing costs. Russell Lynes once said that "it is unlikely that in the entire history of the American book business, any unwilling publisher ever got talked by an author into so lucrative and safe a deal."

FANNIE FARMER'S cookbook has sold more than four million copies since it first appeared in 1896. The copyright is now owned by the Fanny Farmer Candy Company, which originally had no connection with Fannie Farmer (not even a recipe for its candies). It was granted permission to use the name only on the condition that the spelling of "Fanny" should be different from the way Miss Farmer spelled her name. Judith B. Jones, editor at Knopf, publishers since 1980 of the twelfth edition of this true best seller, reports that the cookbook suffered only one major lapse from its well-known high standard "during the noncooking forties when a number of box-top-type recipes slipped in that had to be weeded out for the more sophisticated tastes of today's readers."

Streamlined, with a plethora of ideas for figure-conscious, health-minded contemporary cooks, the fully revised twelfth edition of *The Fannie Farmer Cookbook* had sold three hundred thousand copies by the end of 1980, its first year of publication.

Animal Crackers

Animal Crackers and cocoa to drink,
That is the finest of suppers, I think:
When I am grown up and can have
   what I please,
I think I shall always insist upon these.[1]

Author-editor Christopher Morley was referring to ANIMAL CRACKERS, of course. Officially brand-named BARNUM'S ANIMALS, they were introduced by the National Biscuit Company in 1902 in a small rectangular box imprinted to resemble a circus cage filled with wild animals. Children loved the strip of string tape that made it easy to carry the box around, though that wasn't the original purpose of the string. It was first put there to enable parents of small children to hang the boxes on the family Christmas tree.

ANIMAL CRACKERS was not a totally new item in the American cookie jar in 1902. A similar design had originated many years earlier in England. They were made by several American bakeries before N.B.C. sold them, but never were they marketed with such flair and showmanship. With P. T. Barnum's name on *that* box, who could resist them?

[1]Christopher Morley, *Chimney Smoke* (New York: J. B. Lippincott, 1917).

108

ICE CREAM CONE

BY MOST ACCOUNTS THE ICE
CREAM CONE dates back to the St.
Louis World's Fair of 1904. This
particular fair was organized to
commemorate the one hundredth
anniversary of the Louisiana
Purchase. The fair had a host of
special attractions, including the

John Philip Sousa Military Band,
palaces of art, machinery and
electricity, and a large number of
food-vending concessions.

Side by side in the food area were
a baker who made a waffle-type
sweet pastry and a merchant who
sold ice cream in assorted flavors.

Neither product was entirely new,
but there was something different
about the way customers were eating
them. More than a few had the
bright idea of buying the thin
wafflelike pastry first, putting the ice
cream on top and eating the two
together.

The pastry baker noticed that in many cases the ice cream tended to slide off the flat waffle. So he rolled a few into a cone shape and passed them on to his fellow vendor who filled the pocket with ice cream. It worked perfectly.

Scores of businessmen who visited the fair observed this informal pooling of resources and began to think how it could be done on a larger scale. The only serious obstacle was the difficulty of making the thin waffle pastry just firm enough to be turned into a cone without breaking.

In 1912 an inventor named Frederick A. Bruckman from Portland, Oregon, devised a machine that could perform the cone-making operation automatically. He sold the rights to use this machine to businesses all over the country, including one headed by a mining engineer named Alexander McLaren.

By the mid-1920's, Nabisco Brands estimates, one third of all the ice cream consumed in the United States was being eaten from cones. As a result of a series of mergers in 1925, most of the cones were being produced by McLaren Consolidated Cone Corporation, which three years later joined the Nabisco family of companies.

OREO

BY THE TURN OF THE CENTURY, children could choose FIG NEWTONS, UNEEDA Biscuits or ANIMAL CRACKERS for a between-meals treat. But not until 1912 did Nabisco introduce what was destined to be the world's all-time favorite cookie.

The first hint of its upcoming appearance came in a company memo dated April 2, 1912. "We are preparing," N.B.C. told its managers, "to offer to the trade three entirely new varieties of the highest class biscuit packed in a new style. The varieties are as follows:

"*Mother Goose* Biscuit—a rich, high class biscuit bearing impressions of the Mother Goose legends.

"*Veronese* Biscuit—a delicious, hard, sweet biscuit of beautiful design and high quality.

"*Oreo* Biscuit—two beautifully embossed, chocolate flavored wafers with a rich cream filling."

The company indicated that it

expected great results from Mother Goose and Veronese. No special mention was made of Oreo.

Today, OREO outsells every other cookie in the world. More than five billion of them are sold every year in the United States alone. Mother Goose and Veronese were never a great success. Production of them was discontinued after only a few years.

Since its introduction, the size of the OREO has varied. Today's version is midway between the largest and the smallest. The name has changed too. From the OREO Biscuit it became the OREO Sandwich, then the OREO Creme Sandwich and finally, in 1974, the OREO Chocolate Sandwich Cookie.

How, you might reasonably ask, did two chocolate-flavored wafers with a rich cream filling come to be called an OREO? There's no authoritative answer but it is quite possible that the National Biscuit Company's first chairman, Adolphus Green, who had a great love of the classics, chose the name OREO because it is the Greek word for "mountain" and in early tests the shape of the cookie resembled a mountain. On the other hand, the name may be derived from *or*, the French word for "gold." The original label had scrollwork in gold on a pale green background, and the product name was printed in gold. Whatever the explanation, it was a perfect choice. The *o*'s of the word seem to roll off the tongue with a roundness that is totally appropriate to the product—an ongoing top seller if ever there was one!

BABY RUTH

JUST BEFORE AMERICA'S ENTRY into World War I another enterprising confectioner who sensed the possibilities of the chocolate and peanuts business was young Otto Schnering in Chicago. His approach was to lease a small room over a plumber's shop, install a five-gallon kettle and a rented stove, hire four employees and announce the formation of the Curtiss Candy Company.

For several years the new company just barely managed to survive as Schnering and his associates tried out one candy recipe after another. Among their early efforts were Curtiss Ostrich Eggs, Curtiss Peter Pan, Curtiss Milk Nut Loaf and Curtiss Cocoanut Grove—tasty and wholesome all, but none of them an instant bonanza at the cash register.

Then after the war, in 1920, Schnering hit the jackpot. Almost overnight the Curtiss Company rose from low-volume obscurity to huge-volume industry leadership. The change was reflected in its magazine advertisements, signed by Schnering himself and listing the five cities the Curtiss Company had so rapidly moved into—New York, Boston, San Francisco and Los Angeles as well as the Chicago home base.

The secret of the Curtiss Company's sudden success was a log-shaped candy bar called BABY RUTH. Contrary to popular opinion, the bar was *not* named for the famous baseball player Babe Ruth, who in 1920 had just joined the New York Yankees and had not yet become a celebrity. It was named in honor of the daughter of former President Grover Cleveland. Born in the White House, she had been the nation's pet, and though she was now a grown woman, Americans still remembered her fondly.

The early ads for BABY RUTH candy were mouth-watering examples of early twentieth century copywriting: "the finest peanuts from the South—roasted then toasted"; "the richest chocolate from the East"; "the choicest milk from the prize herds of the North." Curtiss reinforced its ad campaign with a promotion featuring barnstorming biplanes emblazoned like candy wrappers with the words BABY RUTH. The planes peppered the cities and towns of America with thousands of BABY RUTHS dropped by parachute.

It all paid off in spades for the Curtiss Company. Just six years after its introduction, the ad copy could claim that BABY RUTH was "the world's most popular candy," with over five million sold daily.

In years to come Curtiss would add to its roster such favorites as BUTTERFINGER candy bar, JUMBO BLOCK, peanut-butter cups, SUN MAID raisins and CAMP FIRE marshmallows. In 1964 Curtiss took its place in the Standard Brands galaxy of companies later to merge with Nabisco.

MORTON SALT

EVERY CIVILIZATION HAS HAD ITS salt lore, an assortment of superstitions and legends that have been passed from generation to generation, sometimes reverently and sometimes with tongue in cheek.

The early Greeks worshiped salt no less than the sun and had a saying that no one should trust a man without first eating a peck of salt with him, implying that by the time two people had shared that amount of salt they would no longer be strangers.

"He's not worth his salt" is a common expression that also originated in ancient Greece where salt was traded for slaves.

There has never been any great shortage of salt. It is found in vast underground deposits that occasionally thrust up to the surface, and it can be produced by various methods, including solar evaporation and vacuum-pan evaporation as well as underground mining. All of these methods are used by the Morton Salt Company, the world's leading producer of salt for home, food-service, industrial, agricultural and highway use.

Morton Salt, now a division of Morton-Norwich, had its beginning in Chicago, where the company is still based, as a small midwestern sales agency in 1848. It grew as the population headed west and kept growing long after the West was settled.

The firm was incorporated as the Morton Salt Company in 1910. By then it was a manufacturer as well as a merchant of salt. Among its products was a free-running salt in a round package with a patented spout. The company was anxious to promote sales of this product for table use, with emphasis on the fact that the salt was free-running even in damp weather.

The well-known advertising agency of N. W. Ayer & Company was asked to submit a series of twelve different ads to run in consecutive issues of *Good Housekeeping* magazine. The agency's account executives came back with twelve proposed ads and three possible substitutes.

Sterling Morton, then secretary of the newly formed company, was immediately interested in one of the substitutes showing a little girl holding, in one hand, an umbrella to ward off falling rain and, in the other, a package of salt tilted back under her arm with the spout open and salt pouring out.

"Here was the whole story in a picture—the message that the salt would run in damp weather was made beautifully evident," Morton later recalled. Still it needed something. The proposed copy read "Even in rainy weather, it flows

freely." Obviously, that was too long. Suggestions came along for "Flows Freely," "Runs Freely," and then, at last, the old proverb, "It Never Rains But It Pours." When this was vetoed as being too negative, a positive rephrasing led to "When It Rains It Pours." The picture of the MORTON Salt Girl first appeared with those immortal words on the blue package of table salt in 1914.

Though the product in the blue container never changes, the ageless MORTON Umbrella Girl has been given new dresses and hairstyles to keep her fashionable throughout the years. She was updated in 1921, 1933, 1941 and 1956, and finally in 1968 she acquired a hairstyle and outfit so classic that they may last forever.

LIFE SAVERS

IN THE SUMMER OF 1912 Clarence A. Crane was having trouble selling his homemade chocolate candies. It occured to him that at that time of year he might have better luck with a less perishable item, a refreshing hard mint, for example.

As Crane looked over the selection of mints on the market then, he noticed that, in addition to being made in Europe, virtually all of them were more or less pillow-shaped. Crane figured he could make mints right there in Cleveland that would cost less than the European ones, and he could make them distinctive looking as well as delicious. He decided that a round mint would be a step in the right direction, but a mint with a hole in the middle might really attract attention. It required only a little research to find a pill maker to press out the candies and, with a little persuasion, agree to adapt his machine to put a hole in the middle.

The name for the new product followed quickly upon its invention: It looked exactly like a life preserver.

No other name but LIFE SAVER was seriously considered, and it was registered as a trademark that same year. A label design flaunting the slogan, "For that stormy breath," brought LIFE SAVERS onto the market in a paperboard tube which Crane managed to have distributed as far afield as New York City.

In New York, Edward John Noble, an enterprising salesman of streetcar advertising space, happened to see some of the tubular packages in his neighborhood candy store. He was so impressed with the name of the mints, the shape, the taste that he promptly bought himself a ticket to Cleveland to meet the man who made them.

Almost as soon as they met, Noble tried to talk Crane into advertising the mints. Crane was not interested. "My business is chocolates," he declared. "The mint idea was just something to fill in during the summer when chocolate sales fell off."

The two men continued to argue until Crane finally suggested Noble buy the rights and make them himself. "How much are you asking?" Noble replied. "Five thousand dollars," said Crane, naming a figure almost at random.

Noble returned to New York where he discussed the prospective deal with a boyhood friend, Roy Arlen. Together they raised $3,800. Crane agreed to lower his price to $2,900, leaving the young entrepreneurs a $900 balance for working capital.

Almost immediately the partners discovered they had a serious problem. The roll of LIFE SAVERS that had inspired Noble to pledge his faith in the product's future was only one week old. There were thousands of other rolls resting stale and flavorless on retailers' shelves thanks to the cardboard package which quickly absorbed the zesty peppermint flavor.

Noble promptly devised a tinfoil wrapping (a first in the industry) that kept the flavor intact. He then undertook to persuade shop owners far and wide to take a new supply of LIFE SAVERS in even exchange for the old, stale ones. Whenever he met any resistance to trying the new LIFE SAVERS, he simply said, "Just put a few near the cash register with a price card. Then be sure every customer gets a nickel with his change and see what happens."

What happened was that within two years Noble's company had made a quarter of a million dollars. World War I temporarily slowed sugar production almost to a standstill, but the year after the war, with quotas removed, LIFE SAVERS enjoyed a sales increase of more than 200 percent. They have increased steadily ever since.

Life Savers

L ife Savers, Inc., has never underestimated the importance of clever marketing. One famous blooper, however, occurred on the day several groups of men hired by the company appeared on the streets of New York City encased in metal tubes painted to look like rolls of LIFE SAVERS. A party of these men trudged up a hill near Columbia University where they encountered a small band of undergraduates. The students, delighted at the approaching opportunity to liven up a dull day, turned the encapsulated men on their sides and rolled them down the hill again.

On another occasion, the company bought commercial time on a program hosted by radio's irrepressible Henry Morgan. Company officials listening in were appalled to hear Morgan scrap the copy for the commercial and launch dreamily into one of his own inimitable monologues.

"You folks," he began, "are being gypped. That hole in the center of a LIFE SAVER is just so much candy you're not getting. Think of the money they save on those millions of holes."

Apparently the public laughed and went right on buying LIFE SAVERS.

Tank Watch

I nspired by patriotism, Louis Cartier designed the TANK watch in 1914 for the U.S. Tank Corps. The hefty, no-nonsense design, intended to resemble a tank as seen from above, caught on immediately and has never lost its appeal. Yves St. Laurent and Sammy Davis, Jr., both wear one; so do Jackie Kennedy Onassis and Helen Gurley Brown. In solid gold, a TANK watch costs $2,300, or it is available in sterling silver with gold plate for $600.

Lenox China/Autumn

Tops in dinnerware sales since its inception, the pattern called AUTUMN was introduced by Lenox in 1919. The realistic blossoms and delicate gold rim are still hand-painted by Lenox's craftswomen today.

KELLOGG'S CORN FLAKES

A WALK DOWN THE SUPERMARKET aisle in the breakfast-food department reveals a new advertising ploy on the part of the cereal companies: Among the serious health-food products with labels proclaiming ALL natural ingredients, NO preservatives or additives, are boxes marked "No Added Sugar," "High Protein," "Low Sodium," "High Fiber," and "Multi-Vitamin."

We may assume from what Ronald Deutsch tells us about the early days of the cereal industry in his book *The Nuts Among the Berries* (Ballantine Books, 1961), that the founders of the Kellogg Company would be pleased about the recent changes in the cereal business.

According to Ronald Deutsch, the story of Kellogg's begins with Sister Ellen Harmon White, a Seventh Day Adventist wholeheartedly devoted to care of

the body in order to achieve purity of mind and spirit. Toward this end, she recommended a diet of water, fruits and vegetables with occasional nibbles of a stiff bread known as Graham bread, the invention of her predecessor in the health-food field, Sylvester Graham.

Sister White considered herself the true spiritual leader of the Adventist Church in the mid-nineteenth century with a special mission to perform for God. She had been convinced of this since the night she stood waiting on a hilltop in Maine with other devoted Adventists ready to ascend into heaven in their laundry baskets. The fact that nothing happened was a clear sign to Sister White that the Lord still had work for her to do on earth.

Sister White's holy revelations led her to Battle Creek, Michigan, where, she claimed, the Almighty wanted her to build a sanitarium.

The Western Health Forum Institute was duly opened in 1866, unencumbered by any sanctions other than the divine. Only two doctors were associated with it. The institute's most serious enticement was a program based on Sister Ellen Harmon White's recommended diet, guaranteed to make one pure in both body and spirit.

By 1876 Sister White had found the man she wanted to be director of her institute. She chose Dr. John Harvey Kellogg, son of an Adventist broom maker. Kellogg, a graduate of Bellevue Medical College, in New York, had been editor of the institute's magazine, *Good Health*, before he started his medical education. He was also author of two books about the importance of a correct diet. The books were familiar to Sister White who for years had used them as a primary resource for her revelations and theories about health.

Almost as soon as Kellogg moved to Battle Creek, he decided to change the name of the institute to Battle Creek Sanitarium, which seemed to him to strike a more authentically medical note. He hired his younger brother, William Keith (W.K.), as business manager, made his plans and began to build.

In a remarkably short time, the sanitarium (soon known as the "San") began attracting the rich, the famous and the somewhat ailing from all over the country. Henry Ford, John D. Rockefeller, Harvey Firestone and President-to-be Harding came there to be treated amidst the handsome buildings, landscaped lawns, fountains and verandas of this health world Kellogg was determined to create.

The surroundings were beautiful but the regime was Spartan, since guests at the San were expected to observe a strict, vegetarian diet. The kitchen at the San was frequently busy as members of the Kellogg family and staff experimented with new ways to make San food more nutritious and palatable. One of these experiments entailed running boiled wheat dough through rollers to produce thin sheets. Then the wheat dough was toasted and ground into meal. One day, after spreading the boiled wheat in pans for toasting, the cooks were called away from the kitchen. When they returned the next day and saw the unbaked wheat they decided to run it through the toasting rollers anyway. What emerged was not the thin sheets of wheat they expected but many individual flakes. Served up in bowls with milk and sugar, the new wheat flakes were so popular that sanitarium patients who had gone home would often write to Dr. Kellogg asking to have the cereal sent to them by mail. To meet this demand Kellogg started the Sanitas Food Company, for the sole purpose of producing wheat flakes, rice flakes and corn flakes. The corn flakes were not big sellers at first because the corn kernel made them too tough. In time, W. K. Kellogg, general manager of the company and co-partner with his brother, developed a tastier corn flake by using only the grit, or heart, of the corn and adding malt for flavoring. The new recipe proved so successful that W.K. decided to form his own company specializing in CORN FLAKES.

It was a few years before W.K. could devote himself entirely to his new company, for in 1902 Sister White's dire prophecies of a sword of fire hanging over Battle Creek came to grim fulfillment. In that year a series of fires crippled the San. W.K. spent four years helping his brother rebuild it. In the meantime, other entrepreneurs were beginning to see the possibilities of the cereal market. C. W. Post, a former patient at the San, was one of these.

Texan Charles W. Post had decided to try his own approach to capitalizing on health. He planned to start his own "health center," but before he did, he offered his services to Dr. Kellogg to promote a cereal coffee called MINUTE BREW that he had enjoyed while staying at the sanitarium. Preferring to keep the profits in his own pocket, Kellogg turned him down. The possibility of a Kellogg-Post partnership was never discussed again.

Post went on to develop his own cereal coffee, called POSTUM, and he sent it into the marketplace with all the promotional savvy he knew how to muster. You could buy POSTUM in paper bags from a

handcart that roamed the streets of Battle Creek; there were ads for it everywhere Post could persuade an editor to let him say, "It Makes Red Blood." In his copy Post referred menacingly to "coffee neuralgia" and "coffee heart," then offered POSTUM as an alternative. He was inventing a strategy: Threaten an affliction, then offer to heal it or prevent it.

Three years after POSTUM, along came a sibling product, GRAPE NUTS, made from a baked wheat cracker cooked hard as a rock, then broken up into pebblelike crumbs. Post claimed with impunity that it was good for appendicitis, tightened up loose teeth, nourished the brain and was very effective against consumption and malaria. This was no ordinary breakfast food! For the benefit of anyone who was not totally convinced, Post enclosed a free copy of his personal treatise on health, called "Road to Wellville."

By 1901 Post had made his first million and was on his way to more.

Other companies endeavored to follow in his footsteps. Battle Creek turned into a boomtown as entrepreneurs came to seek their fortunes not in gold but in cereal.

When the factory doors opened for W. K. Kellogg's Toasted Corn Flake Company in 1906, there were forty-two cereal companies registered in the Battle Creek area, more than the total number of employees at the original Sanitas Food Plant. W.K.'s company became the leader among the few survivors of the early competition. To guard against any possible confusion, W.K. had his name printed on every package. It is there still, on every package of Kellogg's CORN FLAKES, in W.K.'s own handwriting style, with the explanation, "The original bears this signature."

Five years later, the company was selling more than a million cases of CORN FLAKES annually and, in 1911, had budgeted $1 million for advertising. Part of this fortune was

spent to erect the world's largest electric sign on the roof of the Mecca Building at Times Square in New York, featuring the word KELLOGG'S with a K sixty-six feet tall.

Though Kellogg Company has plants in twenty-one countries around the world, and today sells many other products, from pizza to drink mixes, its chairman and CEO, William E. LaMothe, sees the company's growth in grains. "The food for the future," he calls it. LaMothe predicts that the world's population will exceed six billion people by the year 2000. He told shareholders in 1983 that, "Kellogg Company foresees people turning to one major food category in their diet—one food group that satisfies hunger at minimal cost while providing essential nutrients—grain."

Where cereals are concerned Chairman LaMothe says confidently, "The last seventy-seven years are just the beginning!"

JOLLY GREEN GIANT

By 1921, MINNESOTA VALLEY Canning Company had been raising and canning corn for eighteen years. In the early days it had had to battle a deep-seated color prejudice on the part of Americans who would eat only white corn. "Yellow corn is horse corn," people used to say. Sometime around 1920 the company decided to commit itself to a marketing philosophy stressing

product individuality: It began raising golden corn, which was sweeter and more tender as well as easier to produce than white corn. With bated breath the company put the golden corn on the market in 1924 as DEL MAIZ Brand cream-style corn. To everyone's amazement, it sold very well. DEL MAIZ was followed five years later by NIBLETS Brand vacuum-packed

whole kernel corn and it too was a success. Today yellow corn is the favorite of 90 percent of corn eaters everywhere, whether it's fresh, frozen or canned.

Two years after Minnesota Valley began raising golden sweet corn, Board of Directors-member Ward Cosgrove brought back from Europe a green pea that also challenged the eating habits of the day. It was an

English garden variety called "Prince of Wales"—wrinkled, oblong and, as peas go, huge. Americans customarily preferred "Early June" peas—small, smooth and round. They thought big peas were old and tough. But the brave few who sampled the Prince of Wales could not deny that it had a flavor, sweetness and tenderness Early Junes couldn't match. Minnesota Valley Canning decided to make a marketing feature out of the size of the peas. They packed them in cans with the words GREEN GIANT on the label.

When the company applied for a trademark for the new pea, their attorney, Warwick Keegin, said the words GREEN GIANT were descriptive and therefore not patentable.

Keegin suggested putting a giant on the label as a symbol. By claiming that GREEN GIANT referred to the symbol rather than the pea, perhaps a patent could be obtained.

So the first GREEN GIANT appeared in 1925. Borrowed from a book of *Grimm's Fairy Tales*, he wore a scowl and a scruffy bearskin, not a suit of leaves and a smile. He looked more like a dwarf than a giant and, worst of all, he wasn't even green, he was white.

Later on Keegin came to the company headquarters in Le Sueur, Minnesota, to argue that the giant should be green. He ran into some opposition.

"That's ridiculous, Warwick," future president of the company Bill Dietrich remembers saying. "Whoever heard of a green giant?"

In the years that followed, as ingenious advertising made the JOLLY GREEN GIANT as familiar a figure to American families as the milkman, Minnesota Valley Canning outgrew its original facilities in Le Sueur, expanded into several other states and took the name of the character it had created to signify the whole company.

TINKER TOYS/ERECTOR SETS

WHO SAID TINKERTOYS WERE JUST for kids! There's a two-story fairy-tale castle made from 5,770 Giant TINKERTOY parts in the Museum of North Orange County, California. It took eight *grown-ups* one hundred hours to build. Every year more than a thousand people, including engineers, architects, artists and children who aspire to the design professions, all gather for TINKERTOY Weekend at the Franklin Institute in Philadelphia to bring their fantasies to life by building gigantic and unique TINKERTOY constructions. And in case you think a well-made TINKERTOY construction does not necessarily indicate the builder has a high IQ, it is reliably reported that Indiana Bell Telephone has tested management candidates with TINKERTOY sets and that Lockheed used TINKERTOY as a design model to build an airplane wingfuselage testing system.

It is doubtful whether Charles Pajeau, inventor of the TINKERTOY, ever fully realized the future his creation would have. Pajeau was a stonemason from Evanston, Illinois. Seeing the fun children had making toys with pencils, sticks and empty spools of thread, Pajeau's plan was to supply them with several basic parts that they could combine in a variety of three-dimensional, abstract ways. He brought his

TINKERTOY®

invention to New York in 1913 where it was introduced at the American Toy Fair. Within a year, nearly a million of the sets had been sold.

In 1980, when the nation's construction industry was in a serious slump, TINKERTOYS and its companion product ERECTOR Sets, then made by Gabriel Industries (now by Ideal/CBS Toys), were apparently enjoying a major boom. In December of that year Art Barnett, vice-president of marketing services for Gabriel, reported that retail sales in building toys had doubled to more than *$150 million in five years*! Apparently this is one industry that is "recession-proof."

The inventor of the ERECTOR Set was A. C. Gilbert, a man of many talents. Long before he had the idea for ERECTOR Sets, he had earned a medical degree at Yale, won an Olympic gold medal for pole vaulting (1908) and operated a successful magic-trick business—all before he turned twenty-eight years old.

It was in 1912, while traveling to one of his entrepreneurial enterprises, that Gilbert became intrigued by the sight of workmen constructing a high-tension tower for power lines beside the tracks of the New Haven railroad. Day after day Gilbert watched the tower's progress, becoming increasingly fascinated with the idea of building with girders. One evening at home he cut a few girderlike strips out of cardboard. He had some of these cast in steel at a machinist's shop and soon discovered that when a groove was etched along the sides of the girder, the pieces could be locked together quite securely with bolts and screws. Now, he realized, children could build sturdy constructions in steel, of all shapes and sizes, using small modular parts and nut-and-bolt fastenings.

The ERECTOR Set was first shown at the 1913 Toy Fair in New York City. By this time Gilbert had designed wheels and axles for it, as well as pinions, girders, angles, plates . . . and an electric motor that made many parts of the models move. There was a windmill that actually turned, a bridge that lifted, an elevator that went up and down—and that was only the beginning of the myriad functions children and adults would soon discover ERECTOR Sets could perform.

ERECTOR®

In 1967 A. C. Gilbert's company was acquired by Gabriel Industries, where ERECTOR Sets joined TINKERTOYS as one of the company's big money-makers. Now owned by Ideal/CBS Toys, the designers of ERECTOR Sets have moved into the space age with the Mega Claw Excavator, an Alien Terrain Patrol and a Pod Foot Lunar Patrol to engage the imagination of today's children as earlier models of the toy have in the past.

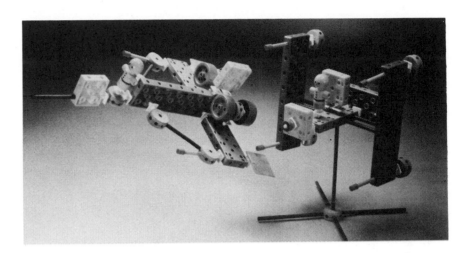

REYNOLDS TOBACCO

"A CUSTOM LOATHSOME TO THE EYE, hateful to the nose, harmful to the brain, dangerous to the lungs, and in the black stinking fume thereof, nearest resembling the horrible Stygian smoke of the pit that is bottomless," declared James I in 1604 on the subject of smoking. He was so violently opposed to the habit that he reserved a special punishment for doctors who indulged in it. They would be banished, he swore, to "the land of the red Indians."

If any doctors were banished, they must have brought their habit with them, for there are few industries in America that have turned larger profits than those that deal in tobacco. The biggest money-maker of them all, R. J. Reynolds, now merged with Heublein, has expanded and diversified since its founding in 1875 into areas as different as packaged Oriental food

(CHUN KING) and container-shipping operations, but tobacco still accounts for 80 percent of its profits.

The R. J. Reynolds Company was not the first to get into the American tobacco business: Philip Morris and Liggett & Meyers preceded Reynolds and have offered stiff competition from time to time all through Reynolds's history. The American Tobacco Company's James Buchanan "Buck" Duke and later George Washington Hill, who made LUCKY STRIKE the most popular smoke in America during the 1930's and 1940's, gave Reynolds a run for its money. But Reynolds, personified by R. J. Reynolds, founder of the company, and his successor, Bowman Gray, never admitted to taking a backseat to anyone.

The story of the Reynolds company and its best-selling brand name begins with Richard Joshua

Reynolds, known as Dick to family and friends. By some accounts, he first rode into the twin towns of Winston and Salem, North Carolina, as a barefoot, illiterate farm boy atop a wagonload of his dad's tobacco. After attending both college and business school, he returned to Rock Spring in southwestern Virginia, where his father grew tobacco, made it into plug for chewing and sold it throughout the South. Dick Reynolds helped manage the factory on his father's plantation and went on peddling expeditions, often driving a wagonload of chewing tobacco as far as Kentucky and Tennessee in search of customers.

On one of these trips, the company history reports, he found times so hard and money so scarce that he resorted to barter. Reynolds returned home with a wagonload of ginseng, tallow, cowhides, bearskins, homespun goods, furniture, rag carpets—and three horses and mules hitched on behind. In his pocket was a gold watch the owner had traded for $30 worth of tobacco.

Apparently Reynolds had given the equivalent of $2,000 in tobacco for all this booty, which he then auctioned off, making more than the tobacco would ever have brought in cash. As for the gold watch, when his brother bid $30, Dick raised the bid to $90 and kept it for himself.

It is not surprising that with this kind of business acumen, Reynolds soon went off to seek his own fortune. In the fall of 1874 he borrowed money from his family to build a factory in Winston, conveniently located on a new railway line and the center for the new flue-cured leaf that made the best chewing tobacco. Reynolds set up housekeeping on the second floor of his factory and a few months later began processing chewing tobacco. In that first season of operations Reynolds and his workers turned out 150,000 pounds; by 1887 there were eighty-six brands of Reynolds's tobacco on the market.

Not long after the turn of the century, Reynolds began experimenting with different formulas for making smoking tobacco, eventually hitting on one he thought was exceptionally good. He named it PRINCE ALBERT, after the popular Prince of Wales who had become the British monarch Edward VII. In 1910 Reynolds hired the advertising agency, N. W. Ayer & Son, to mount a national advertising campaign to promote the tobacco. Soon the slogan "Can't bite your tongue," ads in all the popular magazines and a huge electric

signboard showing Prince Albert surveying New York's Union Square below all called attention to Reynolds's new tobacco.

From there Reynolds, now commonly known as RJR, moved into the arena where his American Tobacco Company rival Buck Duke had preceded him by more than twenty years. Though most smokers still rolled their own cigarettes in these years, there were at least fifty manufactured brands competing for sales. However, they were all made with "straight" tobaccos—either pure Virginian or pure Turkish— and RJR made up his mind to blend a cigarette that people wouldn't be able to resist. With his characteristic savvy he brought out four at the same time in 1913. The one made with a blend of Turkish and domestic tobaccos and a generous amount of sweetening was called CAMEL and was sold in a pack featuring a rather pathetic-looking one-humped beast with pointed ears against an exotic desert background. Twenty CAMELS cost ten cents, half the price of competing brands. They were a success right from the start, and within a decade half the nation's smokers were hooked on them.

When the first pack of CAMELS came on the market, the Reynolds

people weren't quite sure whether their one-humped dromedary really qualified for the distinguished role he was playing. Fortunately, Barnum & Bailey came to town just in time to settle the issue. In the circus menagerie was a bona fide, certified dromedary named Old Joe, who was reluctantly persuaded to pose for the new, revised design of the CAMEL pack.

Pleased by the good response to his cigarette, RJR decided not to bother with regional marketing programs and went straight to national distribution. When World War I broke out, he seized the opportunity to ensure a future market for CAMELS by offering them, free, to all the doughboys in France. But it was several years until anyone hit upon an appropriate slogan to advertise the increasingly successful brand name. Unfortunately, RJR was not around to hear the story of the foursome of golfers taking a break from their game. Fresh out of cigarettes, one of them exclaimed, "I'd walk a mile for a CAMEL." The man to whom he addressed his remark happened to be Martin Reddington, who handled Reynolds's outdoor ad campaigns. Reddington immediately worked the slogan into a series of ads and within months it appeared on billboards everywhere.

R.J.Reynolds Industries, Inc.

Reprinted with permission from "Our 100th Anniversary 1875–1975," © 1975 by R. J. Reynolds Industries, Inc.

RJR died in 1918 and the company went into something of a slump. Reynolds's sons were not interested in running their father's business, and his favorite nephew had already gone off to start a foil-producing venture, later to become Reynolds Metals. Management of the Reynolds company passed into the hands of Bowman Gray, a salesman and protégé of RJR. The Gray family ran the business for the next fifty years, bravely bucking competition from LUCKIES in the twenties and from Philip Morris when Reynolds raised the price of CAMELS at the beginning of the Depression. By means of a massive increase in advertising and promotion, CAMELS managed to win back its Number One position by 1935. The company continued to hold it there through the post-World War II health craze by inviting athletes to endorse the cigarette. The public was only too willing to believe that if CAMELS didn't bother "Big Bill" Tilden, champion of the tennis world, and Gloria Wheedon, aquaplane expert, they couldn't be all that bad for you.

By 1955 the government had stepped into the health issue. The Federal Trade Commission forbade all further health claims, direct or indirect, by cigarette advertisers, and published a set of Cigarette Advertising Guides. Reynolds was ready to usher in a new era of filtered cigarettes with WINSTONS, produced for the first time in 1954, but, seeing the writing on the wall as far as smoking was concerned, Reynolds and other tobacco companies hastened to move into other areas, too. Reynolds amended its charter to permit investment in non-tobacco enterprises and gradually became involved in foil materials, convenience foods and beverages, and containerized freight operations. In 1970 it spent $55 million to acquire the American Independent Oil Company (Aminoil) and, in that same year, created a new parent company, R. J.

Reynolds Industries, Inc., with Reynolds Tobacco Company becoming a wholly owned subsidiary.

Reynolds's SALEM, the first filter-tipped menthol cigarette, had successfully followed WINSTON into the health-minded market of the 1950's, but no competitor in the tobacco industry was ready for the arrival of the MARLBORO Man. Taking a totally new tack in advertising, Philip Morris sent the lean, laconic MARLBORO cowboy onto the nation's billboards in 1954, offering nothing—except an invitation to MARLBORO country. Results soon showed that in a market where, when blindfolded, even the most experienced smokers often can't tell one brand from the other, identification with an image means everything. By the end of the 1970's MARLBORO had become, and still is, the best-selling cigarette in the United States. By 1982, MARLBORO sales were roughly $3.8 billion a year, representing 35 percent of Philip Morris's total annual revenue of $11 billion.

FORMICA

FORMICA BRAND PLASTIC laminate revolutionized the design of kitchens and bathrooms all over America. Since World War II, it has made its way into every room in the house and most public areas, figuring prominently in the streamlined appearance of interiors in the 1970's and, in the 1980's, conforming comfortably with revived interest in texture and color.

One might imagine that FORMICA laminate is a typical space-age product, created specifically to serve the decorating industry. On the contrary, it evolved slowly, sometimes painfully, from a modest beginning in 1913 when two former employees of Westinghouse discovered a new way to make high-quality insulation materials for the booming electrical industry.

Herbert A. Faber and Daniel J. O'Conor launched their new

business on the eve of World War I—not exactly with the blessing of their former employer who recognized the talents of the two young men and would have liked to keep them in the Westinghouse fold. But Faber and O'Conor (commonly known as D.J.) struck out bravely on their own, opening their plant on May 2, 1913, in Cincinnati, without benefit of ceremony or of employees other than themselves, in overalls, filling their first order. That order was from Chalmers Motor Company for commutator rings in which Faber and O'Conor laminate replaced mica. (Hence, *for* "in place of," *mica*.)

Four months after opening for business, the new company had eighteen employees making thousands of insulating parts for electrical equipment just coming on the market. Meanwhile, their own handmade equipment was suffering from overuse. They used C-clamps and baling wire to hold it together. The partners were too broke to buy the machines that would have made their work easier. Many nights they had to decide whether to let Faber take a press apart and fix it or hope that it would hold up for O'Conor to turn out a rush job.

Faced with the urgent need of cash, the young men borrowed on everything they owned and persuaded three businessmen to support them by becoming investors. In October of that first year they incorporated as the Formica Insulation Company with a board of directors made up of Faber, O'Conor and the three investors. Faber, who would subsequently take major responsibility for the design and building of most of the processing machinery, was elected

president. O'Conor, who would be in charge mainly of product development and improvement, was vice-president and secretary. This management organization continued until 1935.

The intervening years were marked with peaks and valleys. One of the latter occurred soon after Faber and O'Conor had decided to go into the making of sheet laminates. The sales manager of the Bakelite Company, supplier of one of the material's most essential components, resin, took D. J. O'Conor out to lunch and informed him that Bakelite had decided that Westinghouse would be permitted to make flat sheet laminates using their material under license, but the Formica Company would not. They would supply resin to Formica for rings and tubes only.

Undeterred, Faber and O'Conor soon found another supplier for resin, Dr. L. V. Redman who operated a small plant in Chicago. The partners enlisted his enthusiastic support, and on July 4, 1914, the first sheet of FORMICA laminate came off the press. Faber and O'Conor were jubilant. They knew they had a great new material which would open up big markets.

Orders came in slowly, but for an increasing variety of product-uses; in 1917 the wartime radio industry discovered FORMICA; as news spread of its unusual combination of strength and pliability, the Formica Company was soon supplying laminated plastic to replace older materials as washer parts, refrigerator parts, timing gears and spinning parts for the burgeoning textile industry.

Not until 1938 did the Formica Company make decorative laminate. In that year a new

melamine resin was incorporated into the manufacturing process, which made the laminate tough and durable enough to use as we do today. For years the company made the only decorative laminate of this type. Today, Formica Corporation commands a 40 percent market share.

In 1978 Formica Corporation found itself embroiled in a stiff legal battle to defend its winning brand name. In May 1978 the Denver regional office of the Federal Trade Commission filed a petition to cancel the registration of the FORMICA trademark. The petition alleged that the FORMICA trademark had become the generic or descriptive name for all decorative plastic laminate. According to the government petition, the name had become part of everyday language, giving the company an unfair advantage over its competitors.

The Formica Corporation maintained that its trademark appeared conspicuously on a variety of decorative plastic laminates and other products manufactured only by the Formica Corporation. Furthermore, it claims that the FTC lacks the authority to challenge trademarks registered prior to the 1946 Lanham Act.

In the proud tradition of its founders, Formica Corporation, now headed by President Gordon D. Sterling, contested the matter vigorously, "until our position was vindicated." Today, the Formica brand name continues as one of the strongest in the country.

KLEENEX

THE KLEENEX STORY IS A CLASSIC illustration of what the right package can do for a humble product.

KLEENEX was one of the first consumer products offered by Kimberley-Clark right after World War I as part of a program to find peacetime uses for Cellucotton, a form of cotton wadding used extensively for surgical dressing in military hospitals. (KOTEX feminine napkins were another such spin-off product.) The tissues, called KLEENEX Kerchiefs, were originally presented as a cold-cream remover—a disposable substitute for facial towels. A package of one hundred sold for sixty-five cents.

The first KLEENEX box was a far cry from today's streamlined package. It was almost square, printed in dark blue with the name and other lettering in white. A narrow band encircled the package and a cross suggestive of the earlier surgical product was centered on top.

Early magazine and newspaper ads for KLEENEX showed Hollywood makeup studios in the background and called attention to the new "scientific way to remove cold cream." Later, endorsements by Helen Hayes, Gertrude Lawrence, Ronald Colman and other stars appeared in the ads, tying in the product with the glamorous world of Hollywood that captivated Americans during the twenties.

The year 1929 is a milestone in KLEENEX history. It was the year that the Serv-a-Tissue box was introduced after a long period of experimentation by its designer, Andrew P. Olsen, of Chicago. The tear-out slot in the top permitting another tissue to pop up, ready for use, has been consistently featured, with fabulous success, in KLEENEX advertising ever since.

Prior to 1930 KLEENEX was advertised almost exclusively to women as a cold-cream remover, but the mail the manufacturer was getting about that time indicated that KLEENEX's best feature might be its usefulness as a disposable handkerchief. In January and February 1930, two newspaper test campaigns were run simultaneously in Peoria, Illinois. Each campaign ran ads of identical size and layout but highlighted distinctly different uses for the product. Half were headlined "We pay to prove there is no way like Kleenex to remove cold cream"; the others stated, "We pay to prove Kleenex is wonderful for handkerchiefs." The pay was a free box of KLEENEX.

To the manufacturer's amazement, the test showed that more than 60 percent of the people purchasing KLEENEX were using it as a disposable handkerchief. Advertising was changed to emphasize this usage, and sales doubled within the year.

During the period 1935–1936, KLEENEX sales practically doubled again as the KLEENEX radio show, *The Story of Mary Marlin*, became a daytime hit. With two commercials a day, five days a week, this program sold KLEENEX for dozens of uses—as handkerchiefs and to remove cosmetics, as well as to dust, polish, clean out pans, drain fried foods and do other tasks in the home, office and car. A 1936 package insert listed forty-eight possible uses.

Another major package change came in 1938 when the solid blue blocks diagonally opposed across the carton were introduced as a background for the KLEENEX name. The new design was acclaimed for its "across-the-store" display value, a prime consideration in modern merchandising, especially in self-service locations.

The revised KLEENEX package won praise in other circles, too, including New York's Museum of Modern Art where it was selected as an outstanding example of modern design. Writing in *The New Yorker*, art critic Robert M. Coates theorized that the KLEENEX box had been "obviously designed with the work of the artist Mondrian in mind." (The company reports that the package designer wasn't sure about that.)

By the time KLEENEX was going into the marketplace in its smart modern package, its price had dropped from sixty-five cents for the two-hundred-tissue carton in 1925 to fifty cents in 1926, thirty-five cents in 1932, eighteen cents in 1934 and thirteen cents or two for a quarter in 1938. It was a perfect illustration of the marketing lesson that the way to higher sales is paved by large volume and low price. The ingenious package and the advertising support behind it had made this possible.

Nothing demonstrated more clearly the heights attained by KLEENEX's ad campaigns than Little Lulu, standing thirty-five feet tall next to a giant KLEENEX box above New York's Times Square in the early fifties. Lulu, created by Marge Buell, had become a famous cartoon character in *The Saturday Evening Post* before her alliance with KLEENEX in 1944. She was introduced at a time when the armed forces were receiving about one third of KLEENEX's curtailed production and competition was beginning to edge in. The partnership of a beloved cartoon character with a tried-and-true product was eminently successful. KLEENEX has confidently dominated the disposable tissue market ever since.

S.O.S Soap Pads

S.O.S pads were first made in San Francisco in 1917 by Edwin W. Cox, a salesman who wanted to add a little luster to his sales pitch for aluminum cookware by giving away one soap-impregnated steel-wool pad to every customer. He made them at home, by hand, dipping the pads countless times to load them with soap, until the demand for the pads outgrew his ability to make them. Then, in order to raise capital to manufacture them on a profitable scale, Cox subdivided and sold his patent rights on a geographical basis. Companies were formed to sell the product in twelve states. Cox took charge of the office in Chicago where, many years later, all S.O.S operations were eventually consolidated.

It is said that Mrs. Edwin Cox suggested the name S.O.S because it was "the universal call for help and also the first letters of Save Our Saucepans."

LINCOLN LOGS

IF YOU'VE EVER ADMIRED THE architectural simplicity of a LINCOLN LOGS creation, it may be because the toy was invented by John L. Wright, who inherited his talent for design from his father, architect Frank Lloyd Wright.

From childhood, John was intrigued by stories of America's pioneer days. In 1916 on a business trip with his father, he passed the time while his father consulted with his client by watching workmen move huge timbers into place for construction of the Imperial Palace Hotel in Tokyo. As he watched, young Wright visualized a building toy that would allow children to duplicate, on a small scale, many of the structures that were part of America's past—log cabins, forts, covered bridges.

When he returned home to Merrill, Wisconsin, Wright worked out the details of the design for his toy and tried to market it, but not until 1924 did American children begin to catch on to the possibilities the toy held for imaginative play. In 1943 Wright sold the rights to LINCOLN LOGS to Playskool, which has enjoyed steady profits from its sales ever since.

original
LINCOLN LOGS®

BAND-AIDS

IN 1920 EARLE E. DICKSON AND his wife, Josephine, were newlyweds living in New Brunswick, New Jersey. Like all brides, Mrs. Dickson had a habit of nicking or burning her fingers while preparing meals in her new kitchen. When this happened, her husband would tenderly bandage his wife's injured fingers with gauze and adhesive, products of the local Johnson & Johnson plant where Dickson was employed as cotton buyer in the purchasing department.

As time went on, Dickson grew impatient with the clumsy, easily lost bandages his wife still seemed to need. He sat down one night to give the matter some thought. He recalled, "I was determined to devise some manner of bandage that would stay in place, be easily applied and still retain its sterility."

Dickson experimented with strips of surgical tape, also from Johnson & Johnson, laying them sticky side up on the dining-room table. Then Dickson made a pad of gauze, stuck it on the middle of the tape and covered both tape and gauze with a length of crinoline cut to the right size. When he realized that his bandages, with their protective layer of crinoline, could be easily stored for future use, he went ahead and made a few dozen more for his wife's needs and took a handful to work with him.

Dickson's colleagues at Johnson & Johnson encouraged him to show his new invention to people in the management division of the company. A little shyly, Dickson took their advice and found his idea was well received. The company's president, James W. Johnson, saw the potential for a new and unique bandage as a basic first-aid product. A decision was made to manufacture it under the trademark of BAND-AID, a name suggested by W. Johnson Kenyon, superintendent of the mill at the Johnson & Johnson plant.

The first adhesive bandages were made by hand and produced in sections three inches wide and eighteen inches long. As in the Dickson home where they originated, removable crinoline protected the adhesive surface. The user would scissor off as long a strip as was required.

At first sales were slow, but believers in the new bandage persevered. One of these was Dr. Frederick B. Kilmer, father of the poet Joyce Kilmer. In addition to heading the company's research department, Dr. Kilmer edited a Johnson & Johnson magazine for druggists. Perhaps an occasional victim of paper cuts, Kilmer became a leading advocate of the BAND-AID Brand Adhesive Bandage. In nearly every issue of the magazine he promoted the product as a means of

preventing infection and speeding the healing of small injuries. Other marketing strategies included supplying Boy Scouts with unlimited free samples and distributing ample supplies of the new bandages to every butcher in Cleveland.

By 1924 further development of the BAND-AID led to the design of machinery to precut three-inch by three-quarter-inch bandages. These met with great enthusiasm from consumers and the sale of BAND-AID Brand Adhesive Bandages soon increased 50 percent.

Product improvements to BAND-AIDS continued over the years. In 1928 aeration holes were added to the pad—and later to the entire bandage—to promote faster healing. Also in 1928, medicated bandages were introduced. A means of

making the whole product sterile was devised in 1938. Today the key to the sterilization process is a huge steam pressure cooker, large enough to contain a small automobile. The boxes of BAND-AIDS are placed in this machine and subjected to sufficient steam to destroy all microorganisms.

Postscript: Earle E. Dickson, the considerate husband who improvised the first BAND-AIDS for his bride, went on to a long and fruitful career with Johnson & Johnson. He was elected to the Board of Directors and named a vice-president in 1932. The company estimates that about 100 billion of his ingenious invention have been sold since Johnson & Johnson introduced it in 1921.

MAIDENFORM BRA

RIGHT AT THE HEIGHT OF THE flapper era when fashions were flat-chested and boyish, Ida Rosenthal was giving away her handmade bras to lift the sales of her custom-designed dresses as well as her customer's figures.

Ida and her husband had an elegant dress shop on Manhattan's Fifty-seventh Street where Ida designed chic little frocks for notable New York ladies. It was the Roaring Twenties and although other designers' clients paraded boldly in shifts and chemises, Ida continued to cater to the shapely figure. She had many faithful customers who

rewarded her well with their patronage.

As Ida struggled over the elegant dresses that were so time-consuming to make, husband William observed the increasing popularity of the "bonus" undergarments which, by now, were creating as much interest as the dresses themselves. He studied the feasibility of producing bras based on a categorization of women into four basic figure types. He concluded that a bra, with built-in adjustments, could be designed and manufactured to fit each type of figure.

In 1922 the Rosenthals gave up the dress shop and, with a capital

investment of only $4,500, started the MAIDENFORM Brassiere Company.

By 1926, William Rosenthal, who was a pioneer of mass-production techniques, had forty machines humming away in the same building that had once housed the dress business.

Forty years later, MAIDENFORM had nineteen factories producing twenty-five million garments each year. Sales were in excess of $40 million per year. Ida Rosenthal no longer merely dreamed of becoming a chairman of the board in her MAIDENFORM bra, she actually served in that role for many years.

I dreamed I was a knockout
in my *maidenform bra*

Arabesque*... *new Maidenform bra*...has bias-cut center-of-attraction for *superb*
separation...insert of elastic for *comfort*...floral circular stitching for the most *beautiful* contours!
White in A, B, C cups, just 2.50. Also pre-shaped (light foam lining) 3.50.

WONDER BREAD

THOUGH YOU MIGHT IMAGINE that the story of large-scale commercial breadmaking began with a humble baker who happened to discover the secret of making a loaf that would stay fresh longer than forty-eight hours, the history of WONDER bread reads more like a chapter in a marketing textbook. The success of WONDER bread's predecessor, known as the MARY MAID loaf, had shown there was an eager market waiting for a commercially produced loaf that wouldn't spoil right away. When WONDER bread came along in 1918, done up in an appealing package with a name everyone could remember, boosted by lavish promotion and a fortune spent in ad campaigns, it was bound to succeed even if it had the taste and texture of KLEENEX.

Before 1910 most bread was made fresh and sold daily at neighborhood bakeries. Mass production came late to the bread-making business because ingredients for bread were so perishable. They could be bought only in small quantities and had to be used quickly. Freshly baked loaves were wrapped in plain paper and tied with string at the time of purchase. Even loaves from wholesalers came unwrapped to the retail outlets; no kind of commercial wrapping had yet been devised that would keep the bread salably soft for more than forty-eight hours.

The advent of motorized trucks changed the bread business radically. With trucks, larger quantities of yeast and flour could be transported rapidly from their sources to the baker's kitchen, and far more loaves could be carried to retail outlets for sale each day.

Another major breakthrough for bread makers was the invention by Henri Sévigné of the first bread-wrapping machine in 1914. The paper used by the Sévigné machines was dry waxed; another machine applied adhesive wax at each end to seal the wrapping. Now bread would keep on the grocer's shelf for several days before turning stale.

Even as America found itself increasingly involved in war abroad, at home wholesale baking was becoming a major industry. Bread bakeries grew in size and number and soon joined the trend toward amalgamation and conglomeration pioneered by manufacturers of other baked goods. One of the first bread bakers to move in this direction was the Taggert Baking Company of Indianapolis. In 1913 this firm sold an unwrapped loaf identified merely by a small sticker. Its successor was a popular one-pound loaf wrapped in waxed paper and trade-named MARY MAID. After the war, on the strength of an intensive ad campaign featuring a folksy lady named Mary who seemed to remind buyers of their mothers—or sisters or favorite aunts—Taggart went on to produce a one-and-a-half-pound loaf. The name WONDER was chosen by Elmer Cline, then vice-president of the company, because it met the requirements that he felt were responsible for the success of the MARY MAID loaf: The name was easy to remember and apparently sparked connotations that he wanted people to associate with the new jumbo loaf. The design theme for the wrapper came to him one evening as he saw the sky near his house in Indianapolis fill up with varicolored balloons drifting

gracefully in the International Balloon Race being held at the Indianapolis Speedway. The pattern of the balloons seemed to symbolize wonder, excitement, novelty—just the concepts that Cline wanted to combine with the suggestion of down-home quality in the promotion of his new bread.

The first WONDER bread wrapper had blue, yellow and red circles with the word WONDER printed on each circle. The vivid colors and strong end design were miles ahead of packages for rival brands and unquestionably gave WONDER bread a valuable sales advantage. Years later, the WONDER name and the balloon design were chosen, from a number of available brands, for national promotion when the Taggart Baking Company joined the family of local bakeries that made up the Continental Baking Company.

For days following the appearance of WONDER bread on the market, company trucks carried cylinders of gas to various neighborhoods where routemen filled balloons for children. Youngsters were given a balloon if they promised to take a letter home to mother. The message, of course, was an invitation to try the new bread. WONDER bread sales, it is said, soon outdistanced those of any other brand in the city—even those of Taggart's long-established MARY MAID loaf.

Under the aegis of Continental, WONDER bread enjoyed continuous growth in popularity, larger and more up-to-date promotions proving over and over again the sales power of the name and package design. Throughout the thirties and forties Continental capitalized on the persuasive powers of big stars in the entertainment world to recommend WONDER bread in print, on radio and later on TV, always with allusions to the bread's nutritive value—the big gun in WONDER bread's campaign. Despite the recent war against white bread, Continental has never hesitated to affirm that WONDER bread supplies minerals, proteins and vitamins in more than adequate quantities for healthy growth and high energy.

Only in 1935 was the design of the WONDER bread wrapper ever markedly altered, and then only to eliminate the cluttered appearance it had taken on since its early days.

Graphic designer George Switzer removed the word "Wonder" from the balloons, which were made smaller in size, and the WONDER bread logotype was repeated top and sides. Since then, with virtually no changes in any aspect of its formula for success, WONDER bread continues to be a winner.

HALLMARK CARDS

IN HIS DIARY, SAMUEL PEPYS mentions exchanging Valentines with his wife in 1664. But apparently other forms of greeting cards did not become popular in England or America until the nineteenth century. In the absence of a postal system, no matter how deeply you might have wished to say "Happy Birthday" or "Merry Christmas" on paper, it was too expensive for most people to pay a messenger to deliver those noble sentiments by hand.

Today, there is scarcely a sentiment, noble or otherwise, that you won't find printed and illustrated on a card that you can purchase for a reasonable sum and pop in the mail at the current postage rate. Joyce Hall, chairman of the board of Hallmark company until his death in 1982, did more than anyone to make this possible.

Hallmark Cards, Inc., is the largest and best-known publisher of "social expression," as it is called in the jargon of the trade. That means

that of the seven billion cards sent annually in America, Hallmark makes approximately *ten million a day*. Six hundred artists and writers come up with fourteen thousand new ideas each year. Cards are printed in seventeen languages and distributed to one hundred countries. In addition, Hallmark manufactures and sells wrapping paper, ribbon, party goods, gifts and stationery.

The story of this gigantic, mostly family-owned business begins in Norfolk, Nebraska, when Joyce Hall was a boy of fifteen. At that age he had already been working for six years to help support his mother, sisters and brothers. He left school in 1906 to work full-time in a bookstore which carried a large stock of picture postcards imported from England and Germany. Hall was intrigued by the postcards, particularly the elaborately engraved ones for Christmas and the lacy Victorian Valentines. He felt they served a basic human need for

thoughtful expression and he couldn't figure out why no one was publishing a type of card that the average citizen could afford.

In January 1910 Joyce Clyde Hall moved to Kansas City, Missouri, and rented a room at the local YMCA. His brother Rollie joined him the following year and the two young men opened a specialty store in downtown Kansas City, selling postcards, gifts, books and stationery. Within eight months, business was so good that the partners were obliged to seek larger quarters which they soon filled. By January 1915 the offices were bulging with frilly Valentines waiting to be sold in February— when fire wiped out the Hall business overnight.

But the promise shown by the young partners in their first five years encouraged a local banker to lend them $25,000 to get back on their feet. By the end of that year they were doing well enough to purchase an engraving firm and

Hallmark Cards

HALLMARK'S "Thinking of You" card was introduced in February 1941 and sold for a nickel until 1974. The current pansy card has a double-thickness "French fold," is slightly larger than the original and sells for thirty-five cents. To date the card, HALLMARK'S top seller, has sold more than twenty million copies.

begin making their own greeting cards. The first two HALLMARK cards came on the market in November 1915.

Another brother, W. F. Hall, came to Kansas City as office manager in 1921 and the three

brothers expanded their operations to Kansas, Oklahoma, Nebraska and Missouri. By 1922, Hall Brothers, Inc., as the firm was known until 1954, numbered 120 people on the payroll and was on its way to gaining a reputation for quality, taste and

originality in social greeting cards.

Association of the HALLMARK name with quality and good taste was always a serious priority for Joyce C. Hall. ("Good taste is good business," he was known to say.) The HALLMARK Gallery on New

York's upper Fifth Avenue was one expression of that philosophy. For more than ten years it operated on the lower level of the company's most posh retail store in Manhattan's high-rent district, across the street from Bonwit Teller and only a (precious) stone's throw from Tiffany's. The purpose was evidently to lure well-heeled shoppers with good taste into the gallery to see the latest exhibition with the hope that they would select a few cards and gift items in the retail store on the way out. The scheme was not a total success; the gallery is gone and the store has expanded into the space that it vacated. But Hall never regretted starting the gallery. It was an elegant showplace for Hallmark, and Joyce Hall always believed that quality is best promoted in quality locations.

The *Hallmark Hall of Fame* is another example of Hallmark's particular brand of promotion. Since 1951 the company has spent millions to produce this series of dramatic "specials." The ratings have rarely been more than mediocre but critics have acclaimed the *Hall of Fame* as "an oasis in television's wasteland." That's the sort of accolade Hall enjoyed most.

Hallmark's Crown Center is the ultimate tribute to the company's success. A $500 million real-estate venture, the project involves the redevelopment of eighty-five once-blighted acres on the southern edge of Kansas City. When completed in the late eighties, this city-within-a-city will include the buildings that make up the company headquarters, additional office buildings, a bank, a large open plaza, a retail complex

with sixty-five stores, apartment houses, a 730-room hotel and a motel. Hallmark has won praise for the project's design and has been credited with sparking a far-reaching proposal to rehabilitate another decaying area nearby in downtown Kansas City.

Both in its broad scope and in the details of the plan's realization, Crown Center is characteristic of the expansive thinking of Joyce Hall and of his son, Donald Hall, now president of the company. It is also a good example of what can be accomplished when control of a company rests in the hands of a few interested individuals rather than with an assortment of outside investors. (In 1982 the Hall family still held 75 percent of the company stock; the rest is in an employee profit-sharing trust.)

P A R T   F I V E

1918–WORLD WAR II

"The man who builds a factory builds a temple. The man who works there worships there."

—CALVIN COOLIDGE

Never have private businessmen been held in such high esteem as they were in the postwar boom that extended into the 1920's.

In 1917 and 1918, the nation's economic might was organized to help win the war. The War Industries Board, headed by Bernard Baruch, took control of the U.S. economy, dictating to manufacturers what to make and what not to make. But after armistice was declared and the soldiers returned home, most major industries returned to "business as usual."

Then, toward the end of the 1920's, as the nation swooned over Rudolph Valentino and Clara Bow, cheered Babe Ruth and danced to the swinging rhythms of Duke Ellington, signs of trouble showed up in skyrocketing stock prices. Almost before anyone knew what was happening, the nation was in the throes of economic disaster.

Caught up in the problems of trying to deal with mass unemployment and labor problems all through the thirties, Congress endeavored to keep America out of the political turmoil in Europe and the Far East. But by 1940 involvement seemed inevitable. Finally, the Japanese attack on Pearl Harbor, December 7, 1941, catapulted the United States into war with Japan and the Axis powers. Industry once again became focused on manufacturing for war.

ASPIRIN

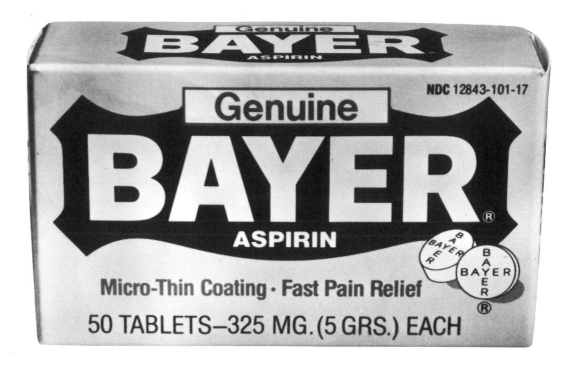

ASPIRIN IS NOT AN AMERICAN invention. It only seems that way because of the strong marketing program mounted by Sterling Drug, Inc., to launch the product in this country after World War I and to keep it selling steadily ever since.

Sterling Drug was originally the Neuralgyline Company, manufacturing only one product, a pain reliever called Neuralgine. Its special talent was not to develop new ideas, processes and products but to buy them from other people and then spend huge percentages of the company's capital assets on advertising.

When the United States entered World War I, the properties of enemy aliens were seized by the American government. Among these properties were the shares of the Bayer Company, Inc., of New York, which were owned at that time by aliens seeking to extend their business into the American market.

A month after the 1918 armistice, the government offered the Bayer stocks for sale at a public auction. To the highest American bid would go a large plant, a relatively little-known product called ASPIRIN, a substantial number of physician's drugs and a line of dyestuffs.

Sterling Drug (renamed since 1917) recognized in ASPIRIN the product it needed to consolidate its position as a specialist in the manufacture of analgesics. It decided to bid, if necessary, as much as the company had earned in its almost eighteen years of existence.

More than one hundred American firms participated in the bidding, which started at $1 million. When the auctioneer finally banged down his gavel, Sterling had acquired the Bayer Company for $5,310,000, about $1 million less than it had earned throughout its entire history. Sterling applied its own expertise to the formulating, tableting and production of the then-powdered ingredients of ASPIRIN, and in a few years the company had earned back its investment many times over.

For a few years ASPIRIN took a backseat to TYLENOL as a pain reliever. Then the problems that beset that product in September and October 1982 and the discovery of new capabilities of ASPIRIN combined to brighten the outlook for the Sterling product.

Raggedy Ann

© Knickerbocker Toy Co., Inc.

One little lady who certainly doesn't show her age is RAGGEDY ANN, who celebrated her sixty-fifth birthday in 1983. She first appeared as a rag doll in Marshall Field's department store window at Christmastime in 1918 in honor of the publication of Johnny Gruelle's collection of short stories. Doting grandmothers and various companies made the dolls until 1964 when Knickerbocker Toys bought the rights. In 1982 these were sold to Hasbro Toy Company, Pawtucket, Rhode Island, who now make the RAGGEDY ANNS that grandmas don't.

Chanel No. 5

Not exactly an American product, but a Big Seller here, is CHANEL NO. 5, so called because it was introduced in France on the fifth day of the fifth month of 1921 and "5" was Coco Chanel's lucky number.

FRIGIDAIRE, 1921

FRIGIDAIRE

THE FIRST SELF-CONTAINED electric household refrigerator, made by the Frigidaire division of General Motors, made its appearance in 1915, marking the demise of the iceman and that classic symbol of better living, the icebox.

For many Americans the refrigerator put an end to a grim series of household chores like emptying the drain pan under the

Frigidaire
One of the White Consolidated Industries WCI

icebox—which frequently spilled all over the kitchen floor—and sniffing all perishable food every day to determine whether it had gone rancid or sour. In the words of the Frigidaire people themselves (the company is now part of White Consolidated Industries, Inc.), "Electric refrigerators brought into the American home a safe, economical and convenient method of food preservation completely unrivaled in the history of the world . . . and helped raise American living standards to heights never before believed possible."

But it was a long way from the bulky unit known as the Guardian,

with its limited food-storage facilities, to the more familiar "cold wall" household refrigerator that many of us, as children, knew simply as the Fridge. Among the obstacles to the evolution of the fridge, in the early days, was the danger of toxic fumes from the refrigerating agents which could cause harm if they were inhaled.

A major breakthrough came in 1931 when Frigidaire was able to use a revolutionary new refrigerant, a safe, odorless chemical called Freon. By the mid-1930's, Freon was used by virtually all manufacturers of electric refrigerators.

Frigidaire pulled ahead of the others in 1939 when the company retained the world-famous industrial designer, Raymond Loewy, to design the 1941 model of the FRIGIDAIRE. Lowey had borrowed details and techniques of style from the automobile industry when he designed the curved COLDSPOT refrigerator, complete with "feather touch" latch connected to a foot pedal, for Sears, Roebuck in 1935. Many of the same features, more highly refined, characterized the 1941 FRIGIDAIRE, which remained in production for twenty years and became the best-selling refrigerator in the world.

BIRDS EYE FROZEN FOODS

THOUGH CLARENCE BIRDSEYE was the first person to figure out a successful means of preserving food by freezing it, he was not the first to try. Sir Francis Bacon, the seventeenth-century English philosopher-scientist, apparently understood the basic concept of freezing to preserve food, but when he undertook to demonstrate it one winter day by killing a hen and stuffing it with snow, he became ill from overexposure to the cold and

died before he could develop his theories further.

There were a multitude of efforts to perfect the refrigeration process after 1626 when Bacon died, but no one found the secret of freezing food on a commercial scale until Clarence Birdseye worked it out.

Birdseye had been sent by the U.S. Geographic Service on an expedition to Labrador from 1914 to 1917. While he was there, Birdseye observed that fish and caribou meat

frozen in the dry Arctic air were still tender and fresh-tasting when thawed and cooked months later. He concluded that the secret lay in rapid freezing at extremely low temperatures as opposed to the slow-freezing cold-storage methods of the past which had invariably led to unpalatable results.

Home again in Gloucester, Massachusetts, Bob Birdseye (no one who knew him called him Clarence) devoted himself to working out the details of the quick-freezing process. He finally achieved the results he wanted by placing packages of fish between two metal surfaces chilled to a sub-zero temperature. He was pleased to find that fish fillets bought fresh from the Gloucester fishermen and frozen in this way developed only tiny ice crystals which did not adversely affect the texture, flavor or nutritional value of the fish.

Within a few months Birdseye was able to muster the financial support he needed to open a small plant in Gloucester, the General Seafoods Company. During this time Birdseye developed his "belt froster" freezing device into a twenty-ton "Quick Freeze" machine, forty feet long. By 1927 he was ready to pack and ship frozen fish to markets thousands of miles away.

As he pursued experiments with the same techniques on meats, poultry, vegetables and fruit, Birdseye began to have a clearer idea of the possible future of the industry he was starting. He organized the General Foods Company to act as the stockholding company for General Seafoods and to control all patents on the belt-froster process.

Then in late 1927 and early 1928 Birdseye ran into some roadblocks he had not anticipated. He could not persuade retailers to invest in the special refrigerating equipment required to store frozen food. And consumers were not showing enough interest in the new product to change the retailers' minds.

As the winter of 1928 approached, most of the seafood Birdseye had frozen the previous summer was still unsold. The business that had seemed to have such a bright future was about to

fail. Birdseye desperately needed help from some company that had the resources and know-how to promote a new product. The Postum Cereal Company came forward.

Postum saw in the General Foods Company an opportunity to add another promising independent company to the group it had acquired since 1895, which included JELL-O gelatin, MINUTE tapioca, and MAXWELL HOUSE coffee. In June 1929, for $22 million, Postum purchased the assets of Birdseye's company and rechristened itself General Foods Corporation. The sale included all patents covering the quick-freeze process as well as the BIRDS EYE trademark.

Almost a year later the General Foods Corporation was ready to begin the marketing blitz that it hoped would make BIRDS EYE frozen foods a permanent part of the American way of life. It started with the most serious obstacle: the retailers' unwillingness to invest in expensive refrigerating equipment. General Foods installed at its own expense custom-built refrigerated cases in eighteen grocery stores in Springfield, Massachusetts. Along with the BIRDS EYE frozen foods storage cases came a team of demonstrators who urged shoppers to taste free samples of chicken, haddock, steak, strawberries. Speakers were sent by the company to home-economics classes and women's clubs. Housewives were interviewed in their own homes by Birds Eye product salesmen to get as much feedback as possible. It was a major marketing campaign. Fortified with advertising, it continued for forty weeks.

But despite General Foods' best

efforts, the public remained reluctant to buy frozen foods. For several years after Postum's acquisition of Birds Eye frozen foods, the company balance sheets showed more losses than gains. But General Foods continued to give the product every possible support: Super-insulated railroad cars were designed to transport the frozen food; a fleet of special Birds Eye frozen foods trawlers was launched; packing plants were opened in areas where fruits and vegetables could be harvested, packed and frozen within a few hours. But still Birds Eye could claim only 516 retail outlets, most of them in New England.

Three years after the first campaign, General Foods marketers decided to change their strategy and go after large-quantity sales to institutions such as hospitals, schools, hotels, restaurants. At the same time the company developed a new kind of freezer case which it was able to offer to retailers for a reasonable monthly rental fee.

This time results were overwhelmingly positive. Through the institutions, greater numbers of people were introduced to frozen foods, and retailers were willing to try the new refrigeration equipment on a short-term rental basis. By 1937 Birds Eye was finally showing a profit, but not until 1940 did national distribution even seem like a realistic goal.

With the specter of involvement in world war looming large over America, in 1940 Birds Eye frozen foods finally made a major breakthrough: Women involved in mobilization had little time to spend preparing food and turned to their grocers' cases for assistance. After Pearl Harbor, processors of all descriptions were threatened with cutback status as a "nonessential" industry, but General Foods managed to persuade the U.S. government that the freezing process was infinitely more economical than canning. ("To can twenty million pounds of vegetables would require twenty-six hundred tons of vital steel.") The government went still further, ordering quick-frozen foods to be listed on the Office of Price Administration charts posted in food stores everywhere, thereby completing the process of public consciousness-raising with regard to frozen foods. Meanwhile, members of the armed forces were becoming accustomed to having frozen foods of a uniform standard of quality wherever in the world they happened to be serving Uncle Sam.

Despite heavy competition, consistently good marketing has kept BIRDS EYE frozen foods selling well since World War II. When Clarence Birdseye died in 1956 after years of supervising the General Foods laboratories he established in Gloucester, he had known the satisfaction of seeing the product he developed become the success he always believed it would be.

BISQUICK

JUST WHEN EVERYTHING economic was taking a nose dive at the beginning of the Depression, a young General Mills executive thought of a convenient way to make baked goods rise.

Carl Smith was traveling by train on a night in early 1930. Having ordered some biscuits in the dining car well past the usual dinner hours, Smith was pleasurably surprised to be served piping-hot, fresh rolls in record time. The secret, he discovered from the chef, was that the dough had been mixed ahead of time and stored in the icebox. Smith was so impressed with the obvious convenience of having a premixed biscuit dough on hand that he could hardly wait to get back to the General Mills lab to discuss the possibility of developing such a mix for the general market.

There were some tricky chemical problems to resolve: How to keep the shortening fresh as it stood on the shelf? How to retain the power of the leavening agent over a long

period of time? And what blend of ingredients could possibly make biscuits as good as, or better than, homemade? One by one, the General Mills chemists found answers to these questions (many of the same technologies would later be used in the first cake mixes), and in 1930 BISQUICK was born.

Other companies immediately recognized the commercial possibilities of ready-made dough, but they did not attend as carefully as General Mills to the solution of the accompanying problems. Within one year after BISQUICK's appearance, there were ninety-five other biscuit mixes on the market. The next year only six remained.

It was soon discovered that BISQUICK could be used to make more than biscuits. In 1933 the partnership of BISQUICK and BETTY CROCKER produced a recipe booklet called *Betty Crocker's 101 Delicious Bisquick Creations*. In the 1950's BISQUICK was known as the 12-in-1 mix that could make pancakes, dumplings, coffee cake, meat pies, waffles, shortcake, cookies, upside-down cake, nut bread, muffins and velvet crumb cake as well as biscuits. Today, fifty years after its introduction on the grocery-store shelf, consumers continue to find new ways to use BISQUICK.

BETTY CROCKER

THOUGH BETTY CROCKER MAY seem as familiar to some Americans as a distant member of their own family, she is a corporate trade character created by the Washburn Crosby Company, a forerunner of General Mills. If she were real, she would be over sixty years old today, for it was in 1921 that the management of Washburn Crosby created the BETTY CROCKER name to be used in replying to homemakers' requests for recipes and solutions to baking problems.

The surname Crocker was chosen to honor a popular, recently retired director of the company, William G. Crocker, and also because it was the name of the first Minneapolis flour mill. The name Betty was selected to go with it "because of its warm and friendly sound." Women employees submitted sample BETTY CROCKER signatures and the one judged most characteristic continues in use today.

In 1904 BETTY CROCKER took to the airwaves on daytime radio's first food-service program. The program was so successful that it was extended to thirteen regional stations, each with its own BETTY CROCKER voice broadcasting from scripts written at the Home Service Department in Minneapolis. Subsequently, the BETTY CROCKER *Cooking School of the Air* became a network program and continued for twenty-four years with more than one million formal registrations by homemaker-listeners.

During World War II, BETTY CROCKER stepped into the breach with a special radio program, *Your Nation's Rations*, offered through the U.S. Department of State. BETTY CROCKER-endorsed booklets on low-cost menus and budgeting also helped wartime families get through the hard times. In 1950 BETTY CROCKER's first full-length (picture) cookbook became a national best seller. Its fifth edition, published in 1978, reflects the changing life-styles of families in which the wife and mother is also a wage earner with limited time for food preparation and greater interest in nutrition and natural foods.

Betty Crocker

1936

1955

1965

1980

The first portrait of BETTY CROCKER was commissioned from Neysa McMein, a New York artist, to celebrate the fifteenth birthday of the BETTY CROCKER name. For it Mrs. McNein allegedly blended the features of early Home Service Department members into an official likeness. The portrait has been updated five times, most recently in 1980, when Betty was given a more casual coiffure and more contemporary clothing.

JOY OF COOKING

ETHAN AND MARK ROMBAUER, heirs to the tradition of editing the JOY OF COOKING, recall their mother, Marion Rombauer Becker, describing how she and *her* mother, Irma S. Rombauer, went about publishing their cookbook. "We simply called in a printer," Mrs. Becker said. "He arrived laden with washable cover fabrics, type and paper samples. In a few hours all decisions were made, and shortly afterward we signed a contract for our first three thousand copies."

This privately printed edition of the first American cookbook ever to seriously challenge FANNIE FARMER as a general guide to cooking appeared in 1931 and offered five hundred tested recipes from which Mrs. Rombauer claimed "inexperienced cooks cannot fail to make successful soufflés, pies, cakes, soups, gravies, etc., if they follow the clear instructions."

In 1936 Irma Rombauer met Lawrence Chambers, then president of the Bobbs-Merrill publishing company, who agreed to look over an enlarged version of the JOY OF COOKING text. His interest was prompted by his pleasant memories of elegant meals served in the home of another member of the Rombauer family, Irma's cousin. After reading the manuscript he was evidently convinced of the Rombauer family expertise in the culinary arts. He published the expanded version of the JOY OF COOKING later that year.

In the fifty years since its first publication, the JOY OF COOKING editors have endeavored to keep up with the times: During the Depression there were recipes for economical use of leftovers; the 1943 edition included recipes for the "war bride"; in 1946 the JOY OF COOKING reflected postwar interest in nutritional values. Recent editions make frequent references to classic continental cuisine and what Marion Becker, Mrs. Rombauer's daughter and collaborator, described as "ingredients which modern science and transport have so miraculously made available."

Today, Irma Rombauer's grandsons, Ethan and Mark, have the responsibility for carrying on the JOY OF COOKING tradition. The updating of what is now a vast compendium could eventually require outside help, but they themselves research and test recipes daily and endeavor always to follow their grandmother's cardinal rule: "to write as though all the JOY OF COOKING readers are amateurs in the kitchen."

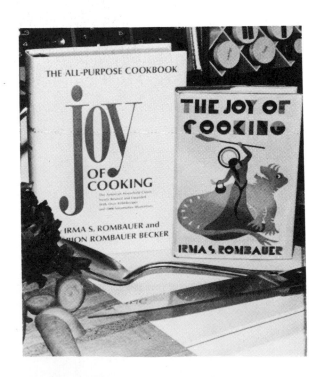

TOLL HOUSE COOKIES

THE LEGENDARY TOLL HOUSE cookie takes it name from a tollhouse built in 1708 on the outskirts of Whitman, Massachusetts, at the halfway point between Boston and New Bedford. It was a well-known haven for weary travelers stopping for food, drink and rest while they waited for a change of horses. The historic building was purchased in 1930 by Mr. and Mrs. Wakefield, who turned it into the famous Toll House Inn.

In addition to serving as proprietress, Ruth Wakefield was the resident baker, highly esteemed for her desserts which attracted people from all over New England. One day, while experimenting with her favorite recipe for butter cookies, she dropped a handful of chocolate pieces into the batter. Half expecting them to melt, she waited eagerly for the result and was pleased to find the bits of chocolate had held their shape, softening just slightly to a delicately creamy texture. Mrs. Wakefield named her discovery the TOLL HOUSE cookie.

The Nestlé Company, whose chocolate she used, was so impressed with Mrs. Wakefield's cookies that it offered to print her recipe right on the wrapper of its Semi-Sweet Chocolate Bar. In addition to other legal arrangements for the privilege of publicizing her recipe, the Nestlé Company supplied Mrs. Wakefield with all the chocolate she could use to make her cookies for the rest of her life.

As the popularity of the TOLL HOUSE cookie grew, Nestlé first produced a special scored bar accompanied by a chopper for cutting the chocolate into small pieces. Then in 1939 it offered the MORSELS in varying package sizes. Today they are used to make any number of chocolate treats . . . in addition to the nearly seven billion TOLL HOUSE cookies baked in homes each year.

RITZ CRACKERS

IN 1934 THE NATIONAL BISCUIT Company took the country by storm when it launched a new product called RITZ crackers. The new cracker differed from the traditional soda cracker in that it had more shortening and no yeast at all. The result was a crisper, less fluffy cracker, whose flavor was enhanced by a thin coat of coconut oil and a sprinkling of salt.

RITZ was introduced as a prestige item, accompanied by such promotional headlines as "Anytime is the right time to serve Ritz," "Tomorrow's cracker today," and "Almost overnight, America's most popular cracker."

There was no doubt about the latter claim. The new product posted a first-year sales record unequaled before or since. Within three years RITZ became, and has remained, the top-selling cracker in the world with more than 40 million sold each day.

PARCHEESI

A POPULAR GAME WITH MEDIEVAL origins is PARCHEESI, Royal Game of India, first played in the court of Mogul Emperor Akbar in the fourteenth century, with slave girls as pawns. Abkar's courtyard was the game board; his throne rested where home is now. The slave girls moved along the lush garden paths according to the roll of marked cowrie shells used as dice. Many of India's most beautiful women vied for the honor of serving their emperor thus, as pawns in his favorite game.

The modern version of the game, with a board that duplicates the paths of the emperor's garden, was trademarked by Selchow & Righter in 1894. No one is sure who actually adapted the game for the Victorian parlor, but by its fourth season in Selchow & Righter's catalog it is described as having "a larger sale than any other game on the market in the same space of time." By 1927 it was considered a classic, with a strong tradition already behind its name.

A newspaper photo taken in the early twenties pictures Calvin Coolidge and his family playing the game during a political campaign. Selchow & Righter reports that Coolidge and another well-known PARCHEESI fan, Thomas Alva Edison, were challenged to play a championship match. There's no record of whether or not it was played.

Clara Bow once declared emphatically that she was giving up gambling in favor of PARCHEESI: In gambling she frequently made the mistake of playing hundred-dollar chips when she intended to put up fifty-cent ones. Her carelessness was getting expensive.

Also in Selchow & Righter's log of PARCHEESI enthusiasts is the elderly gentleman who had a bet on a PARCHEESI game with a fellow member of New York's exclusive Union League Club. One day he presented himself at Selchow & Righter's offices requesting arbitration of a particular rule. Waving a sketch of the playing board at the time of the move in question, he said, "If I am wrong, I take forty people to dinner, but if I am right, then the forty people will dine courtesy of my opponent." He asked a company official to type out the decision in triplicate and have it notarized. When he received the decision, a small smile broke over his face: Dinner was on his opponent.

Another time, a woman complained to the company that the new dice cubes they had supplied for her PARCHEESI set were noisier when shaken than the originals. The sound so disturbed her husband that he refused to play with her. As the lady in question was the wife of a master strategist, General Douglas MacArthur, Selchow & Righter obligingly agreed to test the dice and found they were indeed noisier than the originals. Quieter cups were provided.

Though PARCHEESI boards tend

Emperor Akbar's Guide

PARCHEESI® BRAND
Royal Game of India

to be passed from generation to generation as lovingly as heirlooms, Selchow & Righter's sales records show that PARCHEESI Brand Royal Game of India continues to be one of America's three top-selling games.

Yo-Yo

Like the boomerang, the YO-YO is a harmless plaything that was originally designed to serve as a weapon. The Australian aborigines used a heavier version of the boomerang in armed combat. The YO-YO was devised by sixteenth-century hunters in the Philippine Islands to ensnare the legs of animals. Donald Duncan adapted the design for use as a toy and introduced it to America in 1928.

Did you hear about the cargo ship loaded with YO-YO's that hit a mine left over from World War II off the coast of Hawaii? It exploded and sank—thirty-eight times.

SCRABBLE

THERE ARE TWO FRIENDLY arguments that arise from time to time in the toy-making business. One concerns the matter of the toy bear and whether it was Ideal Toys or Reeves International that first marketed it. The other question is whether MONOPOLY is the top-selling trademarked game in the world, or whether SCRABBLE is.

Selchow & Righter Company, manufacturer of SCRABBLE brand crossword game, says with conviction that there is no contest. Though neither manufacturer has revealed exact production figures, Selchow & Righter maintains that SCRABBLE is selling nearly as well today as it did twenty years ago when it was considered a national craze. To make its point, the company asserts that there are well over a hundred active Scrabble Players Clubs across the United

States and that there are tournaments going on somewhere every weekend. Every two or three years, Selchow & Righter also sponsor a national tournament.

SCRABBLE was invented in 1931 by Alfred Butts, an unemployed architect with time on his hands. Butts's game was made up of one hundred wooden tiles, each having a letter of the alphabet printed on it. The idea was to select random letters out of the pool and form a high-scoring word.

Over a period of a dozen years, Butts developed the details of the game, adding a playing board, giving each letter a point score related to how frequently it is used in the language, and changing the name to Criss-Cross Words. Occasionally, Butts would make a special set for a friend. It was one such set that in 1948 prompted the friend and his wife to help Butts market and produce the game on a larger scale. Their first move was to

rename it SCRABBLE, then they set up a workshop in a schoolhouse.

Selchow & Righter soon found out about SCRABBLE and agreed to manufacture the boards, fully expecting that the market for this trendy diversion would die down as quickly as it had arisen. By 1953, however, orders for the game were still pouring in. At this point, Selchow & Righter took over complete manufacturing and marketing responsibility for SCRABBLE.

Today, the game continues to be immensely popular throughout the United States and around the world. It has been translated into six other languages and is produced in a number of variations, including Braille.

MONOPOLY

LIKE SCRABBLE, MONOPOLY WAS the brainchild of a young man, Charles B. Darrow, who found himself unemployed because of the Depression. An engineer by profession, from Germantown, Pennsylvania, Darrow spent hours working out the details of the game he had invented primarily to amuse himself when there was little else to do. His family and friends enjoyed playing it so much that, like Alfred Butts, who invented SCRABBLE, Darrow made several copies by hand to give to friends. As the demand for more sets grew, Darrow could not keep up with the orders and decided to take it to Parker Brothers in Massachusetts.

At the end of the test game played by Parker Brothers executives, Darrow's proposal was unanimously turned down. George and Charles Parker thought MONOPOLY took much too long to play, the rules were hopelessly complicated and there were at least fifty-two other weak points that they believed ruled the game out as far as they were concerned. Darrow persevered on his own. When Parker Brothers heard, a few months later, that Darrow had received an order for five thousand sets from Wanamaker's in Philadelphia, they reconsidered and offered him a contract.

The Parker Brothers plant was soon producing twenty thousand MONOPOLY sets a week. There were so many orders at Christmastime that they were filed in huge laundry baskets and stacked in the hallways. But despite this enthusiasm, Parker Brothers viewed MONOPOLY as a fad game for adults which would sell for only about three years. (Selchow & Righter had shown a similar lack of confidence in SCRABBLE's long-term future.) On December 19, 1936, George Parker issued instructions to "cease absolutely to make any more boards or utensil boxes. . . . We will stop making Monopoly against the possibility of a very early slump." But the slump never came, and sales have done nothing but

spiral upward ever since. By the age of forty-six, Darrow had become a millionaire from his royalties as the company went on to sell rights to publish the game in twenty-eight countries and nineteen languages. There is even reason to suspect it's being played somewhere in the USSR—ever since all six MONOPOLY sets on display at the American National Exhibition in Moscow disappeared in 1959.

Milestones in Monopoly History

Records for extraordinary MONOPOLY events are documented not only in the files of Parker Brothers but also in the *Guinness Book of World Records*.

There's the longest game played in a moving elevator (16 days) or in a bathtub (99 hours), as well as the longest anti-gravitational game (played on a ceiling for 36 hours). The current world's record for the longest game ever is held by the McCluer North Games club in Florissant, Missouri, whose members played for 1,416 hours, or 59 days straight.

The largest MONOPOLY game on record took place in April 1967, at Juniata College in Huntington, Pennsylvania. The playing board was laid out on an area larger than a city block, using campus streets and sidewalks. The dice were large foam-rubber cubes cast from a third floor fire escape and players were informed of their moves by messengers on bicycles, equipped with walkie-talkies.

One of the most exotic MONOPOLY-playing marathons was held in 1976 when the Lodi (California) Diving School played for 1,008 hours—underwater. One hundred forty people in wet suits played in two-hour relays during 42 days of unbroken play.

PYREX

"COME, RUPERT," SAID THE KING, "show us this amazing piece of glass." The Bavarian prince advanced nervously toward King Charles II of England. "Sire," he said, "I will demonstrate." Rupert knelt and placed on the marble floor a droplet of glass, the size and shape of a polliwog, with a thick body and thin tapering tail. Then he lifted a heavy maul and brought it down squarely on the polliwog's torso.

Nothing happened. Again and again he pounded the small globule. It didn't even crack. Then, as the king watched in total amazement, Rupert asked permission to perform his next feat. The king nodded assent. Rupert gently flicked the thin tail of the glass polliwog. It burst into a thousand tiny fragments. "Truly," murmured the king, "this must be witchcraft."

The tale of Prince Rupert drops, as they came to be known, is told around the Corning Glass Works to illustrate the fact that for centuries people knew that a molten droplet of glass plunged into cold water would yield a substance of incredible tensile strength. Prince Rupert understood the special property of such strengthened glass: It could withstand the impact of a remarkably heavy weight when the impact was spread *evenly* over its surface. His small act of magic proved he knew something was still not right: A minor blow off-center destroyed the droplet. Presumably he did not know why, and it was not until three centuries later that professional glassmakers discovered the secret of using such durable glass and understood the flaw that came with it.

In the last quarter of the nineteenth century, European glassmakers did produce functional glassware strengthened by quick chilling, but the effects were still spotty. Their resilient products were likely to break without warning, in the manner of Rupert's polliwog. Even the most sophisticated craftsmen had scant knowledge of why this happened or what could be done to prevent it.

During the first two decades of this century, science began to catch up with practice. By 1920, studies made mainly by Dr. Jesse T. Littleton led to more information about strengthening tempered glass by rapid chilling. Quite simply, the basic problem seemed to be that the outside of a tempered-glass surface cooled more quickly than the inside, creating a compression that caused the glass to break.

Corning technicians set themselves to resolving this problem. They had good results with tempering lantern globes and insulators, but met repeated failures in trying to produce tempered glass for use in the kitchen. Eventually, Dr. Littleton and his associates were able to spell out clearly the stress relationships caused by sudden chilling. With additional data from Littleton and others about fundamental properties of glass, the way was opened to tempered stovetop glassware.

Even in the depths of the Depression, Corning's scientists continued their mission of developing superstrong glass for the home. The problem was complex, involving as it did not only the process of chilling molten glass but also of heating it up again on the kitchen stove. They experimented with air-chilling but couldn't achieve the pinpoint control they needed. Oil baths were tried and rejected. The glass that emerged from them was not strong enough and it was tainted with a charred residue of oil that created immense cleaning problems.

Then a technique was developed for using molten chemical salts. This was the answer. After months of patient testing, the proper temperature ratios were worked out. More than eighteen thousand pounds of potatoes were boiled and fried in stovetop trials. Finally, in 1936, Corning introduced a totally new line of tempered-glass cookware for the stove, called PYREX.

Throughout the war years and afterward, Corning continued the process of refining its strong, tempered glassware. At the request of the armed services, in 1942 Corning developed a line of strengthened tableware suitable for the rough usage it would get in mess halls. After the war Corning was able to present to the general market decorated PYREX brand tableware, mixing bowls, oven-freezer sets and a host of related products that are now considered staples of most American households.

Though Corning occasionally suffers setbacks as technical flaws show up belatedly in its products, one can't help thinking their labs are full of mighty polliwogs like the Prince Rupert drops. Corning appears to believe that virtually anything is possible in the realm of glassmaking.

Scotch Tape

The brand name SCOTCH Tape dates back to the day the first transparent adhesive tape was tested by an auto painter who used it to mask part of the car's surface. The tape came loose because it was not fully coated with adhesive. Said the painter angrily to the inventor: "Take this tape back to your stingy 'Scotch' bosses and tell them to put more adhesive on it!"

The "Scotch" bosses were the executives of the 3M company in St. Paul, Minnesota. They improved the adhesive, and today, over fifty years later, SCOTCH Tape is used for everything from taking lint off clothing to sealing the cracks in the soft shells of fertilized pigeon eggs.

FRITOS

ONE HOT DAY IN SEPTEMBER 1932 a young Texan named Elmer Doolin stopped in for lunch at a café near the Mexican border. While waiting for his sandwich, he became intrigued with a package of corn chips on the counter. He decided to spend an extra nickel to find out what they were like. To his amazement, Doolin found the chips about the tastiest things he had ever eaten. He promptly sought out the Mexican who had made them and offered him $100 for the recipe. Doolin's timing was good. The Mexican was eager to return to his native land and he needed $100 to make the move.

Doolin borrowed $100 to pay the Mexican and began cooking the corn chips in his mother's kitchen in San Antonio at night. By day he sold them from the back of his Model T Ford. Production capacity on this small scale was only about ten pounds per hour. When he sold a whole night's output, Doolin was able to ring up $8 to $10 a day in sales with profits of about $2. As sales increased, production problems arose. Doolin developed a press that could turn out more corn chips in an hour than the potato ricer he had been using, although it had to be struck with a hammer to separate the strips of dough. Within a year, however, Doolin was ready to move into a streamlined plant in Dallas with up-to-date equipment for producing and packaging the corn chips now known as FRITOS.

Meanwhile, in Nashville,

Tennessee, twenty-two-year-old Herman Lay was selling potato chips for an Atlanta-based company from his 1928-model touring car. Each year he expanded the business, adding new routes and products. By 1934, with six regular snack-food routes, he was rapidly becoming one of the company's major distributors.

Then in 1938 the Atlanta chip manufacturer developed problems. With a little help from his friends and business associates, Herman Lay arranged to buy the Atlanta company and change its name to H. W. Lay & Company. With Lay's expert guidance, the company prospered. New plants were opened and distribution centers enlarged. Business was booming until World War II broke out, calling a halt to further expansion.

In 1945, as business began to return to normal, Lay considered adding FRITOS to his company's product line. He was granted one of the first exclusive franchises to manufacture and distribute FRITOS brand corn chips in the Southeast. As the two companies worked together toward national distribution, a close business affiliation developed which eventually resulted in merger.

In 1965 Pepsi bought Frito-Lay, thereby forming a new company, PepsiCo, Inc. It became the first company ever to reach $1 billion in annual sales of snack foods alone, and with more Americans each day grabbing meals on the run, the outlook for Frito-Lay and its sibling companies (Pepsi-Cola, Pizza Hut, Taco Bell) is bright.

TWINKIES

IF YOU THINK THAT TWINKIES came in with fast foods sometime in the fifties or early sixties, Continental Bakeries, now owned by ITT, will hasten to inform you that TWINKIES celebrated its fiftieth anniversary in 1981. They were invented by Jimmy Dewar, who was eighty-four years old in the year TWINKIES passed the half-century mark.

Dewar joined Continental as the driver of a horse-drawn pound-cake wagon in Chicago and rapidly became manager of the Chicago-area plant. As plant manager, Dewar was aware that the pans Continental used to make shortcakes during the strawberry season were sitting idle all the rest of the year. As the economy was getting tight and the company needed another low-priced item, Dewar began to eye the shortcake pans with concern for getting more use out of them. "I

thought of a two-to-a-pack snack for a nickel," Dewar recalled. "I came up with the idea of injecting the little cakes with a filling to make them a year-round product."

The name for Dewar's new product came to him while he was on a business trip to St. Louis. "I saw a billboard advertising Twinkle Toe Shoes. The name Twinkies evolved from that. Sales took off, and the item was soon the company's top Hostess-line seller."

In the early days TWINKIES sold for five cents apiece, and in the forties when eggs and sugar were neither cheap nor easy to come by, TWINKIES went up in price a mere five cents. The snack cakes were popular and became more so in the fifties when Hostess co-sponsored the popular *Howdy Doody* show. While Clarabell the clown distributed the cakes to children in the studio audience, Buffalo Bob sang their praises for the benefit of at-home viewers. Twinkle-the-Kid,

the cowboy snack-cake character, pitched TWINKIES to the next generation of youngsters and still can be found handing out free samples at parades, fairs, sports events and other festive functions.

Continental prides itself on having had plenty of celebrity promotion for TWINKIES over the years. Rosalynn Carter, former First Lady, was once seen, and photographed, wearing a Continental bakery cap, eating a TWINKIE. A character on the *Sonny and Cher* show had a TWINKIE wedding cake. (Continental has letters telling of real weddings featuring TWINKIE wedding cakes, with guests receiving a TWINKIE instead of a slice of cake.) And apparently it is common knowledge that Archie Bunker never went out without a TWINKIE in his lunch pail.

ITT Continental is not ashamed to report that TWINKIES are baked in a mammoth 190-foot-long oven and

are filled at the rate of 52,000 units an hour, without ever being touched by a human hand. It is not known whether anyone in the company blushed when, in 1979, attorney Douglas Schmidt defended his client Dan White on charges of killing San Francisco's Mayor George Moscone and Supervisor Harvey Milk by introducing the testimony of psychiatrist Martin Blinder who suggested to the jury that White's mental capacity was diminished by his high intake of junk food—including TWINKIES. Schmidt's advocacy must have made some impression: White was acquitted on the murder charge and found guilty of voluntary manslaughter.

Meanwhile, TWINKIES continues to be big business for ITT Continental. As sales of the little cakes continue to climb, the company expects soon to be selling at least one billion TWINKIES a year!

ZIPPO LIGHTER

THE ZIPPO STORY BEGINS ON A muggy summer night in Bradford, Pennsylvania. It was 1932, in the midst of the Depression. George G. Blaisdell, then co-owner of the Blaisdell Oil Company, stepped out onto the terrace of Bradford's Pennhill Country Club for a smoke. There he met a friend lighting a cigarette with a cheap Austrian lighter. It was a cumbersome device with a separate, removable brass top.

"You're all dressed up," Blaisdell chided his tux-clad friend. "Why

don't you get a lighter that looks decent?"

"Well, George," his friend replied, "it works!"

It works. These words would echo in Blaisdell's mind as he set out to make an attractive durable lighter that would work. Success did not come overnight. Blaisdell obtained the distribution rights for the Austrian lighter, but found he could not sell enough to make a profit. He decided the clumsy Austrian lighter needed to be adapted for the

American market. Blaisdell totally redesigned the case of the lighter, making one that was rectangular and would fit neatly in the hand. He attached the top with a hinge and surrounded the wick with a wind hood. Fascinated by the name of another recent invention, the zipper, he called the new lighter a ZIPPO.

In the early days, Blaisdell promoted ZIPPOS by giving them to the long-distance drivers who came in and out of the Bradford bus

station. He offered them to jewelers and tobacconists, telling them to keep the lighters if they could not sell them. But he discovered that retailers were hesitant to stock the product without the support of advertising. In 1937, with $3,000 of mostly borrowed money, Blaisdell ran a full page ad in *Esquire* magazine. When the response was not overwhelming, Blaisdell sought other ways to publicize the lighters.

Between 1934 and 1940, punchboards helped Blaisdell move more than three hundred thousand Zippo lighters. Popular throughout the United States in tobacco and confectionery shops, poolrooms and cigar stands, punchboards were a game of chance that you played for two cents. A player could punch any hole on a one-thousand- or two-thousand-hole board. If the player's chosen number matched a number at the top of the board, the player would win a prize. (In 1940 they were ruled illegal.)

With the onset of World War II, the government stopped production of many consumer products, but Blaisdell arranged to produce Zippos for the military post exchanges. As the original brass was no longer available for nonmilitary purposes, wartime Zippo lighter cases were made of low-grade steel. They were sprayed with black paint and baked to a crackle finish.

There was hardly a serviceman who did not carry a Zippo. They were used to light smoking lamps, and campfires in swamps and jungles, to cook soup in helmets and to save lives as a fire signal. One army pilot maneuvered his disabled plane to safety by using a Zippo lighter to illuminate his darkened instrument panel.

By the end of World War II,

Zippo lighters, like Gillette razors and Coca-Cola had become part of the GI's everyday life. As returning soldiers demonstrated the virtues of Zippos to their friends, sales of the lighters soared. At the height of this boom, in 1946, Blaisdell halted all shipments of Zippos because it had come to his attention that the most frequent repairs Zippos required were to worn flint wheels. The company launched a crash research program to find the toughest material possible for an improved wheel. It cost them $300,000 to lick the problem, but finally Zippo engineers developed what is considered to be the highest-quality striking wheel in the world.

Zippo goes to extraordinary lengths to honor its lifetime guarantee of every lighter. It costs the company more than $200,000 a year to assure its unbroken record that "no one has ever paid a cent to fix a Zippo." Zippo chalks it up to good public relations. It does not advertise widely in the media but attributes 40 percent of Zippo volume to the gains from advertising

other companies' products via Zippo lighters bearing corporate insignia or sales messages. Some of the biggest corporate names in industry regularly order Zippos in huge lots to serve as premiums, promotional handouts, employee awards and sales incentives. The company figures that "every Zippo that pushes another company's products also adds zip to Zippo's sales."

After twenty-eight years of making nothing but lighters, Zippo cautiously diversified its output to include a six-foot flexible-steel pocket rule. Since then it has added such items as a compact pocketknife and nail file, a money-clip knife, a golf ball, a key holder, a magnifier and a letter opener, all of which can be indelibly printed with any symbol or message. Though the odds against any of these products failing to perform are in Zippo's favor, each Zippo metal product comes with the pledge: "If for any reason your Zippo will not work, regardless of age or condition—we'll fix it free." Even the golf ball is guaranteed playable for 180 holes.

Waring Blender

Band-leader Fred Waring and his brother developed the WARING BLENDER in the early 1930's to liquify vegetables for a member of the family who could not eat solid food. The new gadget was considered extravagantly expensive in those days ($40 to $60) and sold well only to others interested in liquified food for health reasons (and to bartenders for making daiquiris). Its usefulness to the gourmet cook became apparent in the 1950's when Waring hired a professional to develop recipes like hollandaise and mayonnaise that could be whipped up, with a blender, in a trice. Waring made the blender still more attractive by reducing its price so that the handy devices soon spun their way into the basic inventory of most American kitchens, where they have remained in spite of the advent of more complex machines like the CUISINART.

PARKER PEN

PRESIDENT HARRY TRUMAN USED one to sign the peace treaty in 1952 between the United States, Britain and France and West Germany.

Physicist Robert Millikan, a Nobel Prize winner, claims to have written most of his eighteen books with his.

When actress Billie Burke toured the country to promote her book *With a Feather on My Nose*—telling of her early theatrical roles, her marriage to Flo Ziegfeld and her experiences in Hollywood—she signed autographs *only* with a PARKER 51.

The PARKER 51 fountain pen, produced in 1939—the fifty-first year after the company's founding—is a top seller that can claim the distinction of being a classic of modern design as well as a highly successful product.

George S. Parker, a teacher of telegraphy in Janesville, Wisconsin, sold John Holland pens as a sideline in 1888. He felt obligated to repair any defective pens for his students, and after tinkering with dozens of them, he decided that with the right tools, he could make a better pen himself. In the next two years, Parker had his first pen patented and took on a partner, W. F. Palmer, a local insurance salesman, with whom he incorporated the Parker Pen Company in Janesville.

In 1894 Parker patented the "Lucky Curve" ink feed for the pen he designed. With this feature, the ink drained back into a reservoir when the pen was in the upright position. The Parker Lucky Curve Pen was the company's principal product until the 1920's.

During World War I, Parker's Trench Pen was used by soldiers on the battlefields of Europe. The pen used ink made in the field by the doughboys, using a pill of black pigment mixed with water in the pen's cap. Thus, the Trench Pen became a "portable ink plant" as well as something to write with.

After the war, Parker sales for all its pen models soared well past the $1 million mark. The company suffered a setback during the Depression but rallied to produce the elegant Parker Vacuumatic in 1933 with 102 percent more ink capacity than any other pen of comparable size.

But it was the PARKER 51 that really took the market by storm, winning acclaim for its sleek design and technical sophistication. The pen represented the culmination of the company's experiments with fast-drying inks and noncorrosive barrel materials: The new synthetic called Lucite used in the PARKER 51 appeared to be a perfect replacement for the rubber sacs which tended to rot from the high alkali content of most inks. Parker invested $250,000 in the development of this pen and the promotion for it; it became an all-time best seller, influencing the design of pens made by Parker and others ever since.

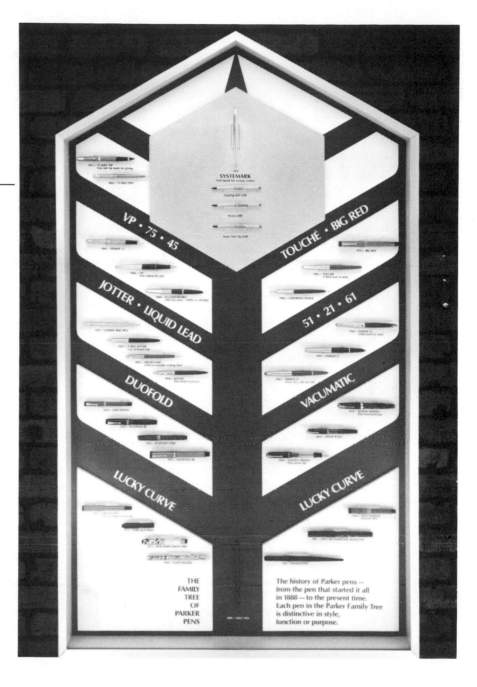

SMIRNOFF VODKA

RUNNING A CLOSE SECOND (AFTER BACARDI rum) for the distinction of being America's Best-Selling Booze is Heublein's star product, SMIRNOFF vodka.

Of course, vodka comes to us by way of Russia, where the Smirnoffs were exclusive purveyors of it to the imperial Russian court. At the time of the Bolshevik Revolution, the secret of the SMIRNOFF process passed with Vladimir Smirnoff first to Poland, then to France. With Smirnoff's permission, Russian-born emigrant Rudolph Kunett, whose family had supplied the grain for making SMIRNOFF vodka before the revolution, brought the SMIRNOFF process to Bethel, Connecticut, where Kunett set up a small distillery.

But Kunett's business did not fare as well as he had anticipated. In 1939, as a favor to Kunett, John G. Martin, president of Heublein, Inc., in Hartford, Connecticut, agreed to sell a few cases of SMIRNOFF vodka under Heublein's name. Several months later, Rudolph Kunett appeared at Heublein's headquarters in Hartford, looking forlorn. Vodka sales had not improved and Kunett was beginning to doubt that they ever would.

"I'm ready to sell the U.S. rights to SMIRNOFF to anyone who'll give me $14,000 and a job," he told John Martin.

Martin thought that sounded like a reasonably good deal and he agreed. His colleagues referred to the new product as "Martin's folly" until one memorable day when John Martin received an order from Heublein's South Carolina distributor for five hundred cases.

Even Martin was staggered. Not that he doubted the good judgment of the distributor, Ed Smith, but he remembered having to twist the man's arm to take twenty-five cases just a few months earlier. Martin decided to visit South Carolina to find out what was going on.

When he arrived in Smith's warehouse he discovered a situation he definitely had not expected. The corks in the bottles of vodka that Martin had originally sent were all labeled SMIRNOFF *whiskey*! Apparently the bottles were part of a final order of two thousand cases that had been produced by Kunett's tiny distillery just before it closed down in Bethel prior to moving to Heublein's headquarters in Hartford. When they ran out of vodka corks in Bethel, someone decided to use up a batch of corks left over from an ill-fated attempt to market SMIRNOFF whiskey. The Bethel people figured that the corks would be covered by tax stamps so no one would know the difference.

As it happened, Ed Wooten, Heublein's sole salesman in the South at the time, was eager to sample this curious whiskey he was being asked to sell. He uncorked a bottle of SMIRNOFF. He sniffed and found it had no smell. He sipped and found it had no taste. He was baffled, but like the good salesman he was, he decided to make the most of the product's unwhiskeylike properties. He had some signs made up: SMIRNOFF'S WHITE WHISKEY. NO TASTE. NO SMELL.

Thomas Fleming points out in *The Smirnoff Story* that the tasteless, odorless "white whiskey" was soon giving other whiskies a run for their money—as Ed Smith's order for five hundred more cases emphatically demonstrated. Says Fleming, "John Martin saw at once that he had made no mistake in believing that Americans could be persuaded to drink vodka. But it was the mistake made by enterprising salesman Ed Wooten that told him why: a substantial number of people liked the relaxation associated with drinking whiskey though they did not really like its taste or smell."

Vodka's increasing popularity was abruptly halted with the advent of World War II, when grain used in the manufacture of alcoholic beverages was diverted to more essential needs. John G. Martin went off to serve for four years in the United States Army. During that time SMIRNOFF vodka was virtually forgotten.

Like other GIs, Martin came home to a nation much changed by the war years. On the positive side, people's horizons had broadened; they were more adventurous in many ways. American servicemen had tasted sake in Japan, the wines of Italy and France, stout and Scotch in Great Britain. Grateful to be home again, they were eager to live well and enjoy life. It seemed the perfect time to reintroduce SMIRNOFF vodka.

Much to his surprise, Martin encountered resistance when he mentioned vodka to potential customers. "Vodka?" they replied. "Who wants to drink that fiery stuff?"

As Martin wondered what approach to try next, he ran into an old friend, Jack Morgan, who was having a similar problem attempting to market a soft drink called ginger beer that he had discovered in Britain. He was finding that

Americans were quite happy with ginger ale and saw no reason to switch.

Martin and Morgan were joined in their problems by another frustrated vendor—a girl friend of Morgan's who had recently inherited a copper factory and was having a hard time finding buyers for the bowls and mugs it produced. The three of them put their heads together and came up with an ingenious plan to convert three white elephants into another kind of highly salable animal—the Moscow Mule. They capitalized on the current popularity of mixed drinks and invented one of their own. It was made by mixing vodka with ginger beer, topping it with a squeeze of lime and serving it in . . . you guessed it! A copper mug!

People soon forgot that vodka was considered fiery. They drank Moscow Mules in restaurants and bars from coast to coast—partly as a result of John G. Martin's personal promotion campaign. The president of Heublein bought himself a POLAROID instant camera and went from bar to bar, gallantly offering to take the bartender's picture. Who could resist the opportunity to be the subject of a finished photograph that one could see only minutes after it was snapped? Bartenders gladly accepted Martin's request to let him take their photograph; they scarcely noticed when he placed a Moscow Mule cup in their upraised hands and a bottle of SMIRNOFF in a prominent position on the bar.

Nor did any bartender think to question why Martin always took a second POLAROID photo, slipping the duplicate into his vest pocket as the bartender's friends gathered round to admire the original. The duplicate was produced at Martin's

next stop to demonstrate how many bartenders were serving SMIRNOFF vodka.

In *The Smirnoff Story*, author Thomas Fleming explains that just as Martin's public-relations program was beginning to pay off, another war intervened. "In June of 1950, Korea exploded, pitting Soviet Russia and Communist North Korea against the United States and its allies, who supported the invaded South Koreans. Americans soon began condemning Russia and all things Russian. The Moscow Mule was a convenient scapegoat. The Bartenders' Union went so far as to stage a parade on New York's Fifth Avenue with the marchers carrying banners that declared: WE CAN DO WITHOUT THE MOSCOW MULE. The message was carried to the rest of the country when the New York *Daily News*, the nation's largest newspaper, ran a front-page picture of the protest march.

"Smirnoff sales would have slowed to a trickle had not Heublein quickly issued a statement . . . that Smirnoff Vodka had long since turned its back on Communist Russia. It was now made in that perennial stronghold of American patriotism—New England."

After the Korean War ended in 1953 Americans entered a new era of affluence and a more relaxed style of living. Vodka was well suited to lounging around the swimming pool, to enjoying Sunday brunch or to taking a leisurely late-afternoon sail. In addition to vodka martinis and the old standbys, vodka and tonic and Bloody Mary, people invented new vodka-based drinks: the Screwdriver (vodka with orange juice), supposedly invented by American engineers in the Middle East who stirred their drinks with screwdrivers; the Bullshot (vodka with bouillon); the Black Russian (vodka with coffee liqueur and cream).

Not unexpectedly, John Martin was standing by ready to promote SMIRNOFF now that its time had clearly come. In the mid-fifties he hired famous photographers including Irving Penn, Gordon Parks and Helmut Newton and sent them around the world to take shots of SMIRNOFF in exotic places. One of the ads that became a classic featured a giant SMIRNOFF martini in the sand with Egypt's Great Pyramid rising dramatically in the background. In those ads as in current ones, the copy always alludes suggestively to that unique quality of SMIRNOFF vodka that Martin had learned from the white whiskey episode: "It leaves you breathless."

GALLO WINE

"WHEN I DEPART FROM THIS earth to appear before the Lord to account for my sins, which have been scarlet, I shall say to him, 'I can't remember the name of the place, I don't remember the name of the girl, but that wine, my God, was Chardonnay!'"

Charles M. Crawford, vice-president of the Gallo winery in Modesto, California, likes to quote Hilaire Belloc's words in making the point that quality grapes and fastidious processing are the secret of good winemaking and the key to Gallo's success. Actually, Gallo's phenomenal success—it is the largest winery in the world, producing and selling as much wine as its next three or four competitors combined—is attributable to many factors.

Ernest and Julio Gallo grew up working on their father's small vineyard within one hundred miles of Modesto. Just about the time Prohibition was repealed, the two brothers decided that now that the nation was off the wagon, the future was rosy for the wine industry. They managed to raise $8,000, rent a railroad shed, buy a $2,000 grape crusher and a few redwood tanks on terms. They supplemented their own winemaking experience with

information from two pamphlets found in the local library. They rounded up enough grapes from local growers to fill their tanks and signed a contract with a distributor in Chicago for six thousand gallons at fifty cents apiece. While Julio Gallo busied himself with the winemaking process, Ernest traveled to the East and eventually lined up enough distributors to buy the company's entire output.

That first year's profit was $34,000, all of which was plowed back into the company to spend on equipment. Their second and third year profits were similarly reinvested.

The Gallos have never relied on quality alone to sell their product. They hired the best salesmen they could find and instructed them to propose any kind of incentive they could think of to persuade retailers to give them the best display space in the store. Another strategy was pricing the wine well below that of other wineries. The result of all this planning was that the wine sold very well.

In 1967, following years of experimentation—at one time more than four hundred different wine-grape varieties were under study—Gallo offered growers unprecedented fifteen-year contracts to plant selected wine varieties in the areas where they grew best. The growers were, however, required to follow specified growing standards.

One of the Gallos' many strengths has been their ability to sense consumers' changing tastes. They introduced many newcomers to wine drinking to table wine with BOONE'S FARM in the 1960's and early 1970's. As these consumers' tastes evolved, Gallo was ready with Hearty Burgundy and Chablis Blanc, the two leading generic wines sold in this country. When customers began demanding drier, more complex wines, the Gallos launched, in 1974, a line of cork-finished varietal wines including Chenin Blanc, French Colombard and Johannisberg Riesling, which have become the best-selling varietal wines at retail in America.

Today Gallo buys more grapes from the prestigious wine-growing regions of Napa, Sonoma, Mendocino and Monterey than any other winery. It has been estimated that 20 percent of the grapes in the Napa Valley, 40 percent of the grapes in Sonoma County and 40 percent of the grapes in Monterey County are crushed by Gallo.

ALKA-SELTZER

AFTER A NIGHT OF OVER-indulgence, W. C. Fields once complained of an ALKA-SELTZER fizzing in a glass of water, "Can't anyone do something about that racket!"

For millions of people, "Plop, plop, fizz, fizz" is a friendly sound, promising fast relief. "Try it, you'll like it," and "I can't believe I ate the *whole* thing" became part of our everyday language when the first ALKA-SELTZER television commercials appeared in the late sixties. But the story of ALKA-SELTZER goes back much farther than that.

Its origin can be traced to the day A. H. (Hub) Beardsley, then president of the Dr. Miles Laboratories, paid a visit to the editor of *The Elkhart Truth*, the daily newspaper in Elkhart, Indiana. It was December 1928 and an epidemic of colds and influenza was sweeping the country. To Beardsley's amazement, not one staff member at *The Truth* had been afflicted, and editor Tom Keene was, in fact, lending healthy linotype operators to a paper in a neighboring town where all the linotypists were down with the flu. How, Beardsley politely inquired, did Keene explain the immunity of his employees to the plague that was affecting everyone else?

Keene replied that none of the newspaper's employees had lost any time on account of the colds and flu. "When a member of my staff shows signs of coming down with a cold, I dose him with aspirin and bicarbonate of soda, and instruct him to continue with this until he is free of symptoms."

It sounded a simple enough prescription, particularly appealing to Beardsley, whose company had specialized in home remedies since its founder first produced a sedative

he called Dr. Miles NERVINE.
Upon his return to the Dr. Miles
Laboratories, Beardsley asked his
chief chemist if he could make an
effervescent tablet containing
bicarbonate of soda and aspirin. The
tablets Maurice Treneer produced
were used around the office with
gratifying success. Beardsley took
some with him when he and his
wife went on a Mediterranean cruise
the following January and
distributed them among the
passengers, who later reported that
they found them as effective for
seasickness as they were against the
cold germs and flu viruses some
fellow travelers had unwittingly
brought on board.

The wonder-working tablet was
offered to the public in 1931.
Though the country was in the
depths of the Depression, Miles did
not stint on advertising, particularly
on radio. Sponsoring *The Saturday
Night Barn Dance* on station WLS
in Chicago gave Miles the

opportunity to achieve major market
penetration. The show and ALKA-
SELTZER remained in partnership
nearly fourteen years, ensuring the
familiarity of the ALKA-SELTZER
brand name in households all over
America. During these years ALKA-
SELTZER also sponsored *The Quiz
Kids* and several other radio shows.
When TV came along in the late
forties and early fifties, ALKA-
SELTZER's advertisers made the
transition to the new medium with
characteristic speed and
effectiveness.

Whether it was through
advertising or plain word of mouth,
in the early thirties ALKA-SELTZER
gained a reputation for being the
best possible cure for hangovers. Its
popularity for that purpose became
clear in 1933—the year the United
States emerged from Prohibition.
Miles's sales increased dramatically
that year and doubled every seven
years thereafter.

In the mid-1970's Ralph Nader

charged Miles Laboratories with
producing "an irrational product
. . . promoted to relieve upset
stomachs when it contains aspirin,
suspected of being a stomach
irritant." The company responded to
the criticism with a new ad
campaign designed to stress ALKA-
SELTZER's power to relieve
headaches and queasy stomachs. As
double insurance against sales loss,
Miles introduced a new ALKA-
SELTZER product containing no
aspirin (ALKA-2 Antacid).

Since early 1978 the Miles
Laboratories have been owned by
the Bayer Company of West
Germany (no connection with
Sterling Drug, makers of BAYER
ASPIRIN). Bayer is the fourth-largest
chemical producing company in the
world, with a research budget that
equals the total annual sales of
Miles, which also makes two other
best sellers: S.O.S soap pads and
FLINTSTONE vitamins.

Stories About Alka-Seltzer

References to ALKA-SELTZER culled from clippings in the Miles company files . . .
• *The Wall Street Journal* mentions a divorce kit, marketed as "Split Decision," which includes the following necessary ingredients for a trouble-free break up: forms for changing mailing addresses and credit cards, a list of legal pointers, and two ALKA-SELTZER tablets—all for just $12.50.
• A sports writer tells of a fisherman who uses ALKA-SELTZER as bait to catch bass. He attached a tablet to the line with a clothespin and gets ready to pull as the fish go for the fizz.
• Perhaps the most inspired idea comes from a magazine article discussing the increasing problem of pollution-born acid in rainwater. The writer suggested that clouds be seeded with ALKA-SELTZER to produce acid-free rain.

P A R T   S I X

1946–1982

The wartime technology that led to the atom bomb spurred intensive research in peacetime uses for scientific advances after 1946. Atomic-powered batteries to run watches, radios and machines of all kinds prompted the development of products for both industry and the home. Government interest in aerospace sparked a series of "high tech" products, notably those related to video equipment and information processing.

Technology played an increasingly larger role in the American household as more housewives also became wage earners. Freezers, food processors, microwave ovens became standard equipment for making life easier, and fast food gained acceptance as an alternative to using even these. Other top sellers included products designed to aid male and female in the quest for health, glamour and fitness—essential prerequisites for the new improved American way of life.

POLAROID

FOR EDWIN LAND, PHOTOGRAPHY was just one of the multitude of applications he devised for the use of polarized light. He expected his early experiments would lead him into involvement with the auto industry, but Detroit turned down the Polaroid process for making sun visors and headlights when it found that polarized sheets deteriorated at high temperatures. Land's company found a good market for its special light-filtering materials during World War II, but after the war that market disappeared. It was then that Land began serious research on an idea he'd had in the back of his mind since 1943.

He remembered snapping a picture of his three-year-old daughter while on vacation in Santa Fe, New Mexico. She had been impatient to see the result, and it occurred to him then that there should be some way to develop and print a photograph inside the camera. By 1947 he had worked out the details of the process and presented the world with the POLAROID Model 95. It weighed slightly more than four pounds, produced in sixty seconds sepia-toned prints of uneven quality and retailed for ninety dollars. Offered a chance to market it, Kodak decided that it was a frivolous item with a limited lifespan and would certainly never enjoy the distinction of products by Kodak. (Later on, when Kodak decided to venture into the area of instant photography, it had difficulty designing a camera that did not infringe on Polaroid's patents. When it thought it finally achieved success, Polaroid sued anyway.)

The Polaroid Model 95 was probably the most popular Christmas present received by anyone in 1948, and with each added improvement, its appeal increased. By 1950 Polaroids were available that made good quality black-and-white prints; by 1960 the Polaroid produced pictures in

fifteen seconds and offered automatic exposure. Within five years you could buy color film for Polaroids and there was a lower-priced model on the market—the Savinger, followed in 1971 by the Square Shooter.

But the SX-70 introduced in 1972 became the best-selling camera ever. According to Moskowitz, Katz and Levering in *Everybody's Business*, Land decided to shoot for the moon with this camera, investing half a billion dollars to bring it on the market. "When it debuted in 1972, the camera was an inch-thick, seven-inch-long, fold-up instant miracle. The most miraculous thing about it was the film. Thinner than the hyphen in SX-70, it contained eight separate chemical sheets protected by an 'opacifier' layer that kept out the sun's rays while the picture developed *outside* the camera. Each of the eight dyed

layers responded to a different light frequency when exposed, resulting in brilliant color. Because the dye used was metallic, the finished product didn't fade when exposed to extreme light for a long period. Kodak, Polaroid's chief competitor, was completely nonplussed, and to this day have been unable to match Polaroid's achievement." [1]

While the SX-70 and variations on it have continued to keep Polaroid in first place in the field of instant still photography, another of Land's long shots—this one in instant movies—did not pan out so well. Many aspects of the instant movie system are still too flawed to invite the kind of spectacular sales that the SX-70 enjoyed. As a result Polaroid stock fell in the 1970's, but with the company's reputation for innovation, the next dramatic development may be just around the corner.

[1] *Everybody's Business.*

CASTRO CONVERTIBLE

The night little Bernadette Castro quietly opened the family sofa bed, climbed in and went to sleep was a turning point in her father's career. Bernadette was only four; the year was 1948. Her father, Bernard, had struggled since the early years of the Depression, when he made his living refurbishing

davenports, to design a sofa bed so simple that even a child could operate it.

The sight of Bernadette asleep in their Castro Convertible inspired Castro to take a gamble on the as yet unproven value of TV advertising. He bought air time on New York's Dumont TV Network

and produced a commercial that was to become the firm's trademark and an advertising legend. The commercial featured little Bernadette herself opening a Castro Convertible.

"At first," reports Castro, "we had practically no results. We were going to cancel our television

contract after the thirteen-week period. We were convinced that our message was a good one, but we didn't think television was helping us get it across. Then, one day around the beginning of the thirteenth week, like magic, customers started asking for the convertible the little girl opens on TV. We extended our contract and the commercial ran for years."

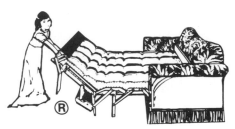

The 1950's saw steady growth for the Castro Convertible Corporation,

enabling Castro to make design changes that have kept CASTRO CONVERTIBLES ahead of their competition ever since. One of these is the development of the "Featherlift" mechanism. Though the device is made of tremendously heavy-gauge steel, it works in such a way that opening a CASTRO CONVERTIBLE is even easier now than it was for Bernadette in 1948.

JOTTER

WHO CAN REMEMBER WHEN BALL-points were not as readily available as small change? Yet, a good quality, low-cost ball-point did not exist in America until Parker introduced the JOTTER in 1954.

Argentinians were using ball-points soon after World War II. The first reasonably successful ball-point pen was invented there, by Lazlo Biro in Buenos Aires. It produced fairly even lines of handwriting, roughly comparable to those of a fountain pen. The secret was a smoothly ground ball rotating in a brass seat in conjunction with a steady flow of ink.

Biro obtained U.S. patent rights on his inventions, then sold them shortly thereafter to Eversharp. As this company was planning an appropriate introduction to the market, an entrepreneur named Milton Reynolds got the jump on Eversharp and at Christmastime, 1945, introduced a ball-point pen to an eager public. The Reynolds pen attracted plenty of attention and sales with its claims of convenience

and practicality. But at $12.50 each, the pens were not really a bargain. The main problem was that the ink flowed too freely or not at all. Competitors developed special gravity-flow ink held in rubber sacs, then in brass tubes, but there were

no major improvements until better inks, increased quality control and more affordable pricing became possible in the early fifties.

After years of research, Parker finally introduced its first ball-point pen in 1954 in the form of the

The ball pen that lets you write beautifully without bearing down

JOTTER, with a variety of point sizes, a rotating cartridge and large-capacity ink refills. Another outstanding feature was the retractable nib with a nylon ratchet that turned the point every time it was retracted, thus solving the problem of uneven wear that had been the undoing of many cheaper ball-point pens.

By 1957, with a few more features added, the JOTTER was able to challenge the long-held record for sales established by PAPERMATE. By 1961 Parker had the top-selling ball-point pen in the world in the over one-dollar category.

As new materials were developed, Parker continued to add refinements—the textured ball, the stainless-steel ball socket—to further improve the JOTTER. Today, nearly seventeen million JOTTERS are sold each year. The ones with a black refill can produce more than 28,000 linear feet of writing—more than five miles—before running out of ink.

TIMEX

THE UNITED STATES TIME Corporation of Middlebury, Connecticut, introduced its first line of inexpensive TIMEX watches to the U.S. marketplace in 1950. Neither American nor foreign watchmakers paid much attention to the new competitor. The industry was already neatly polarized between companies making either high-priced prestige watches or cheap gimmicky ones like the one-jewel watches from overseas.

No one expected the TIMEX watch to sell any better than the current models, nor were they immediately aware that the TIMEX watch represented a totally new concept in watchmaking. Norwegian-born Joakim Lehmkuhl, designer of the first TIMEX watch, had studied engineering at Harvard and MIT. He was convinced that it was possible to capitalize on post-World War II technology to make a quality watch that could be mass-produced.

After studying in the United States, Lehmkuhl had returned in 1919 to his native Norway to direct a small shipbuilding firm. He later

WE MAKE TECHNOLOGY BEAUTIFUL

became involved in Norwegian politics and the publication of an anti-Nazi newspaper. Shortly before the 1940 German invasion of Norway, Lehmkuhl fled with his family to Great Britain. The Germans had cut off all transportation overland so, for the

172 first part of their journey, they traveled on skis. As the youngest member of the family, their five-year-old daughter, could not yet ski, her father pulled her along on a rope.

Finally making it to the North Sea, they set out in a small boat in which they narrowly missed being strafed by the Germans at least three times before they landed in the Orkney Islands. From there, Lehmkuhl contacted the Norwegian government-in-exile which assigned him to organize a Norwegian shipping office in America. Once Lehmkuhl and his family were safely settled in the United States, recognizing that his current assignment was temporary, Lehmkuhl cast about for other business opportunities. He found them in the Waterbury Clock Company, in which he and a group of businessmen acquired a majority interest with the intention of converting the firm to fuse production. The company became the largest producer of fuses in the United States.

After the war, when sales dropped because of disappearing defense orders, it seemed logical now to explore the possibilities of low-cost watch production. Lehmkuhl was convinced that a good, inexpensive watch could be made by combining the precision-tooling techniques used in making fuse timers with a high degree of automation. By 1949 Waterbury's engineers had succeeded in upgrading the mechanism used in children's watches into the prototype of the TIMEX watch. The design was infinitely simpler than that of a higher-priced Swiss watch and it had one outstanding feature that had evolved from the wartime research

effort: New hard alloy (Armalloy) bearings replaced the jewels in the movement. According to the company, this feature made the watch the equal of many jewel-lever models and better than any of the pin-lever models then available.

According to Fred Nelson, former TIMEX vice-president of sales, TIMEX's debut in the early 1950's was modest. "Point-of-purchase displays were not sophisticated and there was virtually no advertising in the first two or three years. Then, as the business grew, we went into magazines, with ads showing people like Ben Hogan (who, the ad said, tested the TIMEX watch with one hundred thousand golf swings) and Mickey Mantle with a TIMEX strapped on his bat."

In 1954 the company introduced a showcase for point-of-purchase display designed to demonstrate in no uncertain terms the durability of the TIMEX watch. The original showcase was fitted with levers that would dunk a TIMEX in water and drop it on an anvil. According to Mr. Lehmkuhl, these promotional tactics accounted in large measure for the rapid rise in sales of the TIMEX in the early 1950's, paving the way for Timex's entry into television advertising in 1956.

"The company became renowned, first at home and then abroad, for its so-called 'torture test.' Its commercials featured news commentator John Cameron Swayze showing a TIMEX which, under varying circumstances, 'took a licking and kept ticking.' In one of the early torture tests, done live, a TIMEX watch was fastened to an outboard engine propeller. In the water, the watch slipped off the spinning propeller, which it was not supposed to do. It was later

recovered, running, and TIMEX watch ended up with yet another highly favorable bit of publicity for its watches."[1]

A decade after the first TIMEX watch came on the market, the company was selling seven million annually. In 1962 an Alfred Politz research study indicated that one watch out of every three sold in the United States was a TIMEX. Only twelve years after the introduction of its product, the company was, according to President Lehmkuhl, "completely free of debt, had financed all recent expansions out of earnings, and intended to continue to do so." The Timex strategy had paid off in dollars and cents.

Throughout the sixties and seventies, Timex (the company became Timex Corporation in 1969) continued to broaden its product line, introducing the seventeen-jewel watch for $17.95, retail; the twenty-one-jewel watch for $21.95; and the electric watch, selling for $39.95, about half the price of its nearest competitor. In 1974 Timex started to manufacture digital watches with the liquid crystal display (LCD).

In 1983 Timex looks to the future optimistically, promising to continue "to make technology beautiful" with new products like its personal computer priced at under $100—the least expensive microcomputer on the market so far. Timex's other stake in the future is its line of home health-monitoring instruments, including a scale, thermometer and blood-pressure gauge, all using digital electronics.

---

[1] Harvard Business School Case Study copyright © 1972 by the President and Fellows of Harvard College.

VELCRO

THERE'S SOMETHING ABOUT VELCRO—two roughly textured surfaces that adhere when pressed together—that seems so simple. One wonders why anybody who has ever come back from a country walk with burrs sticking to his clothes could not have thought of it.

George de Mestral, a young inventor, had exactly that idea one day in 1948 after returning from a hunting trip in the Swiss mountains. Ten years later he could testify that creating man-made burrs was not as easy as it seemed.

De Mestral had been working on several projects when he became interested in burrs. By day he was manager of a small machine shop near Nyon, Switzerland. In his spare time he invented things. One

of the few that he earned any money from was a new type of hygrometer, the instrument used to measure humidity. This invention so impressed an old family friend, Alfred Gonet, a banker in Nyon, that Gonet offered De Mestral the use of a fully equipped workshop on his estate to pursue his inventive ideas. The banker paid him what he had been earning at the machine shop and also provided a house to live in, rent-free.

De Mestral glowed with enthusiasm as he told his patron about his idea for a fastener that would soon replace the zipper. Gonet listened patiently, not wishing to discourage his eager young friend, but he later confessed

that he thought De Mestral's idea was crazy.

Undaunted, De Mestral went on to consult the experts in Lyon, textile center of France. They, too, were skeptical, but one of the weavers took an interest in De Mestral's idea. Working mostly by hand on a small loom he managed to produce two strips of cotton fabric, one with hooks, the other with loops. When pressed together, they clung firmly.

De Mestral found one more supporter in Jacques Muller, a Swiss loom manufacturer who believed as De Mestral did that there had to be some way to produce the strips of "locking tape" in quantity. Eventually Muller was compelled to give up in despair; but he put his equipment and experience at his inventor-friend's disposal. Once again, De Mestral was on his own.

After months of experiments with steam, hot air and ultrasonic sound, De Mestral found that he could make loops of nylon thread rigid by weaving them under infrared light. This was a major breakthrough. The next step was to find a glue that would hold them in place. He spoke with chemical experts in London and finally found an adhesive that worked. Now De Mestral could make, at high speed, ribbons of cloth lined with tiny loops. The problem was how to make the corresponding hooks. He found that if alternate loops were cut by hand, the hooks would adhere securely, but he could not find a way to achieve this result by machine.

Months went by and De Mestral was still unable to resolve the problem. He had lost the support of his backers—even Gonet told him

that he could no longer afford to finance him. In desperation De Mestral retreated to a friend's hunting cabin in the mountains to think the problem through. A few days later he had arrived at a possible solution.

On the way down from the mountains, he stopped to buy a pair of barber's clippers, then went straight to visit his friend Jacques Muller, the loom maker. He explained his new idea of adapting the clipper principle to the job of snipping the loops mechanically. Muller agreed with him that the idea was feasible.

The two men spent the following year working out the details of the loop-clipping concept. A special loom was built and workers were trained to operate it. In 1957 a French-born naturalized American, Jean Ravaud, saw the new product, decided there might be a good market for it and agreed to subsidize the launching of the new business.

Soon after that, someone thought of calling the new fastener VELCRO—Vel for velvet, cro for French crochet, "small hook." By 1959 there were enough looms operating to turn out 60 million yards of VELCRO a year. Today the company's largest plant, in Manchester, New Hampshire, has made over 230,000 miles of VELCRO and there are more factories throughout the world. VELCRO is used for everything from securing the gear on board the space shuttle Columbia to holding ventricles together in artificial hearts. Company sales figures are over $45 million . . . and George de Mestral has been well rewarded for his years of perseverance.

FOSTER GRANTS

Though Foster Grant has been in business since 1919, first as a maker of combs, then as a major producer of the valuable plastic, polystyrene, most people don't know Foster Grant ever made anything but sunglasses. And until the mid-1960's they probably didn't know about the sunglasses either.

The comb business was started by young Samuel Foster in Leominster, Massachusetts, the comb capital of the world in those days. Foster teamed up briefly with a partner, William Grant, then bought him out completely, leaving himself too short of cash to change the name of the corporation they had formed together.

The first big crisis the new company was forced to weather occurred in 1921 when the Hollywood dance star Irene Castle bobbed her hair. Women all over the country followed the starlet's lead and Foster Grant's trade in combs and hair ornaments came to a standstill. The company dealt with this by starting a new line of celluloid products, using the latest techniques for injection molding.

Sam Foster imported from Germany the second injection-molding machine ever to enter the United States. The first had been sold to the Celanese Corporation which had the same problem with its machine that Sam Foster had: They simply couldn't get it to work. Sam tinkered with his, had new ones designed, and finally succeeded in making a series of machines that could produce as many parts for sunglasses in an hour as half a dozen of the original machines could turn out in eight.

The following year Sam Foster took the first step toward his goal of developing his own raw materials for a product he knew would have a market. The company set up research and development laboratories and by 1936 was producing polyvinyl acetate for its own use. By 1950 Foster Grant was the largest user of polystyrene in the world and would soon have a plant to produce all it could possibly need. The company has since built facilities for making the nylon and other raw materials required for Foster Grant products with plenty left over to sell to others.

Perhaps it was the squeeze in polystyrene prices in the mid-sixties, creating a large dent in company profits, that persuaded Foster Grant to think about broadening its market for sunglasses. Mauri Edwards was hired in 1964 as director of advertising and immediately given the assignment of finding a way to promote the sale of Foster Grant sunglasses.

"At the time, we weren't even sure that it was possible to establish a brand identity for sunglasses," recalled Edwards recently. "The business had been pretty much dominated by Cool Ray-Polaroid, which wasn't doing anything too dynamic to push its product." According to Harry C. Richards, who was assistant general manager of Foster Grant's Consumer Products Division at the time, "Cool Ray had everything on its side. It had an established name in the marketplace and it had the polarized lens which was a major selling point." Polaroid was known mainly for its cameras but it had a reputation for quality optics of any kind. Mauri Edwards's job was to get together with an ad agency and think of a way to take the edge off Cool Ray's obvious marketing advantage.

"If 'quality optics' was Cool Ray's hallmark, Foster Grant would have to go a different route," reminisced Mauri Edwards. "We chose to put the emphasis on *glamour*." Edwards pointed out that Cool Ray was committed to buying the polarized sheeting made by Polaroid for its lenses. This was expensive. "We could buy our lens material wherever we could get the best deal. As a result, we were able to offer a greater variety of lenses and styles to customers at a cheaper price."

Armed with this gambit and a very low budget, Edwards approached Peter Geer of Geer, DuBois, Inc. The result of their collaboration was the Sunglasses of the Stars campaign which revolutionized the marketing of the product by achieving the ultimate goal of advertising: to make a brand name synonymous with a generic term.

At the Geer, DuBois agency, Edwards teamed up with Rea Brown, creative vice president, to figure out a way to advertise sunglasses for the mass market while associating them with class, glamour, celebrities. "We felt we had a fashion story to tell," said Edwards, "but we wanted something more—something to generate excitement about the product. We decided to put sunglasses on movie stars to capitalize on the exotic, fantasy world of Hollywood."

The first Foster Grant ads appeared in *Life* and *Look* and featured Peter Sellers in a series of black-and-white photographs. The

175

witty caption under each photo ingeniously associated the product with the movie star wearing the glasses, suggesting that the star endorsed the product. The format of the ads never changed and the campaign was extended into 1967 and 1968 to include Elke Sommer, Anita Ekberg, Woody Allen and others in living color. The ads were so successful that Foster Grant was soon getting calls from agents of entertainment figures to tell them that their clients were available to appear in the ads. People began to imagine that they had seen Marcello Mastroianni, Sophia Loren, Brigitte Bardot wearing the glasses—even when they hadn't.

Successful as the magazine ads had been, Foster Grant decided in 1969 that it was time to try something else. They launched a series of TV commercials that once again featured well-known stars, this time in short scenes filmed on location. Each commercial had a humorous twist and ended with an echo from the earlier ad campaign of . . .

Mauri Edwards never thought the TV commercials were as effective as the first FOSTER GRANT ads. "The campaign was a natural for the print medium and just did not translate to the screen as forcefully as we hoped it would."

More TV ads appeared in the early seventies, as Foster Grant geared up to go after its major competitor, Cool Ray-Polaroid, head on. As soon as the company had its own polarized sheeting for making lenses, the management felt it was ready. Since the mid-sixties, Cool Ray's ads had been very low-key, stressing the scientific benefits of Polaroid lenses. In the mid-seventies, Cool Ray tried to counter Foster Grant by putting more emphasis on fashion in its advertising. Cool Ray was hardly prepared when Foster Grant came back with a one-minute television spot making a hard-hitting comparison between its own polarizing lenses and those of "the other leading brand." The commercial was shown for the first

time during the 1973 World Series and continued to be aired frequently during the fall season that followed.

Mauri Edwards enjoys telling the story of Cool Ray's desperate effort to draw to itself some of the attention that Foster Grant was getting. It seems that somewhere in the Midwest in the late seventies, the Lone Ranger was scheduled to make a personal appearance, and for the first time, he planned to do so wearing sunglasses rather than the traditional but somewhat anachronistic black mask. The sunglasses were happily supplied by Cool Ray-Polaroid in return for the free publicity the company expected to receive. Unfortunately, it didn't plug the brand name fast enough. Everyone assumed the Lone Ranger was wearing FOSTER GRANTS. Even the local newspaper applauded the new look of the Lone Ranger, "behind those FOSTER GRANTS."

The brand name picked up another free plug in the 1979 World Series when Reggie Jackson failed to catch a high fly because the sun was in his eyes. Broadcasters, baseball fans and trivia experts have referred to the "FOSTER GRANT Series" ever since.

If Foster Grant intended to drive Cool Ray-Polaroid out of the market, it may have succeeded. First, in the late seventies, Polaroid decided not to renew the license allowing Cool Ray to use its polarizing sheeting for lenses. Shortly thereafter the American Optical Company, which owned Cool Ray, was sold to Warner-Lambert, Inc. That company decided to separate its professional optical products from general consumer items. Cool Ray sunglasses wound up in the latter division where no one seemed

"Isn't that X behind those FOSTER GRANTS?"

particularly interested in promoting them. Finally, in 1980, Cool Ray closed out the brand name and allowed the patent to expire—"an act of commercial suicide," says Mauri Edwards, innocently refusing to admit that Foster Grant had

anything to do with bringing this about.

Foster Grant's investment in advertising had been well repaid. Not only did the ad campaigns, particularly the first one in the sixties, draw the public's attention to

the FG brand name, they made the name part of the American idiom. "FOSTER GRANTS" became everyone's blasé way of referring to sunglasses. The product is a classic best seller.

McDONALD'S BIG MAC

A McDONALD'S BIG MAC IS AN American product with built-in stability, guaranteed not to vary no matter where in the world you buy it. That's because every year half a million head of cattle are raised and slaughtered, then frozen into little patties that are shipped to all the McDonald's outlets from Timbuktu to Kalamazoo. Eating a McDonald's hamburger is a totally predictable experience: no chance of epicurean delight and no risk of serious disappointment.

When you think of stopping at McDonald's, it's not just the food you will be served in the lily-white Styrofoam containers that you consider. You know, in advance, that the whole place will be more or less spotless—scant danger of a filthy restroom—and your hamburger, french fries and shake will be ready to go in less than sixty seconds. It is this total package of convenience, predictability and security that is really Ray Kroc's Number One best seller.

Ray Kroc didn't invent fast-food restaurants any more than he invented the BIG MAC. He just became The Expert on making it all very appealing. (Even if you hate the food you can love the

convenience.) McDonald's is miles ahead of its nearest competitor, which varies widely depending on which charts you check, and Kroc, now in his eighties, claims that he and the company are "still green and growing."

Kroc was past fifty before he ever thought of getting into the fast-food business. In 1954, after seventeen years of selling paper cups for Lily Tulip Company, opportunity appeared to Kroc in the form of a six-spindled milk-shake machine called a Multimixer. Kroc was convinced that the Multimixer was the key to a new future in the soda-fountain and dairy-bar business. He made the whole United States his sales territory.

When Kroc started getting orders from all over the country stating, "I want one of those mixers of yours like the McDonald brothers have in San Bernardino, California," he became more and more curious. Who were these McDonald brothers and what had attracted so many people to their restaurant?

As Kroc tells it in his autobiography, *Grinding It Out: The Making of McDonald's*, he flew out to Los Angeles one day, made some routine business calls there,

then bright and early the next morning drove the sixty miles east to San Bernardino. "I cruised past the McDonald's location about 10 A.M., and I was not terrifically impressed. There was a smallish octagonal building, a very humble sort of structure situated on a corner lot about 200 feet square. It was a typical, ordinary-looking drive-in. As the 11 o'clock opening time approached, I parked my car and watched the helpers begin to show up—all men dressed in spiffy white shirts and trousers and white paper hats. I liked that. They began to move supplies from a long, low shed at the back of the property. They trundled four-wheeled carts loaded with sacks of potatoes, cartons of meat, cases of milk and soft drinks, and boxes of buns into the octagonal building. Something was definitely happening here, I told myself. The tempo of their work picked up until they were bustling around like ants at a picnic."

After talking with the McDonalds, Kroc was even more impressed. "I was fascinated by the simplicity and effectiveness of the system they described. Each step in producing the limited menu was stripped down to its essence and

accomplished with a minimum of effort. They sold hamburgers and cheeseburgers only. The burgers were a tenth of a pound of meat, all fried the same way, for fifteen cents. You got a slice of cheese on it for four cents more. Soft drinks were ten cents, sixteen-ounce milk shakes were twenty cents and coffee was a nickel."

By the next morning, Kroc had a plan of action. He sat down with the McDonald brothers after the lunch-hour rush had abated and without further preliminaries he proposed franchising the whole operation.

The brothers were leery. They had already sold six franchises in California and thought they didn't want to get any bigger. But Kroc persisted and when he flew back to Chicago that same day he had a signed contract with the McDonalds in his briefcase.

Though the McDonalds brought to their partnership with Kroc everything from an ingenious concept for selling America's favorite food to a name and a symbol (the pair of golden arches) that Kroc admired enthusiastically, the relationship of the three men

was an awkward one. The McDonalds' ideas of efficiency and professionalism did not correspond to Kroc's at the higher levels of business management. In 1961, six years after Kroc persuaded them to sign their first contract, he bought them out for $2.7 million. There were 250 McDonald's restaurants dotted around the United States by then. There are now more than 5,000 in this country and abroad, and Kroc's personal worth is estimated to be close to a quarter of a billion dollars.

KENTUCKY FRIED CHICKEN

TRAVELING IN ANTIGONISH, NOVA Scotia, feeling far away from anything familiar, an American tourist does not expect to run into Colonel Sanders beaming benevolently from a neon sign advertising KENTUCKY FRIED Chicken. But there, as in other remote parts, is Colonel Sanders, side by side with Ronald McDonald, Wendy's, Pizza Hut and Bun 'n Burger, making the entire Western world seem like one giant shopping mall.

It was 1956 and Colonel Harland Sanders had just turned sixty-six when he started his new career.

Sanders had been frying chicken since 1930 as part of the service he offered hungry travelers who stopped by his gas station in Corbin, Kentucky. He didn't have a restaurant at that point. He served folks on his own dining table in a small dining room in the station where he and his family lived. As more people started coming just for the food, Sanders expanded into a restaurant that seated 142 people. Over the next nine years he developed his secret combination of eleven herbs and spices and the basic cooking technique that is still used. After Sanders supplemented his on-the-job experience with a short course in restaurant cooking at Cornell University, the news of the quality of the fare served at the Sanders café spread throughout the state. In 1935 Governor Ruby Laffon made Sanders a Kentucky Colonel in recognition of his contribution to the state's cuisine.

In the early 1940's Sanders added a motel to his services for travelers and experimented with refinements to the basic recipe for his now-famous fried chicken. The real problem was that of cooking time. With more travelers to accommodate, many of them in a hurry, Sanders couldn't keep them waiting while he cooked the chicken the usual way.

Everything improved the day the Colonel bought a pressure cooker and made a few adjustments on it. After a lot of experimenting he found a way to fry chicken in jig time and have it taste as good as the best chicken he'd ever fried. Sanders was now fully prepared to accommodate travelers on a much larger scale.

But it was the eve of World War II. Gas rationing had virtually ended all tourist travel. Sanders was forced to close the motel he had only recently opened.

The motel was reopened briefly after World War II but it was only a few years before a new interstate highway was built drawing travelers away from the Sanders Café and Motel. The Colonel was forced to auction off his equipment to pay his bills. Faced with the prospect of trying to live on his Social Security check, Sanders took to the road with his major assets: a fifty-pound can of seasoning, his beloved pressure cooker and the secret for cooking the best fried chicken most people had ever tasted.

"Let me cook chicken for you and your staff," he volunteered at restaurant after restaurant across the country. "If you like the way it tastes, I'll sell you my seasoning, teach you how to cook it, and you pay me a four-cent royalty on every chicken you sell." That was the deal. If the reaction to his chicken was good, the agreement was sealed with a handshake, nothing more.

By 1964 Colonel Sanders had more than six hundred franchised outlets for his chicken in the United States and Canada grossing $37 million a year. The Colonel was occasionally heard to mutter, "This danged business is beginning to run right over me."

Shortly after that the Colonel sold his interest in the U.S. company for $2 million and gave the Canadian company to a charitable foundation. Under the new owners, John Young Brown, Jr., and Nashville financier Jack Massey, the Kentucky Fried Chicken Corporation grew rapidly. More than thirty-five hundred stores

were in worldwide operation when Heublein, Inc., acquired KFC Corporation for $285 million. Brown reportedly received $35 million in cash and stock for his share of the business, and Massey slightly more.

Until he was fatally stricken with leukemia in 1980, the white-haired Colonel with the twinkling eyes traveled more than two hundred thousand miles a year visiting the outposts of the empire he had founded twenty years before. By the time he died it was some empire, with gross sales of more than $2 billion annually.

PEPPERIDGE FARM

PEPPERIDGE FARM BREAD IS A product that one might imagine was first baked with loving care in a family kitchen before it found its way into the commercial marketplace. And so it was.

As Margaret Rudkin, baker of those early loaves, wrote in her reminiscences of the first twenty-five years of Pepperidge Farm, "I could not convince myself that I wanted my children to have the only kind of

bread commercially available in 1937. I wanted them to have the old-fashioned homemade bread that I had eaten as a child."

Margaret Rudkin had never baked a loaf of bread before she made this decision, but she had a clear idea of the result she intended to achieve and a great deal of perseverance and zeal. She needed this kind of spirit for, by her own admission, the first loaf of PEPPERIDGE FARM bread

ever baked was hard as a rock and about one inch high. The trouble was, Margaret Rudkin had not yet learned to use yeast which requires careful handling and temperature control.

By methodical application of the lessons of trial and error, Mrs. Rudkin was soon producing loaves of homemade whole-wheat bread that her family and friends found infinitely preferable to any store-bought bread. She was fond of telling the story of one conversion: "When I told our family doctor I was making stone-ground whole wheat, he wouldn't believe me. He said it would be too coarse and I would have to add white flour to it. To convince him I brought him some samples and told him exactly what I put in with the flour—butter, whole milk, honey and molasses. He was indeed convinced and wanted to order some for himself and his patients."

With a talent for promotion almost equal to her bread-baking ability, Mrs. Rudkin persuaded the doctor to express his enthusiasm for her bread in writing, as a letter. Armed with this endorsement, she approached other men in the medical profession and soon had a sizable mail-order business on her hands.

In less than two months, Mrs. Rudkin was compelled to move from her kitchen to a remodeled garage and from there to the polo stables that had been empty since Mrs. Rudkin's husband suffered a bad riding accident years before.

But Mrs. Rudkin was not to enjoy the luxury of "working at home" much longer. By the time she moved the bakery into the polo stables her product line had grown to five items and production was in excess of twenty thousand loaves a week. The Pepperidge Farm Bakery would soon move into rented buildings in Norwalk, Connecticut, before finally becoming established in modern quarters in that same town.

The more her business grew, the more Margaret Rudkin thought in terms of developing it still further. When she decided the time had come to find a retail outlet in New York City, she simply went to the specialty shop she had in mind and asked to see the manager. He came out, she reported, "looking rather skeptical to see a woman with a package under her arm, another package in one hand (a quarter pound of butter) and in the other a bread knife. I was petrified with fright and he probably was also when he saw my knife—but I told him about my homemade bread, and the doctors' patients who were ready-made customers that I could send to him."

When the manager continued to hesitate, Margaret Rudkin put down her bread, cut off a slice, slathered it with butter and handed it to the man. She went home with an order for twenty-four loaves the next day.

Having cracked the New York market, Mrs. Rudkin had to deal with the problem of making deliveries there. For several weeks, her husband toted a twenty-five-pound package of loaves with him each morning on his way to Wall Street. He arranged to have a porter meet him in Grand Central and for twenty-five cents take the package across the street to the specialty shop where the bread was sold.

Soon thereafter the Rudkins discovered the advantages offered by Railway Express. They went on to invest, cautiously, in delivery trucks and, eventually, bakery facilities in other states to service their ever-broadening market.

As facilities expanded, so did the product line. In the late fifties frozen baked goods were added to the already impressive roster of PEPPERIDGE FARM products. Downington, Pennsylvania, was chosen as the site of the new frozen-food plant where turnovers, strudels and other puff pastries would be made.

In a move to ensure future growth and security, Pepperidge Farm became affiliated with Campbell Soup Company in 1961. Mrs. Rudkin was a member of the Board of Directors until her death in 1967.

M&M's

THE DIVISION OF MARS, Incorporated, that manufactures M&M's was opened in Newark, New Jersey, in 1940 by a pair of candy-family scions. One was Forrest Mars, son of the founder of the Mars Candy fortune, who had lived for nearly a decade in England where he became acquainted with SMARTIES, a sugar-coated candy with a chocolate center made by the Rowntree Mackintosh firm. The

PLAIN CHOCOLATE CANDIES

other founder of the new M&M division was Bruce Murries, son of a former president of the Hershey Chocolate Company. When Mars and Murries opened their factory (with the blessing of Rowntree Mackintosh) they used HERSHEY chocolate for the center of their candies. In the process of improving the M&M formula, they stopped doing business with Hershey and made their own chocolate centers instead.

According to authorized M&M/Mars sources (and these are limited due to the reluctance of the company to disclose much information about the family-owned business), M&M's were first introduced partly to meet a practical need for a candy GIs could carry in their K rations that would not melt like block chocolate. M&M's—"The milk chocolate that melts in your mouth—not in your hand"—were the result. In the years that followed, intensive TV advertising of the new product helped to propel Mars to the top of the American candy industry.

Today, M&M's are available in economy-sized bags containing a big enough assortment for all the members of the family to choose their favorite colors. Only people who always loved red M&M's are out of luck: When the federal government banned Red No. 2 food dye in the mid-1970's, Mars experimented with other red coloring and failed to find any satisfactory substitute. So it just stopped making red M&M's altogether.

SARA LEE

UNLIKE PEPPERIDGE FARM'S Margaret Rudkin, who did not initially dream of marketing her stone-ground whole-wheat bread on a very large scale, SARA LEE's Charles W. Lubin thought in terms of big business from the moment the first SARA LEE Original Cream Cheese Cake (named after his young daughter) met with overwhelming success in 1949.

Lubin had started his career in baking shortly after World War I as a fourteen-year-old apprentice in Decatur, Illinois. In 1935 Lubin teamed up with his brother-in-law, Arthur Gordon, to buy and manage three Chicago bakeries, known as the Community Bake Shops. For fourteen years they sold baked goods over the counter in Chicago neighborhoods, but Lubin could not resist thinking of how the scope of the business could be extended.

He was convinced that there was a substantial market for high-quality baked goods that could be sold in supermarkets. His thinking tied in with housewives' eagerness to be relieved of kitchen duties, and when Lubin began adding more items to his bakery line—Pecan All-Butter Coffee Cake, then All-Butter Pound Cake—they were welcomed with as much enthusiasm as the Cream Cheese Cake.

The Sara Lee Company grew so fast that several times in the 1950's production had to be moved to larger facilities. As the company grew, Lubin experimented with new forms of food packaging, the most notable being the aluminum-foil pan, permitting products to be baked, sold and warmed up in the same container. Another of his experiments proved that it was possible to freeze baked goods

SARA LEE billboard art in the 1940's

straight out of the oven, thus opening up opportunities for mass distribution—a major marketing breakthrough which led to mass distribution of SARA LEE items from one central production point and permitted absolute quality control.

By the early 1960's, frozen SARA LEE products were available nationwide.

Charles Lubin's talent for management eventually extended to the establishment of the company's international headquarters in

Deerfield, Illinois. Here a bakery that is a credit to twentieth-century technology—using computers and all the latest methods of automation—turns out baked goods at a rate that exceeds even Lubin's wildest dreams.

THE CUISINART

WHEN THE CUISINART FOOD processor was unveiled at the Chicago housewares show in January, 1973, it scarcely could have been called a hit. Indeed, myopic department-store and kitchen-shop buyers failed to see the machine as anything more than a souped-up blender with an exorbitant price tag. In other words, a white elephant.

Some white elephant. In just ten years it has spawned scores of imitations and turned America into

a food-processor society. No one knows (or to be more accurate, *no one will say*) how many millions of food processors have been sold across the country since CUISINART's inauspicious debut, but what is known is that there are some thirty different brands on the market today, not to mention more models and attachments than you can shake a whisk at.

All because Carl G. Sontheimer, a retired electronics engineer and dedicated amateur chef from

Connecticut, haunted the French housewares show in Paris in 1971 looking for a project to occupy his spare time. That project turned out to be a powerful, compact French machine that could grind, chop, mince, slice, purée, pulverize, mix and blend with stunning speed. Sontheimer and his wife Shirley were fascinated. They tracked down the machine's inventor, Pierre Verdun, who had also invented its precursor, Le Robot-Coupe, a heavy-duty restaurant machine dubbed "the buffalo chopper" by American chefs.

Sontheimer secured distribution rights for the machine in the United States, then shipped one dozen back to Connecticut to tinker around with in his garage. He took them apart, reassembled them, took them apart again, analyzing their strengths and shortcomings. He kitchen-tested them, his wife kitchen-tested them, and he tinkered some more. He refined the French processor's design, improved its slicing and shredding discs, incorporated safety features and rechristened it the CUISINART.

Undaunted by the CUISINART's tepid reception in Chicago among the housewares buyers, Sontheimer set out to demonstrate his machine and to convince America's best-known food gurus personally that it was indeed a miracle worker. It won their unanimous blessings[1] . . . and was praised so lavishly that anyone with the slightest interest in cooking could not fail to pay attention.

Though every competing manufacturer eventually offered refined and improved machines with tantalizing extra buttons, blades, attachments, motors of multiple horsepower and avalanches of

---

[1] From *Jean Anderson's New Processor Cooking* (New York: William Morrow, 1983).

promotion, all the food processors in fact followed CUISINART's lead. ROBOT-COUPE came charging onto the American scene with a household kitchen model to rival the CUISINART, and a short time later, KITCHEN-AID, maker of quality electric mixers and other appliances, finally introduced its processor in 1982. Only a detailed comparative examination of sales figures could establish the leader, but certainly CUISINART appears to be ahead, even with these two recent strong contenders in the market.

What is certain is that the food processor itself is a top-selling phenomenon.

183

NIKES

PHIL KNIGHT OF NIKES FAME IS A good example of a contemporary entrepreneur who knew how to seize an opportunity and run with it.

Running was something he was accustomed to do, having won a reputation for himself as a miler while an undergraduate business student at the University of Oregon. It was there that he became acquainted with Bill Bowerman, Oregon's track coach, who had very definite ideas about the design of running shoes. Bowerman claimed that American-made shoes were too heavy and clumsy; no serious runner would think of wearing them.

Knight pondered this matter at Stanford, where he went on to earn a graduate business degree. He stayed in touch with Bowerman, keeping him informed of his idea

that it might be possible to find a big market in the United States for well-designed running shoes made in Japan. Two years after Knight's graduation in 1962, the two men went into partnership. They each invested $500 for three hundred pairs of Tiger running shoes made by Onitsuka of Japan and stored them in the basement of Knight's father's house. They started by selling them only in western states, but met such good response that they soon went international.

When the Olympic trials were held in Eugene, Oregon, in 1972, Knight and Bowerman capitalized on being in the right state at the right time. They produced a pair of shoes they had designed themselves and persuaded marathoners to wear them so they could advertise that

NIKES were on the feet of "four of the top seven finishers." (The ads did not mention that the runners who placed first, second and third were wearing West Germany's ADIDAS shoes).

The February 15, 1982, issue of *Time* magazine tells of the day Bowerman first tried out his idea for a new kind of sole for NIKES shoes. Apparently, in a flush of inspiration, he stuffed a piece of rubber into his wife's waffle iron. He wrecked the machine but produced an example of the waffle sole he had in mind.

With similar gusto, the company kept coming up with new products to meet the demand that accompanied the craze for running in the 1970's. The company also added to its executive staff some professionals with pretty good track

records. Neil Goldschmidt, Secretary of Transportation under Jimmy Carter, and a former Portland mayor, is among them.

Though most of Knight's suppliers are in China and Southeast Asia, he has done his share to keep the American shoe industry alive by establishing plants in Exeter, New Hampshire, and Saco, Maine. Even if Americans stopped jogging tomorrow, Nike Inc. would still be selling hundreds of millions of dollars worth of shoes—for basketball, tennis, football, soccer, volleyball, wrestling, hiking and just plain walking.

ATARI

A TOTALLY NEW ELECTRONICS industry was born in California's Silicon Valley, just south of San Francisco, in 1972 when a young graduate computer engineer named Nolan Bushnell combined his knowledge of microprocessing with a penchant for having fun. The result was PONG, the world's first popular video computer game.

Nolan Bushnell is the son of a Clearfield, Utah, cement contractor. Always passionately interested in electronics, his first business was repairing radios, television sets and washing machines. In 1968 he earned a degree in electrical engineering from the University of Utah. From there, he went on to computers.

Bushnell came up with PONG in

1971 and started selling it as a coin-operated game in 1972. It was such a success that Bushnell pressed on to found ATARI. (The word is a Japanese expression of conquest.) The business, which produces a variety of video games, grew at a rate Bushnell had not anticipated. In 1976 he sold the company to

A Warner Communications Company

ATARI, Fuji Design and Pong are registered trademarks of Atari, Inc.

Warner Communications for $28 million. Bushnell stayed with Warner for a while; then, uncomfortable within the giant corporation, he went on to new ventures, including a chain of pizza parlors featuring video games and, later, a company "to mass-produce small companies" which provides new businessmen with services such as accounting and advertising—in return for shares of their stock.

Meanwhile, Atari sees a future for itself that goes beyond video games and computers. In the words of its chief executive officer, Raymond E. Kassar, "Atari is a consumer-oriented company that converts high technology and state-of-the-art electronics into *products that people want.*"

APPLE COMPUTER

IN 1976, STEPHEN WOZNIAK, A child of California's Silicon Valley, spent most of his spare time working to build a small, easy-to-use computer. He finally made one that satisfied him: It was smaller than a portable typewriter, but it could perform the feats of much larger machines.

To Wozniak, the minicomputer was simply a new gadget to show his colleagues at Hewlett-Packard, the big electronics firm where he worked as a designer. But one of his friends, Steven Jobs, saw in Wozniak's invention the commercial possibilities of a machine that could help families organize their personal finances and offer some businesses a way to control inventories. He proposed to Wozniak that they form a company to market the computer.

By selling Jobs's Volkswagen Micro-Bus and Wozniak's Hewlett-Packard scientific calculator, the two young men raised $1,300 to begin manufacturing operations. They christened the new computer APPLE, for reasons that differ depending on which source you consult: According to *California* magazine, Jobs thought APPLE sounded friendly and nonthreatening; former company president Mike Scott says the computer was named APPLE because Jobs was a fruitarian at the time.

APPLE started making money from day one, partly because of Jobs's smooth-talking marketing savvy and partly because the timing of its arrival on the market was so good. Established electronics firms had been reluctant to get into the computer business, fearing they would be competing with themselves. The microcomputer industry was ready and waiting for a few talented individuals to capitalize on the possibilities.

Compared to earlier microcomputers, the APPLE was a work of art. The basic design was simplicity itself and easy to manufacture. "It went together with ten screws and weighed barely twelve pounds. It seemed so empty," said Michael Scott, "that for a while there was serious discussion of adding sash weights so that when people picked it up they would have the sense they were getting full value for their dollar."[1] The prototype was redesigned to appear on the market as APPLE II, which came to the consumer with clear, concise instructions that made it remarkably

---

[1] Paul Ciotta, "Revenge of the Nerds," *California* magazine, July 1982.

easy to use. Sales surged from $2.7 million in 1977 to $200 million in 1980.

Rapid growth, however, brought its share of problems. The introduction of APPLE III, successor to APPLE II, was a fiasco. Apple reached its all-time low in 1981 when some forty employees were fired and the project manager of APPLE III resigned. After that things changed, as sales of an improved APPLE III went up as did those of the less expensive APPLE II PLUS.

As hints of the company's future plans for more advanced microprocessors begin to emerge, one can only imagine the challenges that lie ahead for Apple—from aggressive competitors who have profited from Apple's contributions to the field and are going on to blaze new trails, and from its own

organization where expert management will be required to continue building the company that started from a hobbyist's toy and became a major corporation.

Apple faces the same obstacles that loom large for all new businesses starting out today. (In 1981 587,000 were incorporated, 80 percent more than in 1975 and 53,000 more than in 1980.) Their products are flooding the market at a rate unprecedented in American history. But it is too soon to know which ones will be the enduring top sellers of our time. In an age when the potentialities of invention seem greater than ever before in human history, it is tempting to speculate on what creations will follow ATARI video games, the BETA MAX and the APPLE computer. Will these masterpieces of technology have staying power equivalent to that of the KODAK camera, the GILLETTE razor, the TIMEX watch? And will the discoveries that they engender lead to other products with even greater commercial application?

Time will tell.

Index of Products
with Credits and Sources

ALKA-SELTZER, *pages 163 and 165:* Miles Laboratories, Inc. (Robert Pattillo); *Everybody's Business, An Almanac,* edited by Milton Moskowitz, Michael Katz and Robert Levering (San Francisco: Harper & Row, 1980). Copyright © 1980 by Harper & Row Publishers, Inc.

ANIMAL CRACKERS, *page 107:* Melvin J. Grayson, *The History of Nabisco Brands, Inc.,* Nabisco, Inc., 1981.

A.1. SAUCE, *page 24:* Heublein, Inc. (Erik J. Pierce).

APPLE Computer, *page 185:* Joan Downs, "At Home with Computers," *The Dial* magazine; Paul Ciotti, "Revenge of the Nerds," *California* magazine, July 1982; "The Seeds of Success," *Time* magazine, February 15, 1982.

ARM & HAMMER Baking Soda, *page 39:* Burson-Marsteller (Marsha Cade).

ARROW Shirt, *page 26:* Cluett, Peabody & Co., Inc. (Robert Clark).

ASPIRIN, *page 136: See* BAYER ASPIRIN.

ATARI, *page 184:* Atari Incorporated (Karen Esler); "Sagas of Five Who Made It," *Time* magazine, February 15, 1982; Bernice Kanner, "Can Atari Stay Ahead of the Game?," *New York* magazine, August 16, 1982.

AUNT JEMIMA Pancakes, *page 77:* The Quaker Oats Company (Edith Dexter); Arthur F. Marquette, *Brands, Trademarks and Good Will* (New York: McGraw-Hill, 1967); Moskowitz, Katz, Levering, *Everybody's Business.*

AVON Lady, *pages 61 and 62:* Avon Products (Linda Occidentale); Moskowitz, Katz, Levering, *Everybody's Business;* Stephanie Bernardo, *The Ethnic Almanac* (Garden City, N.Y.: Doubleday, Dolphin Books, 1981).

BABY RUTH, *page 110:* Melvin J. Grayson, *The History of Nabisco Brands, Inc.*

BACARDI Rum, *page 48:* Bacardi Imports, Inc. (Diane Galarza).

BAKER'S Chocolate, *page 14:* The General Foods Company (Eugene Ritchie).

BALL Jar, *page 39:* The Ball Corporation (Joan Herbert and Larry D. Miller); Frederic A. Birmingham, *Ball Corporation, The First Century.* Copyright © 1980 by The Ball Corporation.

BAND-AIDS, *page 127:* Johnson & Johnson (James A. Murray).

BASS Shoes, *page 54:* G. H. Bass & Co. (Cheryl Anderson); Lord, Geller, Federico, Inc. (Marcia Simpson).

BAYER ASPIRIN, *page 136:* Sterling Drug, Inc. (Terry G. Kelley).

BETTY CROCKER, *pages 142 and 143:* General Mills, Inc. (Pam Becker); Edwin McDowell, *New York Times.*

BIRDS EYE Frozen Foods, *page 139:* The General Foods Company (Judy Klein); David Powers Cleary, *Great American Brands* (New York: Fairchild Publications, 1981). Copyright © 1981 by Fairchild Publications.

BISQUICK, *page 141:* General Mills, Inc. (Pam Becker).

BON AMI, *page 59:* Faultless Starch/Bon Ami Company (Gordon T. Beaham III and Christopher A. Charlton).

BUDWEISER, *page 55:* Fleishman-Hillard, Inc. (Joseph T. Finnigan); David Powers Cleary, *Great American Brands;* Moskowitz, Katz, Levering, *Everybody's Business;* Sandra Salmans, "Budweiser Still No. 1 in Sales," *New York Times,* February 16, 1982.

BUSTER BROWN Shoes, *page 89:* Brown Shoe Company (Marilyn Nenninger); David Powers Cleary, *Great American Brands;* Moskowitz, Katz, Levering, *Everybody's Business.*

CAMPBELL'S SOUP, *page 40:* Campbell Soup Company (Herb Baum); Barton Batten; Education Department, New Jersey Historical Society; David Powers Cleary, *How the Great American Brands Were Built,* Dartnell, 1978.

CASTRO CONVERTIBLES, *page 169:* Castro Convertibles (Donna Rollins and Lois Sheaff).

CHANEL NO. 5, *page 137:* Chanel, Inc. (Suzanne Urban).

CHANTILLY SILVER, *page 81:* Ted Materna Associates, Inc.

Chewing Gum, *page 94: See* WRIGLEY'S Chewing Gum.

COCA-COLA, *page 65:* The Coca-Cola Company (C. Randy Humphrey and Randy Donaldson).

CRACKER JACK, *page 44:* Borden Inc. (Christine Shama Tilton).

CRAYOLA CRAYONS, *page 50:* Binney & Smith, Inc. (Reynolds Girdler, Vice-President, and Russell J. McChesney, former Chairman of the Board); David Powers Cleary, *How the Great American Brands Were Built.*

The CUISINART, *page 182: Jean Anderson's* New *Processor Cooking* (New York: William Morrow, 1983).

EBERHARD-FABER Pencils, *page 63:* Eberhard-Faber, Inc. (Russell H. Williams).

Electric Razors, *page 83:* Stephen Bayley, *In Good Shape* (London: Design Council, 1979).

ERECTOR SETS, *page 118:* Schwartz Public Relations Associates, Inc. (Emily Whelan).

EVEREADY Flashlights, *page 96: See* LIONEL Trains.

FANNIE FARMER, *page 105:* Alfred A. Knopf, Inc. (Judith B. Jones); Russell Lynes, "Fannie Farmer."

FIG NEWTONS, *page 95:* Melvin J. Grayson, *The History of Nabisco Brands, Inc.*

FLEISCHMANN'S Yeast, *page 38:* Melvin J. Grayson, *The History of Nabisco Brands, Inc.*

FORMICA, *page 122:* Formica Corporation (Robert H. Kilbury).

FOSTER GRANTS, *page 174:* Foster Grant Corporation (Mauri Edwards); Jesse Rotman, "What's Behind Those Foster Grants?," *Marketing Communications,* January-February 1977; American Hoechst Corporation, *Pronounced Success, America and Hoechst, 1958–1978,* copyright © 1979 by American Hoechst Corporation.

FRIGIDAIRE, *page 138:* Frigidaire Company (D. J. Hughey); Stephen Bayley, *In Good Shape.*

FRITOS, *page 153:* Frito-Lay, Inc. (Al Raya).

FULLER BRUSH Man, *page 61:* The Fuller Brush Company (Pam Gray).

GALLO WINE, *page 162:* E. & J. Gallo Winery (Daniel J. Solomon); Charles M. Crawford, *Vinicultural Research and Gallo Winery;* Moskowitz, Katz, Levering, *Everybody's Business.*

GILLETTE Razor, *page 82:* The Gillette Company (John J. Folan and Gregory R. Niblett).

HALLMARK Cards, *pages 131 and 132:* Hallmark Cards, Inc. (Sally Hopkins); Harlan S. Byrne, "The Greeters," *Wall Street Journal,* August 22, 1973; Barbara Bartocci, "The House That Cards Built," *Flightime* magazine, copyright © 1980 East/West Network, Inc.

HEINZ Ketchup, *page 68:* H. J. Heinz Company (Beth Adams).

HERSHEY'S Chocolate, *page 91:* Hershey Foods Corporation (Susan A. Graham); Katherine Shippen and Paul A. W. Wallace, *Milton S. Hershey* (New York: Random House, 1960).

HOOVER Vacuum Cleaner, *page 103:* The Hoover Company (Lynn S. Dragomier); Moskowitz, Katz, Levering, *Everybody's Business.*

HUDSON'S BAY POINT BLANKETS, *page 16:* Pearce Woolen Mills, Inc. (Sylvia R. Barth); L. L. Bean, Inc.

ICE CREAM CONE, *page 108:* Melvin J. Grayson, *The History of Nabisco Brands, Inc.*

IVORY Soap, *page 57:* The Proctor & Gamble Company (Patricia M. Jent).

JELL-O, *page 28:* General Foods Corporation (Ken Defren); Dr. Burton Spiller, "The Jell-O Story," *Spinning Wheel*, March 1972.

JOHNSON'S WAX, *page 79:* Johnson Wax (Vina D. Jacobs); Moskowitz, Katz, Levering, *Everybody's Business.*

JOLLY GREEN GIANT, *page 116:* Green Giant Company, *Memories of a Giant*, 1978; The Pillsbury Company (Shelly Regan MacArthur).

JOTTER, *page 170: See* PARKER Pen.

JOY OF COOKING, *page 144:* Harshe-Rotman & Druck, Inc. (Linda Miller).

KELLOGG'S CORN FLAKES, *page 114:* Kellogg Company (Diane M. Dickey); Ronald M. Deutsch, *The Nuts Among the Berries* (New York: Ballantine Books, 1961); Moskowitz, Katz, Levering, *Everybody's Business.*

KENTUCKY FRIED CHICKEN, *page 178:* Kentucky Fried Chicken (Clara Lamkin); James Stewart-Gordon, "Saga of the 'Chicken' Colonel," condensed from *Louisville* magazine, January 1975, by *Reader's Digest*, February 1975.

KLEENEX, *page 124:* Kimberly-Clark Corporation (Ron Goudreau); "Kleenex," *Modern Packaging* magazine, April 1950.

KODAK BROWNIE, *page 88:* Eastman Kodak Company (Darlene J. Aiken).

LENOX CHINA/AUTUMN, *page 114:* Ruder & Finn (Marcia Bain).

LEVI'S, *page 32:* Levi & Strauss & Company; John Brooks, "A Friendly Product," *The New Yorker*, November 12, 1979; "Jean-makers to the World," *Newsweek*, August 27, 1973.

LIFE SAVERS, *pages 112 and 113:* Life Savers, Inc. (Thomas M. Asher and Darci D. Goldstein).

LINCOLN LOGS, *page 126:* Stephanie Bernardo, *The Ethnic Almanac.*

LIONEL TRAINS, *page 96:* Fundimensions (Brenda Schweiger); *On the Right Track: A History of Lionel Trains*, Fundimensions Division, General Mills Fun Group, Inc., 1975.

LIPTON Tea, *page 64:* Thomas J. Lipton, Inc. (Marie McDermott).

LISTERINE, *page 63:* Warner-Lambert Company (Walter Weglein).

LOUISVILLE SLUGGER, *page 43:* Hillerich & Bradsby Co., Inc. (Bill Williams); Martin Abramson, "Batter Up!," *Friends* magazine; "Batter Up! The Louisville Slugger Story," *Relay*, April 1970.

LYDIA PINKHAM'S VEGETABLE COMPOUND, *page 59:* Sarah Stage, *Female Complaints*, W. W. Norton; Jean Burton, *Lydia Pinkham Is Her Name* (New York: Farrar, Straus, 1949).

MAIDENFORM Bra, *page 128:* Maidenform, Inc. (Marilyn Zelinsky); Stephanie Bernardo, *The Ethnic Almanac.*

McDONALD'S BIG MAC, *page 176:* McDonald's Corporation (Stephanie Skurdy); Ray Kroc, *The Making of McDonald's* (Contemporary Books, 1977); Moskowitz, Katz, Levering, *Everybody's Business.*

M&M's, *page 180:* M&M/Mars (Risa Shimoda); Moskowitz, Katz, Levering, *Everybody's Business.*

MAXWELL HOUSE Coffee, *page 85:* General Foods Corporation (Eugene P. Ritchie).

MONOPOLY, *page 150:* Parker Brothers (Carol City).

MORTON Salt, *page 111:* Morton Salt (R. W. McDonald).

NATHAN'S Hot Dogs, *page 46:* Stephanie Bernardo, *The Ethnic Almanac.*

NESTLÉ, *page 145:* The Nestlé Company, Inc. (Marie-Claude Stockl and Adair D. Sampogna).

NIKES, *page 183:* Alexander L. Taylor III, "Striking It Rich," *Time* magazine, February 15, 1982.

THE OLD FARMER'S ALMANAC, *page 18:* Harshe-Rotman & Drock, Inc. (Maryellen Conroy).

OREO, *page 109:* Melvin J. Grayson, *The History of Nabisco Brands, Inc.*

PARCHEESI, *page 146:* Selchow & Righter Company (John W. Nason).

PARKER Pen, *page 159:* The Parker Pen Company (Lauren Schuller); Stephen Bayley, *In Good Shape.*

PEPPERIDGE FARM, *page 179:* Pepperidge Farm (Doloris C. Cogan); Margaret Rudkin, *The First Twenty-Five Years,* 1962.

PLANTERS Peanuts, *page 70:* Melvin J. Grayson, *The History of Nabisco Brands, Inc.*

POLAROID, *page 168:* Polaroid Corporation (Pamela Wright); Moskowitz, Katz, Levering, *Everybody's Business.*

POTATO CHIPS, *page 30:* Stephanie Bernardo, *The Ethnic Almanac.*

PYREX, *page 151:* Corning Glass Works.

QUAKER OATS, *page 73:* The Quaker Oats Company (Edith Dexter); Arthur F. Marquette, *Brands, Trademarks and Good Will;* Moskowitz, Katz, Levering, *Everybody's Business.*

RAGGEDY ANN, *page 137:* Knickerbocker Toy Co., Inc.

REYNOLDS Tobacco, *page 119:* R. J. Reynolds Industries, Inc. (Thomas N. Walker); David Powers Cleary, *Great American Brands;* Moskowitz, Katz, Levering, *Everybody's Business.*

RITZ Crackers, *page 146:* Melvin J. Grayson, *The History of Nabisco Brands, Inc.*

SANKA, *page 87:* The General Foods Company.

SARA LEE, *page 181:* Kitchens of Sara Lee, a Consolidated Foods Company (Peg Ransom).

SCOTCH Tape, *page 153:* The 3M Company (Anne Ludcke and Raymond K. Merle).

SCRABBLE, *page 148:* Selchow & Righter Company (James A. Houle, Vice-President); Brouillard Communications (Richard D. Badler).

SEN-SEN, *page 49:* F & F Laboratories (Len Matulewicz).

SHREDDED WHEAT, *page 71:* Melvin G. Grayson, *The History of Nabisco Brands, Inc.*

SINGER Sewing Machine, *page 30:* The Singer Company (Martina Laetsch); Moskowitz, Katz, Levering, *Everybody's Business; New York Times,* February 19, 1982; Gilbert Burck, "Singer: Hardening of the Assets," *Fortune* magazine, January-February 1959, © Time Inc.

SMIRNOFF Vodka, *page 160:* Heublein, Inc.; Thomas Fleming, *The Smirnoff Story.*

SMITH BROTHERS Cough Drops, *page 20:* F & F Laboratories (Len Matulewicz).

S.O.S Soap Pads, *page 125:* Miles Laboratories, Inc. (Robert N. Pattillo).

STEINWAY Piano, *page 24:* Manning, Selvage & Lee (Bernard Groger); Stuart Segal, "Pianomaker Henry Steinway," *Town and Country* magazine, December 1977; Helen Epstein, "Steinway: When the Best Demand the Best," *Companion* magazine, May 1977, copyright © East/West Network, Inc.

STETSON Hat, *page 34:* John B. Stetson Company (David H. Harshaw, Vice-President); John B. Stetson IV; Elbert Hubbard, *A Little Journey to the Home of John B. Stetson,* 1911.

TALON Zipper, *page 84:* Talon (Margaret Hoh and Gani Perolli); *Talon, Inc.: A Romance of Achievement,* an abridgement of the manuscript by James Gray; Stephanie Bernardo, *The Ethnic Almanac.*

TANK Watch (Cartier), *page 113:* Les Must de Cartier (Fernanda Gilligan and Helen Greene).

TEDDY BEAR, *page 90:* Reeves International, Inc.; Stephanie Bernardo, *The Ethnic Almanac.*

TIDE, *page 59:* Moskowitz, Katz, Levering, *Everybody's Business.*

TIMEX, *page 171:* Timex Corporation (Fred Nelson); Harvard Business School Case Study, copyright © 1972, by the President and Fellows of Harvard College; "Timex Gearing Itself for the Future," *National Jeweler* magazine, February 1971; *New York Times,* December 5, 1971, July 14, 1982.

TINKERTOYS, *page 118:* Schwartz Public Relations Associates, Inc. (Emily Whelan).

TOLL HOUSE Cookies, *page 145: See* NESTLÉ.

TOOTSIE ROLLS, *page 95:* Tootsie Roll Industries, Inc. (Ellen R. Bordon, President).

TWINKIES, *page 155:* ITT Continental Bakery Company, Inc. (Gloria Rascoe).

UNEEDA Biscuits, *page 102:* Melvin J. Grayson, *The History of Nabisco Brands, Inc.*

VASELINE, *page 53:* Chesebrough-Ponds, Inc. (James L. Ladd); Moskowitz, Katz, Levering, *Everybody's Business.*

VELCRO, *page 173:* VELCRO USA Inc. (K. J. Christie); George Kent, "VELCRO: Newest Magic Fastener," *Reader's Digest*, February 6, 1959.

WARING Blender, *page 158:* Waring (Sally Kreeda).

WEBSTER'S DICTIONARY, *page 16:* G & C Merriam Company, publishers of Merriam-Webster reference books; Anna M. Rosenberg Associates (Duncan G. Steck).

WEEJUNS, *page 54: See* BASS Shoes.

WITCH HAZEL, *page 14:* The E. E. Dickinson Company (George E. Dyslin).

WONDER Bread, *page 130:* ITT Continental Baking Company Inc. (Gloria Rascoe and Bonita K. Wagner).

WRIGLEY'S Chewing Gum, *page 93:* William Wrigley Jr. Company (Joan Brunner); "William Wrigley Jr., American," *Fortune* magazine, April 1932; "Wrigley Reasserts Itself in the Gum Market," *New York Times*, May 16, 1982; David Powers Cleary, *Great American Brands*; Moskowitz, Katz, Levering, *Everybody's Business.*

YO-YO, *page 148:* Stephanie Bernardo, *The Ethnic Almanac.*

ZIPPO Lighter, *page 156:* Zippo Manufacturing Company (William W. Jones).